# Simulation, Planning, and Society

Books by Melville C. Branch

*Federal Aids to Local Planning* (Editor), 1941

*Urban Planning and Public Opinion*, 1942

*Aerial Photography in Urban Planning and Research*, 1948

*The Corporate Planning Process*, 1962

*Planning: Aspects and Applications*, 1966

*Selected References for Corporate Planning, Annotated, with a Partial List of Companies with Corporate Planning*, 1966

*Comprehensive Urban Planning: A Selective Annotated Bibliography with Related Materials*, 1970

*City Planning and Aerial Information*, 1971

*Urban Air Traffic and City Planning: Case Study of Los Angeles County*, 1973

*Planning Urban Environment*, 1974; Russian Edition, 1979

*Urban Planning Theory* (Editor), 1975

*Comparative Urban Design: Rare Engravings, 1830–1843*, 1978

*Continuous City Planning: Integrating Municipal Management and City Planning*, 1981

*Comprehensive Planning: General Theory and Principles*, 1983

*Comprehensive City Planning: Introduction & Explanation*, 1985; Indonesian Edition, 1995

*Regional Planning: Introduction & Explanation*, 1988

*Planning: Universal Process*, 1990

*Planning and Human Survival*, 1992

*Telepower, Planning and Society: Crisis in Communication*, 1994

# Simulation, Planning, and Society

MELVILLE C. BRANCH

PRAEGER

Westport, Connecticut
London

Library of Congress Cataloging-in-Publication Data

Branch, Melville Campbell, 1913–
    Simulation, planning, and society / Melville C. Branch.
      p.  cm.
    Includes bibliographical references and index.
    ISBN 0–275–95403–X (alk. paper)
    1. Planning—Simulation methods. I. Title.
  HD87.5.B732  1997
  361.2'5—dc20       96–26291

British Library Cataloguing in Publication Data is available.

Library of Congress Catalog Card Number: 96–26291
ISBN: 0–275–95403–X

First published in 1997

Praeger Publishers, 88 Post Road West, Westport, CT 06881
An imprint of Greenwood Publishing Group, Inc.

Printed in the United States of America

The paper used in this book complies with the
Permanent Paper Standard issued by the National
Information Standards Organization (Z39.48–1984).

10 9 8 7 6 5 4 3 2 1

# Contents

# Preface

In previous books and professional papers, the author reported on numerous applications and discussed many aspects of planning. These works were directed toward identifying planning as a distinct intellectual discipline and field of knowledge, as a research and educational emphasis, a professional concentration, and an established occupation. They signify the author's conviction that planning is inherent in natural evolution and all human affairs.

Favorable prospects for Homo sapiens depend on successful planning more than any other of his activities, subject to the dictates of nature and the universe, which we can never comprehend completely. We can irrevocably affect the earth by radiological and biological contamination to the point where we can no longer survive as a species. There is little we can do in the long run, other than genetic manipulation, to direct and manage nature according to our desires. At best, we can improve our prospects of survival and societal advancement by actions directed to this end, affected by evolutionary developments in nature or thwarted by cataclysmic events we cannot anticipate. We can work with or against nature.

We do not know whether the prospects of human society will be enhanced by our behavior during the next several hundred years. This appears to be a critical period with respect to peace, population, poverty, pollution, and the other serious problems confronting us today. It may take a much longer time to estimate our more distant prospects: how people will interact with nature, with other animate life, with the global atmosphere within which we exist, and with unexpected earthly events. We can plan continually to improve our prospects to the extent possible. We can fail to take collective action with respect to the future and accept the consequences.

We can destroy ourselves as a species by inadvertent or misguided activities. We can rely on chance or our collective predilections of the moment without any collaborative effort to direct our affairs and prospects.

This book discusses simulation: an aspect of all human activities, and the single most important element in the art and science of planning. It involves formulating a representation or analytical conceptualization of the entity that is being planned. The entity itself cannot be manipulated at will to test the feasibility of proposed actions, procedures, policies, and plans. No object, organization, or process can function successfully, or at all, if it is continuously altered to observe the consequences of events, presumed conditions, endless minor problems, and constant proposals. Periods of relative stability are required for successful operations. When continuity is desirable and when significant changes are needed varies with different organisms and events affecting their operation.

An analytical simulation cannot represent all of the component parts of an object or organization. There are too many, and their interrelationships are too numerous and complex to portray analytically; for it is known that all organisms and their progressively smaller parts interact among themselves and with their environment in some way, closely or remotely as the case may be. Total simulation is actually and theoretically impossible. Any attempt to be more complete than is needed for planning and management purposes is prohibitively costly, takes too long, and is not worth the resources required for the effort.

Conceptually and analytically, simulation is a very complicated subject. It is present in all the arts and sciences. Complex considerations are of interest to those concerned with research on the technical aspects of the subject, such as: How many and what kinds of descriptive elements are needed to represent different organisms for planning purposes? Or, how are the interrelationships between disparate elements determined and expressed, especially between those that can be represented by numbers and those that cannot?

Fortunately, simulations which treat the primary elements of an organism, without attempting to be all-inclusive, can serve planning purposes successfully. They need not cover the large number of secondary factors and minor considerations which do not normally affect operations significantly. They provide a sufficient analytical base to evaluate existing, expected, and assumed conditions, events and decisions, and also proposals relating to planning and operational management.

The perceptions of the outside world which we internalize continuously in our conscious minds and preconscious memories influence our attitudes and actions. We produce a host of literary and artistic works, mechanisms, and concepts which simulate a wide range of occurrences, situations, and feelings we experience or imagine occurring within us or in our environment. To what extent do ever-present images in our conscious and preconscious minds, and our interpretations of external happenings, represent the real world as it actually exists? What is the reality we comprehend, react to, and cope with, hopefully to our personal benefit and societal success?

Much has been reported involving various uses of mathematical simulation in science and engineering. But little has been written about simulation as a universal means of representation and analysis, its present and potential employment in planning and management, and the consequences for society. The significance of simulation in the everyday life of individuals, the collective activities of people, and society at large has received little attention.

The author makes no statement he cannot justify by research conducted for this book and the substantive material he has accumulated during more than a half century of reading, research, teaching, and experience in business and governmental planning. Rather than a list of corroborative sources, a generally illustrative bibliography is included as a more useful reference. It covers the most important observations concerning simulation and planning made by the author throughout this book.

The author wished for someone to review the manuscript as it progressed. The several people who might have done so are no longer alive, and the author was unable to find someone who viewed the subject as broadly and could provide helpful comment and constructive suggestions. Accordingly, the usual acceptance by authors of their responsibility for the contents of their work is especially relevant in this instance.

# Simulation, Planning, and Society

We are all captives of the pictures we have in our heads.

Walter Lippman, quoted on the *NewsHour*, 4 October 1996

# Chapter 1

# Fundamental Mechanism

## BASIC REFERENT

According to dictionaries today, "simulation" is synonymous with "feigning": forming a mental image or abstraction of something that is unreal, false, a sham, a pretense.

This negative connotation has been superseded by a much broader, more widespread, and generally accepted use of the term today which refers to simplified representations of the form and functioning of entities, situations, processes, and other phenomena. Simulations are used to visualize, plan, and operate whatever they depict in abbreviated form. In some cases the entities simulated may not exist in the real world, may constitute new versions of known phenomena, or are pure products of the imagination. For planning purposes, the simplified representation of an organism or activity as it exists or is visualized is sufficiently inclusive and accurate to provide a basis for analysis, decision, and action. To portray organisms completely in all their aspects and characteristic complications is not only conceptually and analytically impossible, but unnecessary for successful planning and management.

The concepts in our minds as we plan our daily activities or some purposeful endeavor are simulations. The itinerary prepared by our travel agent depicts our intended trip for planning purposes, specific scheduling, and making reservations. Monthly statements indicate our financial situation at the bank: showing deposits, withdrawals, special charges, beginning and ending balances. Profit and loss, operating, and cash flow statements, together with the balance sheet, depict the financial condition of smaller businesses sufficiently for crucial planning and operational purposes. They may also suffice to evaluate the financial condition of larger enterprises. The plans and specifications produced by architects and engineers enable us to visualize the completed structure, evaluate how it will function, estimate its cost; and they provide a basis for construction and mortgage loans. They are used in the field as references by contractors and workmen to ensure that the structure is erected as planned. For very large and complex installations, such as oil refineries, small-scale models supplement working drawings at the construction site.

Shaketables replicate the movements and shocks of manhandling, transportation, earthquakes, acceleration, and other physical forces which many objects must endure. Wind tunnels and water tanks simulate the effects of aerodynamic and hydrodynamic forces imposed on aircraft and ships, on buildings, and other objects under actual operating conditions in the real world of atmospheric and aquatic space. Miniature models of bays, estuaries, harbors, and other water bodies are constructed to simulate the tidal, wind, and water conditions which affect bordering land use, shoreline construction, environmental protection, pollution, marine traffic, or other considerations and plans. Sophisticated flight simulators—originally called Link Trainers—are employed regularly to train, test, and monitor the skill and performance of aircraft pilots under ordinary and emergency conditions, which would be impossible, impractical, costly, and dangerous to conduct with operating aircraft under actual weather conditions. Occasionally, they are used in connection with investigations of aircraft crashes. Similar but simpler simulations train and test the pilots of supertankers to maneuver these huge vessels whose size, large displacement, deep draft, and enormous momentum underway present unique navigational difficulties. Much simpler versions are used for automobile driver tests and training.

Mathematical, computer-generated models simulate all sorts of objects, conditions, situations, and procedures which can be expressed numerically and manipulated quickly, economically, and effectively for the purposes in mind. With the rapid advances being made and expected in computer technology—such as virtually experiencing and traveling through three-dimensional space created in the mind with special headgear or on the computer screen—computers will be the main mechanism for formulating analytical simulations in the future.

If they think about it at all, many people associate simulations with mathematical statements composed of numbers and symbols manipulated on computers. They believe that statements that are not quantified are ipso facto less accurate and therefore less reliable. But novels and other literary works represent the situations and events they depict. Poetry and music symbolize emotional sensations expressed in these ways. Operas combine plot, narrative, acting, song, visual effects, and orchestral music in scenarios simulating imaginary or actual happenings. Most religions incorporate concepts of a spiritual afterlife and the behavior on earth required to experience it. Mathematical and logical abstractions depict theoretical advances in basic knowledge concerning quantum dynamics, chaos, turbulence, superstrings, self-organizing criticality, and other abstruse subjects.

## REALITY

Most simulations symbolize matters in the real world. What is the real world? It may not be necessarily what we believe it to be, because we know that our perceptions of what actually exists or is occurring "out there" are neither uniform nor consistent. The optimist sees things more favorably than the pessimist; the glass is half full rather than half empty. We often hear about witnesses who viewed the same crime, but differ radically in what they are certain in their own minds took place. Everything in our conscious mind is processed through our personal nervous system, affecting our emotional reactions, subjective evaluations, and consequent conclusions. There is no such thing, therefore, as an absolute objective reality, within or outside our subjective comprehension, which can be described and identified positively as such. There are only relative realities that represent a consensus of individual reactions and conclusions by many people.

These often prove mistaken or in need of revision. Witness the belief by most people at one time that the earth was flat, that there was no such thing as an unconscious component of the human mind, that there was a sound barrier in upper atmospheric space which could not be safely breached by high-flying aircraft. Scientific advances regularly refute the established beliefs of most scientists. For example, almost all geologists refused to accept the theory and factual evidence of plate tectonics when it was first introduced. There are hundreds of millions of people who believe firmly in what they consider to be one religious reality, and hundreds of millions of different people who consider another spiritual reality as the true verity.

Generally accepted limits are repeatedly revised and extended, such as the elementary particles and portions of living cells which can be seen with the most powerful miscroscope, or the most distant object in the universe which can be seen with the best telescope. The only realities we know are the images we internalize. Each of us exists in a world represented consciously and unconsciously within our minds. Each of these individual simulations is different. They are subject to change depending on our experience, education, attitudes, beliefs, and other personal characteristics.

The external natural world is not a universal *absolute reality* most of us can comprehend and refer to with certainty. No ultimate reality exists apart from our internalized conceptualization and comprehension of what we can visualize and experience. There is no absolute reality which can confirm conclusions, decisions, and actions by people who formulate plans and manage operations, those who approve or disapprove them, and the much larger population affected by them.

*Perceived realities* are those we are aware of in our minds and that are most real to us as individuals: important in planning when they are shared by most people and constitute a consensus. They affect the reactions and actions of the key individuals engaged in planning who influence or determine its content and outcome. They pose a special problem for planning in general because of our built-in preference for internalized images and recollections that are satisfying rather than disturbing. As noted previously in a different connection, we do not want to live with awarenesses that cause us concern, persistent problems, or pessimistic prospects. Hope and a positive attitude spring eternal within us, making it easier for us to face the ordinary vicissitudes of life. By accentuating the positive we avoid considering distasteful facts and figures.

These tendencies underlie our reluctance or refusal to acknowledge realities that are emotionally distressing, those we wish did not exist, and those we would like to ignore because of the actions they require and the gratifications they preclude. At the present time in the mid-1990s, there are a host of disturbing and frightening realities throughout the world: wars and civil conflict, crime, individual and societal violence, tribal animosities, dissolution of the family, overpopulation, poverty, pollution, epidemics, overindulgence in the present which overburdens the future. They cannot be minimized or ignored forever. They will not disappear or resolve themselves. People must perceive these problems as actual realities before remedial action can be planned and undertaken, unless the need for or a purpose for planning is established for other reasons.

New electronic techniques are allowing advertisers to insert their pitches into television images[;] that makes them indistinguishable from physical reality.

*Los Angeles Times*, 16 September 1996, p. D1

# Chapter 2

# Characteristics

---

## ANALYSIS

Everything consists of components, except the ultimate subatomic particle or other indivisible entity which has not yet been discovered. The different elements of mathematical statements must be correlated according to generally accepted or special means and methods of interconnection. Determination of the interrelationships between the different physical features and dynamic forces operating in a small-scale model of an actual body of water, referred to previously, are an essential part of the simulation. Between the water surface and underwater configurations, between the nature and form of the shore and tidal effects, between weather conditions and hydrodynamic forces, and between shoreline land uses, human traffic, water quality, and marine life. Simulations do not work if there is a contradiction in terms which prevents correlation of their components.

Identifying and measuring the interrelationships between the primary elements of the organism define its functioning. They are the most difficult of the essential operational components to express, measure, and manipulate analytically. Accurate simulation is not achieved unless these interactions can be calculated with different assumptions concerning the primary elements of the object, organization, or process. When a half dozen or so primary elements are considered, the number of interactions is very large. They present the most difficult analytical requirement in simulation.

The terms of comparison need not be the same. Quantification is the main means of correlation, but there are many crucial matters in human affairs that cannot be expressed meaningfully with numbers. Political factors, legal statements, public attitudes, and human reactions are examples.

In many situations, factors that are numerically indeterminate are more important in planning and managing an activity than those that can be enumerated and compared directly with numbers. Written materials can be judged subjectively and ranked in some order by an individual or by a group. But discourse concerning conditions, events, people, and other portions of a simulation cannot be expressed in numbers and analyzed mathematically. The number, type, and frequency of the words used or the average length of sentences and paragraphs can be counted. But such calculations describe literary form. They have nothing to do directly with substantive content other than relating it to the structure of the writing. By their nature, literary simulations are normally broader and more inclusive in their informational content, richer in meaning, more intellectually complete, and much longer than mathematical formulations.

There is always the difficulty of selecting words that express what the speaker or writer has to say, and that mean the same thing to most people. Not only does the meaning and significance of words vary among people, they are different at different times for different individuals, depending, for example, on how often and in what ways they are being used regularly, or on personal experiences that accentuate one of several alternative meanings or some aspect of the same commonly accepted meaning. Dictionaries are not always up-to-date. Sometimes a word is defined by referring to the same word as an adjective or noun without clearly explaining either one. As noted at the beginning of this book, the most common use of the word "simulation" is not included in its definition in dictionaries today. The imprecision of simulations that are formulated with words rather than numbers does not make them less meaningful or important. It does require the most careful selection and use of terms. Clarity and uniformity in the choice of words are as essential to the accuracy and comparability of written statements as statistical accuracy is for numerical elements.

With spoken and written words we can treat feelings, sensations, attitudes, conditions, actions, and events which cannot be portrayed in numbers. In many situations, at certain times, or in some particular respect, emotional considerations may influence planning much more than numerical analysis, which is scientifically more precise but more limited in scope.

Numbers are important in today's world and will become more so as science and technology with their increased use of mathematics affect the human scene. Numbers are not substances in themselves, but adjectival descriptors of the objects, organizations, processes, and other realities or imaginary concepts to which they refer. They are the most accurate means of quantification, immediately comprehensible and comparable with other entities expressed in compatible units. They depict interrelationships more readily and exactly than any other method. Numbers and symbols are the essence of mathematical analysis, which has expanded enormously in recent years with the proliferation of computers and computer programs.

One of the first provisions in Article I of the United States Constitution calls for the "enumeration" of the population to provide the basis for political representation. Since then, the decennial and supplementary censuses have become the most extensive operation in counting in the world, involving almost half a million temporary employees and several billion dollars. These numerical data provide the basis for a multitude of studies in many fields. They are generally accepted as the definitive and official demographic referent. In recent years, however, census statistics concerning minority economic and ethnic groups in large cities have been challenged as undercounting the correct numbers. Except in this respect, census data are accepted without question for planning purposes.

As a form of simulation, statistical sampling supports planning in various ways. In manufacturing operations, a small representative number drawn at random from a much larger quantity can be tested as a measure of the quality of the entire output. The measure is not exact, but has a small plus or minus range of error which can be calculated precisely. It would slow the productive process almost to a halt and greatly increase the cost of manufacturing ball bearings if each one were tested. Every car in an automobile assembly line is not tested to determine if it is one of the defective cars to be expected every so often. To compensate for this reality in the mass production of automobiles, some states have passed "lemon laws" which enable the purchaser of the occasional defective car to obtain a replacement free of charge.

As well as measuring the features of large numbers of inanimate objects, scientific statistical sampling simulates the attitudes, opinions, preferences, or intentions of entire populations or categories of people. Quantifying the results of judgments concerning matters that cannot be expressed directly in numbers is important in planning and simulation because they occur frequently and are often very significant elements in the analysis. Sample surveys have become almost a staple of information concerning the reactions, attitudes, beliefs, and speculative conclusions of an entire population or groups of people, relating to political and socioeconomic affairs, products and services, personal preferences, and behavior. Public opinion polls are taken continually as part of the American political process and the marketing of commercial products. Most people pay attention to and accept without question the results of such surveys. Focus groups are formed to meet and evaluate proposed products, identify personal predispositions, or conduct research into human reactions.

Few people are aware of the care required in collecting and analyzing information by scientific sample survey. First, a sample of the population being examined is selected which represents proportionately the different characteristics of people that affect their responses to the questions asked: age, sex, marital status, children, ethnic group, education, religious affiliation. The sample must be large enough to provide the statistical accuracy that is necessary or desired. If these requirements are met, it is surprising to those who are not familiar with the process how small a percentage of the total target population yields meaningful results.

The questions to be asked must be carefully composed to avoid any bias or potential misunderstanding built into the language of the query. Questions are often pretested on a sample of people to discover if the wording is ambiguous or favors a particular answer. Careless or deliberately misleading formulation of a question or misuse of language can produce false results which are accepted by the public as scientifically and statistically reliable because they are not alerted to the subtle effects of precise wording. Whether the survey will be conducted by interviewer, mail, telephone, fax, or some other method of questioning and answering must be decided. The method selected can affect the accuracy of responses.

The results from different regions are weighted to reflect the actual population surveyed—to take into account household size or the numbers of telephone lines if the survey is by telephone—and adjusted for individual characteristics and experience. Sample surveys cannot produce the exact calculation which results from certain types of surveys. Reliable polls report the range of error—percentage significance—of sample survey results. If the range is plus or minus 3 percent, in 19 of 20 cases the results will not differ more than this amount. If a percentage range of results is mistakenly reported as a single arithmetic mean, the correct figure is within plus or minus twice this amount. If categories of people within the usual sample are examined separately—such as those with more than a high school education or those identified with a particular religion—the statistical range of error is often too large to serve a useful purpose. The alternative is to increase the size of the sample to produce a smaller range of imprecision for categorical as well as total results.

The worth of numbers in general depends on their accuracy and timeliness. Like statistical samples, many are approximately accurate. Not always, however, is this imprecision noted, and most people accept the approximately accurate figures as exact. Few people can judge the reliability of most of the numbers they use and refer to, not knowing in what manner and how accurately they were formulated. Nor do most people realize that carrying numbers to several decimal places is deceptive if the nature of what is being counted or the method of calculation does not permit the exactness suggested by the decimal places.

The most disruptive difficulties dealing with numbers are our own doing, mainly because of ignorance or carelessness. By their nature, numbers seem to us more exact and likely more accurate than words. They reflect the care presumably taken in counting. We tend to ascribe to statistics a significance and validity they may not have. Often, in discussions, the person who cites the most numbers to support his or her position is likely to prevail, whether or not the numbers are accurate or even relevant. Overconfidence in numbers may be accompanied by underestimating the importance of verbal statements which can have far-reaching political, legal, economic, or religious effects on the organization and conduct of human affairs and various aspects of everyday life.

There is also the problem of numerical overkill: presenting so many numbers or a few so rapidly that they are unintelligible, or employing numbers that are incomprehensible to most people without prolonged explanation. There are times when decision makers cannot understand scientific, technical, or other particular terms and numbers. Or they are saturated with a flood of numbers which they understand but cannot absorb and analyze in their minds in the time available. In these instances, formal evaluation of the numbers and the conclusions to be drawn should be deferred until they can be appraised, or referred to those who can understand them and have the time to study them. Too many decision makers refuse to acknowledge such situations to themselves or to other people who assume that they have the requisite capability.

As human knowledge expands and deepens, specialization and the use of particular terminology increases. There is more and more knowledge and information, which most of us cannot understand without specific study. In time, surrogate intelligence can perform certain reviews and analyses of data which have been programmed in the computer to replicate our personal method of deduction and decision, enabling us to concentrate on the most critical problems and crucial decisions. At least for a long time to come, surrogate intelligence cannot replace the specialized knowledge which is essential in human affairs but understood by a smaller and smaller percentage of the population.

Instinctively, we tend to cling to beliefs derived from numbers even when the numbers are suspect, to find order or relationships where none exist. On the one hand, if we toss 100 consecutive heads of a coin, most of us expect the next toss is likely to be tails. Actually, the chance of its being heads or tails is equal. On the other hand, we expect some streaks of good luck to be followed by more of the same. In general, we find it hard to accept some of the facts, features, and consequences of random chance that run counter to our preferences and beliefs. In a disorderly array of objects, or in the shape and pattern of an object in nature, we may discern some regular form which satisfies our instinctive sense of, or our conscious desire for, order. Or we observe in the disorderly array of objects some image previously implemented or formulated in our mind. We tend to see what we want to see, believe what we want to believe. We are tempted to consider the ambiguous as certain, or to interpret it so that it conforms to our personal concepts, theories, preconceived expectations, desires, or favored images. We are prone to transform these tendencies into beliefs and ultimately into convictions that may impair our performance in planning and management.

Inevitably, knowingly or unknowingly, we base some of our beliefs, conclusions, and actions on information which is erroneous or incomplete, or because it supports our predilections. The effects of the misinformation may be cumulative since its consequences are likely to affect other people. We can transform rumors, which are the worst form of misinformation, into accepted facts until the rumor is eventually forgotten or dispelled. Emotionally and intellectually, we favor the positive over the negative because it is reassuring and comforting rather than disruptive and disturbing. It favors the status quo and does not call for critical review and possible corrective action. Accentuating the positive supports our preference to postpone consideration of problems and to pass them on to the next generation. We resist acknowledging new problems; there are enough already that we cannot ignore.

Certainly, we prefer to share beliefs and actions with others. The lone and lonely juror or committee member would prefer not to be the holdout in an otherwise unanimous decision. We resist the situation which finds "everybody out of step but me". Belonging and acting with a compatible group brings a sense of personal security and an appreciation of the convivial contact, shared beliefs, and collective activities. As a member of a group we feel we have an advantage over those who do not have this supportive affiliation. We are prone to believe what others believe, to share common misconceptions, to act in concert, to avoid being the "odd man out". The ultimate manifestation of this tendency is the willingness of moral, normally law-abiding citizens to join at times in riots, vandalism, and emotional frenzy.

In different ways and to different degrees, these human traits present problems for planning and simulation. They affect our acceptance, understanding, and use of information, our beliefs, our concept of the reality we confront. Our reactions, intentions, objectives, and actions are the product of a constant contest between individual and societal needs and desires. With recent research indicating that Homo sapiens is less than 300,000 years old, there has not been much time in the billions of years of evolution of animate life for us to acquire the characteristics conducive to planning in general, much less simulation with its particular analytical requirements. This applies to those who formulate plans, those who implement them, and the much larger number of people who are impacted by them.

The most crucial matters in most planning, and the components most difficult to treat in simulation, require language. The numerical results of scientific sample surveys are calculated statistically, but the content and responders' understanding of the questions they are asked cannot be stated in numbers. The votes of supreme and appellate courts, juries, legislatures, and corporate boards of directors are counted, but the substance and consequences of their actions require words. As do individual and collective political attitudes, forces, and decisions. Philosophical, moral, legal, and religious concepts, theories, and pronouncements are conceived and assimilated by society with words.

Since the most important elements in most simulations cannot be composed, counted, and compared with numbers, they are assigned a rank, weight, value, or other quantification which permits their comparison with numerical components. Or non-numerical and numerical components may have to be considered separately, and the conclusions reached for each category integrated by some form of overall judgmental resolution and decision. Such amalgamation can be based on past experience concerning relationships between disparate elements, or on the best judgment of the individual responsible, or on a structured consensus. The accuracy of the analytical effort can be reviewed by comparing results in the past: recognizing that underlying conditions may have changed, or some unknown or previously disregarded or mistaken factor could produce a different outcome. Correlating dissimilar analytical components is an important subject for research in planning.

The reliability of a simulation depends on the accuracy of the information used to construct it. It may be expertly formulated to depict the primary elements of the organism and their interrelationships, but it is useless or misleading if it is based on inaccurate information. The adage often quoted in connection with computers in general—"garbage in, garbage out"—is especially relevant for simulations of socioeconomic organizations such as government agencies and business corporations composed entirely of information expressed in numbers and supplementary statements. The usefulness of these simulations depends entirely on the accuracy and significance of the numbers, which are several simulative steps removed from the quantities and values they represent. There is no direct physical or experimental simulative evidence.

Many simulations include mechanical elements: wind tunnels, aircraft flight and automobile crash simulators, hydrodynamic water tanks, centrifuges. Their usefulness depends in large part on the accuracy with which the mechanical device simulates the situation considered. The fan in the wind tunnel must reproduce within the chamber the velocities, turbulence, and other forces and effects in the earth's atmosphere which it depicts. Flight simulators duplicate the cockpit controls of the aircraft involved, external meteorological conditions, movements of the aircraft, the views that would be seen through the cockpit windows, even the odors associated with the events being simulated. The experience is so real that pilots show the same physiological symptoms that occur under similar conditions in actual flight.

The reliability of simulations employing mechanical devices depends on whether the information required to adequately represent the reality has been accurately incorporated in the mechanical device. For example, simulators have been developed over the years to evaluate car crashes and produce safer cars. Every year General Motors enacts about 500 intentional car collisions. Sleds carrying cars with dummies inside simulating people are accelerated along tracks from standstill to 30 miles per hour in a fraction of a second. The dummies are designed and built to represent people in size and bodily proportion, with skull construction, rib deflection, bone porosity, and plastic skin reacting in a car crash as would our bodies. The dummies contain numerous transducers simulating our nervous system and measuring the impacts and injuries we would receive. Clothing provides the friction on the car seats which would apply in real life. During a crash lasting about one-half a second, 31 continuous measurements are recorded by sensors in a computer as 4,000 streams of data.

As more and more accurate information concerning car crashes and their effects on the bodies of adults, teenagers, children, and babies in the womb accumulate and are incorporated in the mechanical simulation, its reliability for planning purposes increases. For automobile designers and manufacturers, governmental requirements and regulations, the safety and comfort of automobile drivers and passengers, insurance companies, and medical practice.

Whenever we drive late-model cars, a microcomputer continuously monitors the mechanical system for us far better than we could. Such simulations may include fuel metering, spark timing, exhaust gas recirculation, gear shift, suspension, steering, ride height, and even our geographical location when our car breaks down, to direct the repair vehicle to our rescue.

## PROJECTION

The purpose of planning is to adopt policies and to take action with respect to the future: a function incorporated in the definition of the word and its meaning for just about everyone. In a very fundamental sense, the present does not exist. We are planning and acting with reference to the future all the time. The past and the future comprise a continuous flow of time, in which the present is actually an infinitively small transitory moment between the past and the future.

Practically speaking, planning always involves the future, since it takes time to effect any action. Consideration must be given to conditions as they are expected to exist when the plan is implemented. To some degree or in some small way, conditions will be different within the organism being planned and the external environment affecting it. "Nothing is permanent but change", particularly as we look further into the future. The plans and specifications for new construction are a good example, referred to previously to illustrate simulation. If construction starts immediately and the plans are drawn with forethought, labor and material costs, the interest rate on construction loans, the availability of the materials and equipment needed, and the permits required will not have changed significantly. If construction is delayed for several years, we know that the plans and spec- ifications should be reviewed to corroborate or revise estimated costs, iden- tify any necessary design or scheduling changes, and confirm the feasibility of the project under the conditions that then exist.

There are many words relating to the extension of the present into the future: forecast, forethought, prediction, prognostication, prophesy, antic- ipation, each with its particular meaning concerning intent and method. *Projection* is the term adopted for general use in this book: "the act of throwing or casting forward". Projecting into the future has always been part of human existence, essential for survival, necessary to attain desired objectives, and required for society to function. All the more as society becomes technologically more complex and intricately interrelated. As a single example, anticipating the seasons and local growing conditions have been part of agricultural practice since earliest times.

Projections are based on past experience. An analogy with a comparable situation in the past may be sufficient for planning purposes, recognizing that an undetected difference between the situations could completely nul- lify the comparison. If periodic data reveal a definite trend and the forces underlying it have not changed appreciably, the trend can be extrapolated to forecast the situation in the future which would result from a continu- ation of the same trend. Demographic, economic, financial, political, sci- entific, and other available data constitute a vast array of statistical information, which may serve as a basis for projection concerning many different things.

If numerical data are not collected and processed consistently over the years, they may not be comparable and statistical analysis is impossible. Sometimes, adjustments can be made so that they can be correlated statis- tically, if this is not too costly and can be done in the time available. To be able to extrapolate data collected in the past for planning purposes is a strong argument for consistency in operational reporting. Inconsistencies in the data or changes in the forces affecting a trend may preclude precise extrapolation, but permit projection within a plus-or-minus range of ac- curacy similar to the results of scientific sample surveys. For some planning and simulation this may be accurate enough or at least provide a useful indication.

There are aspects of organisms which cannot be expressed and calculated with numbers, but function according to a logical structure of non- numerical elements and interrelationships. For example, a network of po- litical power centers in a state or municipality may determine what laws, rules, and regulations are legislated. There are numbers connected with such situations: how many people and how much money are involved; how many benefit and how many lose; data concerning operations. But the prin- cipal actors, their interconnections, and the determinative forces involved are personal and political. A logical formulation of the interactions and dynamics of the network portrays the situation. If it has existed and functioned consistently for a period of time, its projection into the future may be as valid an analogy for planning as the extrapolation of established statistical trends. Logical formulations are part of projecting future events and behavior.

As game theory develops, its postulates may be incorporated in planning to a much greater extent than is the case today. If there is an intrinsic tendency proposed for organizations to progress from their beginning, through a period of successful maturity, to gradual decline, failure, or reformulation, it can be considered in the analytical simulation. If chaos theory provides signs of impending breakdown, specific indicators can be incorporated in the analytical scenario of the organization.

The accuracy of projections employed in planning and simulation varies, of course, with what is being predicted and how far into the future the particular prediction is made. No future event can be predicted with absolute certainty. Although the sun has been shining on earth for billions of years, no one can guarantee it will rise tomorrow. Physical and astronomical scientists tell us that it will eventually consume all its energy some billions of years from now, which presents a unique problem for the longest-range planning imaginable. Although physical phenomena cannot be predicted with absolute certainty, there are many of them that can be projected with almost total certainty, including the sun rising tomorrow, the effects of gravity and magnetism, the movement of numerous celestial bodies, the interaction between many elementary particles and between numerous chemical substances. Many biological organisms, including social insects, act in predictable ways. Most reputable scientific projections are reliable enough for planning purposes if they meet two criteria of scientific validity: replication and "the ability to predict". Meeting these criteria often requires limiting the scope of the scientific inquiry.

We know that natural events which involve diverse physical forces are more difficult to project. For example, weather forecasts do not yet meet the needs of agricultural and construction interests. Despite continuing efforts of meteorologists to develop mathematical models which will accurately predict the weather—aided by global, regional, and local reporting of weather conditions by satellites, aircraft, radar, automated instruments, and human observers—farmers, builders, and related interests want to know how the weather will affect their operations tomorrow, next week, and during the forthcoming year or more.

Regular weather forecasts affect agricultural and construction activities, the availability and price of agricultural products, construction costs, financial interests, and market forces involved. They become increasingly important as trading volume increases on agricultural commodity and energy financial markets. Extreme weather conditions and catastrophic events—tornadoes, hurricanes, floods, droughts, volcanic eruptions, earthquakes—can have devastating effects. We do not know when or how frequently they will occur. Meteorologists do the best they can to establish an average expectancy for extreme weather from historical records, observations, and scientific analysis, in order to determine what building requirements are justified to reduce loss of life and physical damage caused by natural disasters, and what protective insurance is desirable and feasible.

Mathematical formulations are the main means for simulation employed today in forecasting the weather, calculating the likelihood of an earthquake and its intensity, or the probable geographical path and dynamic features of a hurricane. Mathematical simulation is an important part of the aerodynamic design of aircraft, but a very different form of simulation has been devised to determine the effects of birds sucked into their jet engines while both are in flight. To deliberately fly aircraft into the migratory routes of large birds seeking a collision between the two, in order to discover the consequences, is patently impractical and potentially destructive and dangerous. In "bird ingestion tests" which simulate on the ground what presents a hazard in flight, an eight-pound bird is fired from a cannon into a jet engine operating at full throttle. The results are observed directly and measured. In a gruesome simulative experiment as part of the Holocaust, the Nazis exposed a sample of humans to freezing water until they died or suffered permanent injury, to test the tolerance of people to frigid weather conditions. It is reported that there were also tests in the United States on human subjects, without their knowledge, to ascertain the effects of radioactive fallout and test various medical treatments. Simulations are conducted in many ways for different purposes.

The accuracy of projections depends in part on how far into the future they extend. Extrapolation of a past trend of corporate profits for one year is usually more accurate than extending the trend over ten years. Unexpected developments affecting the trend may occur immediately, but they are more likely to occur at some time during the next ten years than in the first. The loss of fertile topsoil by erosion during the forthcoming year can be forecast quite accurately if the loss rates in past years have varied very little, or show a definite trend. If there is no applicable record of the past, projection by analogy may be as short as a year. If circumstances have not changed, corporate profits and topsoil erosion will remain about the same.

Of course, an extraordinary event or an unexpected development can nullify a well-reasoned projection. With sufficient meteorological and agronomic historical data, the product of "tree farming" can be projected accurately enough to be part of a long-range strategic plan. It will be 30 to 60 years until harvest, depending on the species of tree selected. There is always the chance that the trees will be damaged or destroyed by disease, pests, or man-made contamination, adverse weather conditions, or a natural catastrophe.

Recent history suggests that major intellectual advances in a field of knowledge are made every twenty years or so, or at longer intervals for some fields. It appears that after such an advance, there is a period during which the new knowledge is absorbed into the subject content of the field, followed by a period favoring new discovery and formulation of the next intellectual "quantum jump" forward. If this timing suggested by recent history is accepted, the likelihood of an intellectual breakthrough in a field of knowledge increases after it has absorbed the previous intellectual advance. Organizations can promote research and be especially alert at such times to advances in fields of knowledge affecting their productive activities.

Fortunately for human affairs, successful planning does not require infallible, precise, or even closely accurate, longer-range projections. Most human activities function effectively and survive for some time. Some prosper without attempting to look into the distant future. Short-range projections are most important because they are needed to support management decisions that must be made continually to conduct current operations and to realize plans which have been adopted but only partially implemented. The continued functioning and survival of the organism depends on the essential requirements of tomorrow more than the probable or possible needs of a distant day. Strategic forecasts are part of determining the best general direction for long-range development, but the continued existence of the organism is a necessary precondition. This depends on short-range projections. Although there are exceptions as noted previously, most phenomena cannot be predicted reliably over an extended period of time; but they evolve so gradually that shorter-range projections can be made with confidence.

This is the case in many situations. For example, in the short term, interest rates conform closely with the expectations of those financially concerned and informed. Were it possible to predict interest rates over a period of years, we could all invest with the certainty of substantial profit. Plans simulating the physical form of a community twenty or so years hence project little change in residential, commercial, industrial, and other land uses during this relatively short period in the life of cities. Short-range projections by the military services concerning the supplies and equipment they need to maintain combat readiness are much more reliable than long-range projections for new weapons systems that take ten to fifteen years to design, produce, and incorporate in the armed forces. During this longer period, the new weapons system is likely to be changed in some way, extended, or cancelled.

The general direction of development indicated by frequent short-range projections is sufficient to successfully plan most socioeconomic organisms. They provide the information needed to manage current operations, and they identify particular conditions and reveal trends in time for adjustments to be made. If these adjustments accumulate and begin to have a compound effect, the trend with which they are associated is revised or abandoned for projective purposes.

Longer-range forecasts are introduced into planning, operations management, and analytical simulation when they can be made with the desired degree of confidence. They are necessary when a business considers a new product, or a military service a new weapons system. Some products take years to design, develop, test, produce, and market. They require commitment of a significant portion of available resources. Much can change during the long gestation period, and with each passing year the money already spent and the funds committed for the next several years represent a larger and larger loss if the project is abandoned.

Automobile companies have faced this problem for years. It takes five or more years to decide on the general features, to design in detail, test, manufacture, and distribute a new model of a car. Manufacturers must estimate buyers' tastes, preferred options, manufacturing requirements and costs, gas prices, sticker price, dealer preferences, environmental requirements, and the competition to be expected years hence. The Chrysler Airflow and Ford Edsel were forecast failures, but the preponderance of sound market projections has enabled the major automobile companies to survive and prosper.

The largest aircraft manufacturers were faced in the mid-1990s with deciding whether their next primary product would be a "superjumbo jetliner" carrying 600 or more passengers, or a 300–seat high-speed "supersonic airliner". A single manufacturer cannot produce both at the same time during the ten years or so required for research, development, manufacture, test, and certification. Advances in simulating aircraft on computers are reducing the time required for their production and certification, as well as enabling many more alternatives to be considered. But the projection into the future is still long enough to make or break a company.

## RESOLUTION

As the main means of analyzing socioeconomic organisms, simulations are the analytical core of master plans that guide current activities, identify desirable policies, set objectives, and devise programs of action to attain the desired results. Master plans must be realistic, indicating what can be achieved rather than the wishful product of overoptimism or false hopes. They represent the organism being planned with sufficient accuracy to serve as the main analytical mechanism for directing its future. Those considerations that are not directly represented in the simulation may be disregarded if they are relatively unimportant. Or they may be associated with or made part of one of the primary elements or one of the interactions among elements. One set of elements and interrelationships includes those that can be calculated mathematically. The other set consists of those that are expressed in words: statements, judgments, logical formulations.

The simulation and master plan are kept up-to-date: modified, revised, or completely replaced as need be. They are based on information that is considered reliable but is checked periodically. Longer-range strategic projections are included and acted on when appropriate. The policies and objectives that are adopted reflect the degree of risk the decision makers are willing to accept. An allowance is made for those variations of quantitative results and verbal statements that are characteristic of certain factors. Flexibility is built in to reduce the possibility of unexpected events which could immediately invalidate an overprecise simulation or a rigid master plan. Continuous feedback provides a check on the accuracy of projections, and compares intentions with the actual results of plans as they are implemented.

Decisions are made by individuals and groups of people who are responsible for reaching conclusions and resolving the key questions involved in management. They may be assisted by surrogate intelligence, if they are confident that a process of reasoning they understand and accept has been accurately simulated and programmed for the computer. Humans must make the final analysis and ultimate decisions. Intelligence, knowledge, experience, and initiative are among the capabilities associated with successful decision makers. Personality is important: whether he or she is an optimist or pessimist, has a positive or negative attitude in general, can work effectively with people, has a sense of humor. Any one of such traits can subtly influence every decision or be the deciding factor in any one of them at times.

Innate and acquired predispositions can affect people's reactions, actions, and decisions, as noted earlier. Unrecognized and unacknowledged prejudices can adversely affect personal and ethnic relations among people and the treatment of subject matter. Reluctance to undertake or accept change can be an emotional reaction rather than a thoughtful conclusion. For some people the indefiniteness of the future compared with the definiteness of the present may inhibit planning ahead. The comfort and relative security of present practices may favor the status quo. Some people do not have the self-confidence to admit their own limitations to themselves much less to others, to defer to someone else on matters they do not comprehend, or refrain from making decisions out of ignorance. There are those who are prone to deny or minimize societal realities that are personally disturbing to them. Others, almost unknowingly, put self-interst or self-satisfaction ahead of the collective best interest.

Some people believe that "what is past is prologue", others that "history never repeats itself", depending on personal predilections more than thoughtful consideration. There are people inclined to accept what is presented to them, out of goodwill, confidence in fellow man, or because it eliminates any need to inquire further or to actively investigate. Skeptics are inclined to question everything, which is generally disconcerting and troublesome but useful in planning because it encourages constructive caution when making critical decisions. To the extent that decision makers are aware of their predispositions and compensate for them, analytic evaluations are more objective and conclusions more accurate.

It is at the top level of governmental and private decision making for the nation and society as a whole that successful simulation and planning are most difficult to attain. Improvement involves some of the most fundamental characteristics of people and the state of major institutions in our society. Critical societal problems cannot be resolved by a single or several isolated actions which we delude ourselves into thinking can cure complex problems. Rather than facing these problems head-on and realistically, we persist in believing that much less than is actually needed will somehow do the trick. We prefer remedial relief to surgical cure.

Most people are unaware of the function of planning in their daily lives, and the fact that it consciously or intuitively directs almost their every action. We do not appreciate the necessity and inevitability of planning by our government, foremost private enterprises, and the military services, which together shape the future for individuals and the prospects for our society. Planning is not yet recognized as a distinctive process by the scholarly community, much less by the body politic. Unless we want to leave this crucial activity in the hands of a delegated few, the public must be informed about planning as it is about other critical societal processes. This can be accomplished over time by the mass media, the computer networks, the educational system, and other means and methods. When the public is aware of and knows about planning it can react and act constructively as the final arbiter in a democratic society.

The mass media are a major force affecting planning and just about every other activity in the United States. They are the principal source of information for most people. They affect our awareness, reactions, attitudes, and actions by the choice of subjects they treat. As a consequence, more than any other force, the mass media formulate the political agenda, the prospects of candidates for political office, and the reputation of elected incumbents. They determine in large part which subjects and issues receive attention, public opinion on many matters, and those of our individual and collective attitudes and actions that are influenced by what we see on television and computer screens, hear on the radio, and read in newspapers.

Most important and as yet largely ignored and unstudied is the impact of television and radio on our concept of reality. The effect of newspapers is less pronounced. Television selects or devises programs that are emotionally appealing, visually enticing, or entertaining in order to attract and hold viewers. It treats activities and events dramatically for the same reason. This built-in dynamic to enhance audience ratings creates on the television screen a reality which is in part imposed and artificial with respect to what is represented or is actually occurring. It certainly affects planning and simulation to the extent that the altered images may prevent or make it difficult for planning to consider events as they actually occurred or situations as they really exist. Planning and simulation must deal directly in their analyses and conclusions with the images in the minds of the public which are the product in part of media enhancement or alteration. The combined and cumulative effects of the mass media of communication on all forms and every aspect of planning are self-evident to the thoughtful observer. What happens to human society, how it uses planning, and the benefits derived from its forethought depend on the mass media more than anything else.

As organisms become more complicated technically, the educational system will determine in large part which activities the leaders of tomorrow can conduct effectively. Whether the followers of tomorrow will participate positively depends not only on the extent to which they are excluded by the complexity and specialization of human affairs. It depends also on whether people can realize their basic self-interests and fulfill family and societal mores. A sense of personal opportunity and social responsibility must be accompanied by interest in and knowledge of public affairs.

An educational system to meet future needs will have to be vastly superior to what we have today. Our educational deficiencies in the United States worsen with each passing year. The percentage of high school students who drop out before graduation is increasing. More and more children receive only rudimentary schooling or none at all. As the traditional family disintegrates, education at home largely disappears. University education without student subsidy is possible for a smaller and smaller percentage of the population. The mass media play almost no constructive part in the educational system. We are creating an underclass of uneducated and undereducated people who will be unemployable except in low-wage, menial jobs, and will require economic and social support to contain civil unrest and prevent serious public health problems.

The improvements in performance that are needed for our society to function successfully in the future will not come about by chance or natural evolution. Problems will overpower capabilities to cope with them unless extensive remedial activities are undertaken. The possibility of societal breakdown lurks in the background if major problems are not attended to. At present our three levels of government operate by partisan politics and political self-interest, with little or no comprehensive planning in the general public interest. Business corporations assume their societal responsibilities are fulfilled by performing successfully in a competitive marketplace with minimal participatory requirements or responsibilities. Their planning is directed toward maximizing their self-interests and those of their stockholders.

Our economic welfare, our societal situation, and our collective and individual behavior depend on comprehensive planning in the general public interest by the two functional pillars of our society, government and business, and on the collective will of the people.

There are motivations and forces in our society that promote comprehensive planning by government and private enterprise working together in the general societal interest, directed by less partisan and more enlightened leadership than is now the case. These motivations and forces operate regardless of which political party is in power. Self-interest favors planning if people believe it makes human activities more rewarding and enjoyable. As these activities become more complex and technically specialized, and as they incorporate scientific and technological advances, they require a high level of planning for their initial design, operation, and executive management. There is also a growing recognition by many people that our most severe social problems—poverty, an increasing disparity between the haves and the have-nots, educational deficiencies, crime and violence, racial tensions—will not be remedied as an automatic consequence or by-product of an affluent, materialistic society. Specific plans and programs are required to guide and integrate the forces that are applied toward their resolution.

The problems and requirements for improvement associated with planning and simulation for socioeconomic organisms have been noted because they affect many people and impact society at large. The simulations for these organisms are the most complex, but most of them involve relatively few elements and interrelationships which must be taken into account in comprehensive planning.

A number of studies show that simulation in corporate and military settings increases learning significantly.

*New York Times*, 6 September 1995, p. zB1

A university in which teachers and students will obtain reading materials not just from libraries, but also from databases; where term papers will be handled by e-mail, and where classes will meet in on-line collaborative sessions, perhaps using video and voice links as well as keyboards . . . integrated with traditional educational settings.

*New York Times*, 25 June 1996, p. zA9

# Chapter 3

# Forms

## PICTORIAL

### Gesticulation

Gestures are one means of communication among animals. A sudden halt in their movement, often accompanied by a raising of the head or some other motion, signals danger. Among monkeys, apes, and many other animals, threatening or submissive gestures establish a relative rank or "pecking" order: an important aspect of their collective behavior which favors evolutionary "survival of the fittest". Some young animals can be imprinted on a surrogate mother simulating the parental relationship to such an extent that the young respond and act as they would with their real mother. For example, grey goslings and sea otters on a human individual, or condor chicks on an artificial reproduction of the head and neck of a mature female condor.

Human gestures include many different bodily motions: movements of the hands, a nod of the head, shrug of the shoulder, grimace, wink or roll of the eyes, pout, holding one's nose. Many of us emphasize a point or accompany an explanation with a gesture of the hand. Or we may express anger, irritation, or emphasis by striking our fist on the table. The use of gestures must have predated communication by expressive sounds followed by spoken language. Using gestures to indicate their emotions and thoughts, primitive people could communicate among themselves concerning events crucial to their survival: signaling fear, warning, hostility, friendship. A sequence of gestures could simulate certain basic actions in obtaining and preparing food, constructing shelter, and other activities. "Body language" is said to represent certain emotions within people. It was developed into an art form by the renowned pantomimist Marcel Marceau. He could climb a ladder, enter a window at the top, walk to a table tripping on a rug on the way, pick up an identifiable object, and return by the same route to the ground, by pantomiming bodily movements and expressing reactions without moving from a fixed position on the stage. The ultimate in simulative communication is the sign language of the deaf.

Gestures relate to planning to the extent that they provide supplementary information concerning the reactions and actions of individuals who formulate plans, and those who are affected by them or are concerned with the process.

## Art

Since earliest times art has been a creative endeavor, a personal statement, and a particular competence. Cave paintings made 20,000 years ago bear witness to art's longevity and importance as a means of individual expression, and as a representation of collective activities and societal beliefs. *Ars longa, vita brevis est.* Since primitive people adorned the walls of caves, art in one of its many forms has provided personal fulfillment, heralded powerful people and their achievements, symbolized and sanctified religious beliefs, beautified public and private monuments and grand structures. It is an element in the design of personal adornment, manufactured products, consumer goods, entertainment, medical therapy, cultural and archaeological research.

Painting, sculpture, music, and dance combine two simulations. One is the actual or "photographic" appearance of the organism being portrayed in the external world as it is seen by most people. The other is the internalized image of the organism as visualized and interpreted within the mind of the artist and represented in his work of art. For example, the realistic painter minimizes his transitory emotional reactions to the object or scene he is portraying. They could interfere with the visually precise reproduction he desires. The abstract painter seeks to express his feelings and internalized concept of what he is simulating on canvas, using line, shape, shade, and other basic forms of graphic expression. He deliberately avoids reproducing it with the exactness of a photograph. Another painter may combine realism and abstraction, interpreting and modifying what he sees with his eyes to simulate a particular element, aspect, or interpretation of reality that requires more than copying the object or scene.

Artists have developed various ways of simulating the third dimension of depth on two-dimensional surfaces: by showing objects in the background at smaller scale; inventing linear perspective to approximate what we view in space; casting shadows as they would appear in three-dimensional space; and incorporating the eye in frontal view on the side view of faces as in ancient Egyptian sculptured reliefs, or by Picasso's showing side view elements of the human face seen from the front.

Sculpture involves the same dual simulation of the external world and the internal response or interpretation of the artist. Similarly, dance expresses the imaginary conceptions of the choreographer as well as movements and sensations observed in the real world. As the "loftiest of the arts", music translates into sound the feelings and thoughts of the composer, the best of whom can hear their compositions in their "inner ear" as clearly as when they are actually performed. Some sounds of the real world resonate in the most abstract music. It is the direct human involvement in simulation that produces the duality in artistic expression. It is not found in mechanistic simulation such as wind tunnels, hydrodynamic water tanks, or centrifuges, unless artificial human intelligence is incorporated to provide feedback and automatic adjustment.

Art simulates most directly when it tells stories, depicts events, explains phenomena, fantasizes. It reflects conscious thought and unconscious emotional dynamics in different ways and to different degrees. Response to an artist's work involves the viewer's emotions as much or more than his mind. When a work of art has almost universal appeal because viewers react to it favorably, it becomes an icon with widespread effects. When listeners resonate favorably with a musical composition, it becomes a classic played frequently and affecting many people. Any one of many emotions may be the sensuous tie between the simulation and the viewer or listener.

Art is a powerful force in our lives providing sensual and cognitive enjoyment and influencing our behavior. It has limited application in planning compared with other forms of simulation. It can be used directly for illustrative purposes. It is an element in many comprehensive plans, important in some, incidental in others. It affects planning indirectly through its effects on the people involved and its use in presenting plans to others.

## Graphics

Graphics are ubiquitous. Several familiar examples appear every day in newspapers, newsletters, periodicals, books, and other written communication. The "pieces" or "slices" in circular "pie" charts show the different components that comprise an organization or some other entity, such as the number and relative size of the different operational units in a company, the allocation of the funds available among different activities, or the different categories of a population. This information may also be portrayed in "bar" charts, with the length of each bar drawn to scale to represent the size and proportional interrelationships among different components. Another form of graphic shows a line representing the numerical value of an element of information by relating it to scales along two sides of the chart. These are familiar methods of portraying the number, size, and interrelationships of the elements or aspects of the entity that is being considered.

Graphics simplify and clarify information which is more difficult to understand in any other form. In some instances, they are the only means of elucidating, for all but a very few people, highly complex or esoteric knowledge. They are widely employed because they can be seen and comprehended at a glance, rather than recorded, formulated, and interrelated entirely within the mind from a list of numbers. They fulfill the ages-old Chinese proverb: "A picture is worth a thousand words".

Clarity and ease of understanding are important in planning and management because the performance of decision makers and analysts is improved when they can readily and clearly absorb and comprehend the information they need to reach analytical conclusions and make decisions. Frequently, they must act under the pressure of time constraints, confronted with great quantities of relevant data. The same graphics that make management's tasks easier or possible when there exists a flood of information which must somehow be excerpted or simplified, can be used to explain material to the public, to stockholders or other people concerned, and for the mass media.

As the term is used in this book, graphics should not be confused with "graphic arts": etchings, engravings, lithographs, silk-screen prints, and other multiple copies of works of art. Any of the technical methods employed in the graphic arts can be used to produce graphics. And some graphs are so well conceived and executed that they are considered works of art. The scientific notebooks of Leonardo da Vinci are prime examples.

Some subjects require graphic simulation if they are to be comprehended by more than a few people familiar with the mathematics, other language, or special notation adopted by a particular specialization. Also those subjects which require inordinate time and study if there is no graphical explanation or simplification. A simple example, familiar to many people, is the organization chart of large companies which show the units into which they are divided for management purposes: starting with the governing body or chief executive at the top, proceeding downward on the chart showing first the primary operational units of the organization, and at lower levels the subordinate units at the next lower levels. Staff units associated with different levels of management, regular consulting connections, particular support or services, and other special arrangements are also shown. For all practical purposes, the disposition of organizational parts and the many interconnections between them established for management and planning purposes by large corporations cannot be visualized and comprehended unless they are represented graphically.

Familiar to many people are the charts recording the movement of the pen mounted on a seismograph, indicating the frequency, spacing, and amplitude of earthquake tremors appearing as "spikes" above a base line on a continuous roll of paper. Long ago, the fate of Napoleon's army invading Russia in 1812 was graphically described by the French engineer Charles Joseph Minard (1781–1870), in what some observers believe is the best statistical graph ever drawn. It employs the width of linear bands to trace the progressive reduction in size of Napoleon's army from the invasion of Russia in June 1812 with 422,000 men until it retreated into Poland in September of the same year with 10,000 survivors. Four variables are plotted: the size of the army, its location, direction of movement, and the temperatures on various dates during the retreat from Moscow. Presentation of the same information in written form would require many pages of text and considerable study to sort out the many facts and figures involved. Graphics are typically used to describe military operations. For example, in every descriptive account of the movements of armies during the American Civil War, which are still studied as classic examples of strategic and tactical maneuvers by military historians and officers on active duty.

Graphical simulation is often helpful or necessary to explain complicated matters. For example, net return on investment for a large corporation—the most important measure of profitability in business—can be expressed by mathematical equations, difficult or impossible for most people to follow. Its formulation can also be shown graphically as a sequence of steps involving the addition, subtraction, and division of quantities which most of us can perform.

The location of fragmented mineral deposits underground—discovered by exploratory drilling and remote sensing—can be fixed in space mathematically with reference to geographical coordinates derived from a satellite system placed in orbit for this purpose. Few people can visualize the underground mineral deposits from the mathematical description. When this is translated into graphic form, the configuration of the deposits is immediately apparent to all.

Feynman diagrams enable physicists to understand complex events among nuclear particles which are difficult and time-consuming to calculate mathematically. Developed by the late Nobel Laureate Richard P. Feynman, they use lines to represent the histories of nuclear particles and nodes to indicate their interactions, with minimum supplementary notations. Abstract symbols are used by scientists and engineers to explore ideas or express concepts. This is such a common process that blackboards are usually included in their offices. The occupants can quickly work out graphical formulations on their blackboards, change them easily as they are developed, and replace them with new thoughts. They are usually filled with the last round of such notations and previous graphics preserved for future reference.

Besides the symbols used regularly in mathematics, chemistry, biology, and other specializations, there are a few general graphical notations. Arrows indicate direction or force, straight lines direct connection. Curved, wavy, zigzag, folded, interrupted, and other irregular lines express the forces suggested by their graphical form and treatment. A star or an encircled period may represent a point of emphasis or importance, an asterisk a halt or indication of an accompanying reference or remark. Lines enclosing a space portray enclosure, containment, boundaries, grouping, or emphasis. The equal sign and arrowheads meaning "greater than" and "lesser than" employed in mathematics are used generally. A superposed diagonal line or cross cancels what is underneath.

Coaches in American football devise graphical simulations using such simple notations as circles, crosses, lines, and arrows to indicate precisely what each man on the offensive team should do to execute his role in the particular play. The "play book" or "operating manual" for the team includes all the plays which might be called by the coach on the sideline or by the quarterback. It is invaluable for training new recruits and as a ready reference as plays are modified, discarded, and new ones introduced.

Although many people are not able to read them accurately, most people know that architectural and engineering schematics and working drawings are complex graphical representations of the structures they portray. The most intricate graphical simulations may be the templates required for the design and manufacture of electronic computer chips. They can involve thousands of circuits and connections in smaller and smaller microscopic sizes. A system has been developed which enables an automaker to simulate on a computer every step in the design and manufacture of cars and trucks before the first machine tool is built. Aircraft designers can simulate commercial airliners on the computer screen with sufficient clarity and precision that mock-up models are not necessary, and the time required for design, development, and production is significantly shortened.

### Remote Sensing

Remote sensing refers to images that were first created with the earliest cameras many years ago. They are the most remarkable of visual simulations. They are more realistic than any other form of simulation. The "photographic likeness" they produce is closest to what we see with our eyes. They are close approximations of what is being portrayed, but they do not have the three-dimensional form, the tactility, graduated spatial depth, and scent of the reality on earth. Furthermore, the scale of the images differs slightly in different parts of the picture unless they are photogrammetrically corrected. The depth perception attained by viewing two slightly displaced photographs side by side through a stereoscope is optically exaggerated and not the same throughout the photograph. Laboratory processing may produce photographic negatives and positives that differ from each other, and from what is seen with the eye.

The different shades of grey, or "densities", in a "black and white" image produced in remote sensing can be transformed into gradations of a single or different colors, if this facilitates the photo interpretation of certain features. The most widespread use of this technique employs images recorded on heat-sensitive infrared film, which shows vegetation in "false-color infrared". This facilitates and extends its interpretation; important, for example, in land use classification, resource inventory, agricultural and timber forecasts, vegetative disease identification and control, and project planning. Since red is not the natural color of vegetation, false-color infrared is an artificial simulation added for interpretive purposes to the simulation of the scene on the ground represented by the remote sensing image itself.

High resolution satellite images, which normally appear as seen from directly above in a vertical view, can be transformed on a computer into different perspective views of the same scene on the ground as seen from different angles and from different directions.

"Virtual reality", another recent technical advance in simulation, produces an illusion so real that the viewer seemingly enters and moves about in three-dimensional space on the ground. At the present time, this requires special ocular equipment attached to the head, or special eyeglasses worn in a specially equipped room or "cave" built for the purpose. Whether the basic technique of achieving simulative, three-dimensional illusion can be developed for use as a normal part of aerial imagery remains to be seen.

Remote sensing began with the first photographs taken by Daguerre and Nipre in 1839. Some twenty years later, Gasparde-Félix Tournachon, a Parisian photographer, took pictures with his camera from a balloon. During World War I, some 50 years later, occasional surveillance of the tortuous trench systems which characterized the conflict was carried out with cameras carried aloft by balloons. During World War II aerial photography was expanded enormously for military purposes: mapping for terrain and target identification, aerial reconnaissance for geographical detail, damage assessment, and special military missions. The money spent for these purposes during a war that lasted some four years was many times what would have been allocated in peacetime during several decades. Cameras and film were greatly improved, special photo reconnaissance aircraft were designed and built, and the processing and interpretation of aerial photographs vastly expanded. The expanded role of air forces in military operations during World War II provided hundreds of platforms in the sky for aerial cameras.

The military services have played a central role in the history of remote sensing. Besides the advancements noted in the previous paragraph, infrared film was developed and manufactured to detect from the air installations on the ground covered with camouflage netting. Radar was developed as a simulative instrument on the ground which detected aircraft at considerable distances and aimed anti-aircraft guns to destroy them. Miniaturized and incorporated as a "proximity fuse" in an anti-aircraft shell, radar eliminated the necessity of a direct hit by triggering the explosion at a lethal distance from the aircraft. "Side-looking" radar was developed for remote sensing of terrain features through cloud cover and at night.

The military continue to play a vital role, although information concerning many of their activities is classified. Sooner or later it is declassified or revealed, and applied for civil purposes. Military aerial reconnaissance satellites provide strategic intelligence concerning the situation and activities in countries around the world, and monitor to the extent possible specific indications of hostile intentions as well as aggressive actions. These same images supply general geographical and precise terrain information important for tactical operations and updating maps. A global positioning system of satellites provides the exact location of army vehicles and equipment, naval vessels at sea, and aircraft in the air.

Mapping from remote sensing images was first inaugurated by the military to provide reliable cartography where it was non-existent, inaccurate, or inadequate for operational purposes, but might be needed in the future. Later on it was used to determine exact geographical coordinates for the targeting of ballistic missiles and other weapons. To be effective, reliable inertial guidance systems require exact geographical coordinates to which they can be directed. Digitalized topographical mapping has become so accurate that cruise missiles launched to follow the terrain to reach targets miles away, are reported to have a 50–50 likelihood of striking within four to six feet of the target. All so-called "smart weapons" incorporate remote sensing in their guidance systems. There are active systems of military surveillance such as the network of acoustical receivers-transmitters placed in the ocean to detect submarines and immediately transmit the information by satellite to information and command centers.

Since World War II, the scope and quality of remote sensing have advanced markedly. The multiband camera and the multispectral scanner have been improved, recording wavelengths in the electromagnetic spectrum of radiation from the surface and objects on earth which are longer or shorter than the narrow range of wavelengths visible to the human eye. Certain wavelengths record certain features on earth better than other wavelengths, permitting more diverse and accurate photo interpretation than if the camera or scanner recorded only the wavelengths we can see. Digitalizing remote sensing images permits superimposing on stored images changes in the same scene which occurred since it was last photographed or scanned. This makes it much easier to update maps to include changes in the natural landscape and new or altered man-made structures. Radar and false-color images have been improved. Always technically complicated, remote sensing has become a complex subject involving optics, electromagnetic radiation, computers, physics, chemistry, mathematics, interpretive techniques, photogrammetric correction, film and print processing. Few people are familiar with this technology outside the military services and intelligence agencies, and civilians involved with aerial reconnaissance.

Orbiting satellites, which did not exist during World War II, have expanded the spatial coverage and increased the frequency of remote sensing. In 1983, the Soviet Union and the United States had each launched about 1,000 payloads into orbit, with 102 and 183, respectively, still in orbit today. Including remnants of satellites and debris, there are now more than 6,000 objects in orbit that are being tracked. Some satellites cover latitudinal swaths around the world. Those in polar orbit cover a longitudinal area as the earth rotates underneath. Those in geostationary orbit record the same area continually. General reconnaissance satellites are used for a wide variety of purposes as suggested below. For example, travelling at 17,000 miles per hour, 438 miles above the earth, LANDSAT's scanners record 1,100 images every day, each covering 10,000 square miles, at six different electromagnetic wavelengths. Each image registers 256 shades of grey. Objects more than 100 feet in dimension can be differentiated for interpretive purposes. Aerial cameras are reported to exist which can differentiate between the pickets in a fence or the numbers and letters in an automobile license plate. Remote sensing platforms now include low-flying helicopters, balloons, light aircraft, specially designed "spy" aircraft operating at over 60,000 feet of altitude, NASA shuttles, and meteorological satellites orbiting 22,300 miles in space.

Gravity-mapping with radar from a satellite in orbit 500 miles high reveals the topographic configuration of the ocean floor: 71 percent of the earth's surface containing plains, fissures, ridges, mountains, volcanoes, and other features. This information, released to the public in 1995, is of interest to commercial fishermen in locating concentrations of marine life, industries concerned with the geological formation of minerals, and to scientists studying plate tectonics, currents and circulatory patterns in the deep ocean as they may relate to meteorology, and the fundamental processes that drive our planet.

The interpretive information and uses of remote sensing are almost without limit. It is far and away the most extensive means of acquiring information in the world today, simulating a wide range of conditions, situations, and events locally, regionally, and globally. It is employed continually or frequently for many different purposes by government, private enterprise, and the military services. No other method of simulation gathers anywhere near as much information that can be used in connection with so many activities. The U.S. Census, big as it is, does not compare with remote sensing in the volume, variety, and import of the information it collects, although certain information can be obtained only by personal interviews or written response in the home. There are those who believe that in certain situations more accurate population estimates can be derived from remote sensing than by traditional census survey. In some countries, no other method may be possible because of cost, cultural restrictions, or other limitations on ground survey.

Probably the most universal application of remote sensing is identifying and determining the different uses of land which represent and shape human activities. They are the primary consideration in local, regional, and national land use planning, in the selection of transportation and other routes, and the location of projects of all kinds and descriptions by governmental bodies, private enterprises, and the military services.

Nowadays almost all maps are made from remote sensing images. In the past, the features shown on maps were recorded as part of the geographical ground survey: woodlands, open land, waterways, water bodies, urban areas, and some man-made features. With remote sensing images these characteristics of the countryside can be identified and delineated more exactly, with additional information it would be impossible or impractical to obtain from ground survey. Geographical Information Systems (GISs) can include information obtained from remote sensing with the land-use information they record and display on computer screens for urban and regional planning purposes. The combination can be brought up-to-date at regular intervals.

Topographic differences as small as a few centimeters are detected, and variations in elevation in the open ocean as large as 60 feet. Deciduous and coniferous trees can be identified within the interior portions of woodlands, visible in remote sensing from above but hidden from view on the ground along the borders of the woods. Certain species of trees and crops can be identified on a polarized image sensing a particular wavelength, or more usually with successive images collected at intervals over several months. Major crop estimates are now made more accurately by remote sensing than they were previously by ground survey. To confirm their accuracy, in 1977, American intelligence agencies compared their estimates of the Soviet wheat crop derived from satellite reconnaissance with official Soviet reports of actual production obtained by ground survey. Preliminary and final estimates were 94 and 99 percent accurate, respectively. LANDSAT can now discriminate between 29 types of vegetation, and between fields that are fallow, freshly plowed, newly sown, or bearing crops.

First noted with potato blight almost twenty years ago, certain crop blight and tree diseases can be spotted by remote sensing before they are observed on the ground, as can certain underwater features such as shallow sand bars, rocky shoals, and dredged channels. Remote sensing can record extremely thin oil slicks on the ocean surface, caused by schools of fish beneath, which are not visible to commercial trawlers looking for them. Traces on the surface of open land reveal the outlines of ruins of archaeological interest which are several feet underground. Floods, earthquake faults, lava flows, volcanic ash deposits, and conditions within volcano cones can be monitored, as can sources of acid rain, air and water pollution, algae, and other surface contamination. In one instance, a plutonium production plant discharged heated effluent underwater into a nearby river, which could not be detected on the surface by remote sensing with ordinary film but was revealed on infrared film registering heat radiation. Certain damage caused by natural and technological disasters can be assessed quickly and accurately by remote sensing. The movement of animals carrying radio-transmitter collars can be recorded by remote sensing.

Radar can view through clouds, haze, smog, and most rain which preclude aerial photography and obstruct or interfere with images registering certain wavelengths of electromagnetic radiation. It reveals distance, size, slope, roughness, and other characteristics of the terrain. It differentiates between water and land, plowed fields and forests, urban and non-urban areas, man-made structures and natural features. In dense woodlands, such as rain forests, radar often yields more details concerning the land surface beneath the tree canopy than aerial photography or multispectral scanning. It can detect watersheds and rocks as much as twenty feet below the surface of open land. It can be used to map regions or smaller countries normally covered with clouds.

There is usually a much longer wait than most people realize for clear weather conditions permitting photographic coverage of an area on the earth below. During the wait, aircraft and equipment must stand by unused at considerable cost. On the average, two-fifths of the earth is covered with clouds. To ensure that a particular area of ten to fifty square miles is cloud free, some ten satellite passes over the area are required at 24–hour intervals.

The interpretation and use of remote sensing images will continue to be improved by those who use them, those who would like to employ them for their particular purposes, and those concerned with the materials and equipment involved. For example, an experimental radar has been developed which is expected, after field test, to detect from aircraft the 110 million undetected and unexploded antipersonnel land mines which have been sown in 64 countries during hostilities, and the millions more planted every year. Technical advances will be made in recording instruments, film, photogrammetric correction of distortions, production processing, and computer-generated images. The accuracy of new interpretations will be checked by comparing them with what they simulate on the ground. As they are confirmed they will be added to the impressive list of interpretations of features on and below the ground whose accuracy has been established.

Determining "ground truth" corroborates the accuracy of image interpretation. This is achieved in different ways. For example, cameras mounted on a tall tower recorded the long shadows of horses, cattle, sheep, and other animals cast on the ground in the early morning or late afternoon, to find out if they can be identified by their shadows and accurate counts made of different animal populations from aircraft or satellites. Examination on the ground after the surrender of the Nazis in World War II revealed that photo interpretation by the Allies of the destruction caused by air bombardment and its impact on the German war effort was exaggerated. Factories which appeared devastated in aerial photographs and inoperative for a long time were quickly restored to at least partial production, and railroad yards which appeared totally destroyed were back in service much sooner than expected. Except in hostile or restricted territory, ground truth can be determined in most cases by comparing the interpretation of particular features shown on remote sensing images with what actually exists on the ground.

Far more has been learned about planet earth in the past fifteen years than ever before, mainly because of remote sensing. It has provided views from satellites and spacecraft never before available: ecological regions, vast expanses of land, complete coastlines, entire oceans, and whole continents in single images. For the first time in human history, people throughout the world can see their global home as a whole photographed from spacecraft, and closer views of the earth portraying the geographical habitat, environmental conditions, and natural resources on which our future as a species depends in large part. The multitude of realities revealed have not yet been absorbed and fully comprehended by most of the world's population. By means of instruments positioned in outer space, remote sensing has also greatly increased our knowledge of the earth's outer atmosphere and the vast universe beyond. It has brought about new knowledge in just about every field alphabetically from archaeology to zoology.

All planning begins with information concerning what is being planned; it provides the basis for analysis, reaching conclusions, making decisions, and taking action. Remote sensing is now the world's most important means of simulation and source of information for many planning purposes by government, business, and the military services. This fact is not only unrecognized by people in general, it is not yet accepted by those most concerned: graduate educational programs in corporate and other business planning, urban and regional planning, and intellectual disciplines directly involved in planning. A graduate course has not yet been developed which concentrates on the availability, procurement, evaluation, and interpretation of the many sources of information that provide the essential first step in planning. The most crucial initial ingredient for successful planning is not yet specifically identified and addressed in education.

## LOGICAL—MATHEMATICAL

As part of our daily lives, we are constantly thinking through a condition, a situation, or a process which we want to consider and to understand. We may wish to confirm or modify an intuitive response or an emotional reaction, or to plan what we will do after we have thought the matter through. Intuitive evaluation and logical reasoning are both forms of simulation. We develop in our minds a concept representing the reality in the external world we are considering. Research indicates that an identification of significant elements, a sequencing of ideas and events, and causal connections among them take place in our preconscious minds before we consciously and deliberately examine what is in our minds. Our conscious deliberation may be based on logical inference and deduction, intuitive conclusion, or even guess work, if we can think of no way of reaching a reasoned resolution.

Logical reasoning is the analytical stem of constructively managing an activity and directing it toward agreed-upon objectives. It underlies mathematics: the means of expressing elements and their interactions which can be stated and manipulated with numbers and symbols. With the proliferation of computers, mathematical models are widely employed to simulate a vast range of investigation in just about every field of knowledge and human activity. With the increasing speed, memory, and other capabilities of computers at decreasing cost, calculations can be made which were impractical or impossible not long ago. The most knowledgeable experts formulate the mathematical basis for computer simulations which can be used by the rest of us to investigate further and develop new understanding of what is represented. The accuracy and value of this new knowledge depend on the validity of the mathematical formulation which constitutes the simulation. And only those quantities and interactions which can be represented by numbers and symbols can be treated.

Mathematics will continue to make its unique computational contributions to planning theory, process, and applications. Theoretical advances now almost entirely limited to a few logicians and mathematicians will gradually develop to the point that at least some aspects can be applied to planning and management in practice.

Very few people are versed in the symbols and languages of formal logic. It is a highly specialized field with a handful of researchers and practitioners. Except for the simplest arithmetic, only a very small percentage of the population and a somewhat larger percentage of those with a college education understand the language of mathematics. The American people in general are deficient in mathematics compared with a number of other industrialized nations which have much higher mathematical requirements in their educational curricula, beginning at an early age. As a consequence, in the United States most of those who make the decisions in almost all forms of planning do not comprehend the mathematics which are part of most simulations and operational analyses. To a somewhat lesser extent, this is also true for decision makers in countries with higher educational requirements in math, since the mathematics underlying most computer programs employed in planning is complex.

As an illustration of what decision makers can be confronted with in the way of incomprehensible language and questionable process, consider the following.

Because adding a new highway lane, whether for HOVs [High Occupancy Vehicle] or not, generates many effects that are difficult to measure—such as route shifts, start-time shifts, induced shifts, and new bottlenecks—I combined queuing theory and mode-choice theory to develop a simulation model that requires but little observed data. The model does not predict what actually will happen when a lane is added because it assumes away route and start-time shifts and makes other simplifying assumptions. However, because these assumptions either favor an HOV lane or do not alter the ranking of the two alternatives, the model can be used to compare their benefits. Whenever the model shows less delay with a general-purpose lane, this is really the case. But when the model shows less delay with an HOV lane, this is not necessarily true—there actually may be less delay with a general purpose lane. The model calculates the number of vehicle- and person-trips and total vehicle- and personal-delay, along with the final proportion of high-occupancy vehicles. The proportion of people who will use high-occupancy vehicles during any time increment is estimated with a logit discrete-choice model.

Comprehensive planning, particularly for socioeconomic organisms, involves interrelationships among elements, shorter-range projections, and other types of analyses that are expressed and calculated mathematically. If a government agency or a business organization has to do with a special field of knowledge, the specific language of that field is a necessary corollary. For example, the U.S. Geological Survey is concerned with thrust plates, anticlines, orogenic sediments, Cretaceous rocks, magnetic anomalies, Tobler fine sandy loam, Rego Gleysol, and ivas. Law incorporates many terms with precise meanings, such as nisi prius, certiorari, nexus, mandamus, tort, codicil, distrain, surrejoinder, demurrer, remainder, writ. Those engaged in planning and managing business organizations must be familiar with at least one field of specific knowledge and nomenclature: petroleum and pharmaceutical companies with chemistry; precious gem cutters with crystallography; banks with economics and finance; metal processors with metallurgy. Every substance, product, and service relates to some field of knowledge and its terminology. Each of the armed services, discussed in a later chapter, has its version of a military vocabulary.

Decision makers at the different levels of planning and management must approve, disapprove, or modify matters they cannot comprehend because they know little or nothing about the field of knowledge involved. In some businesses there may be a number of different substantive fields pertinent to its activities. No one person can comprehend the content and special language of all of them. As our society becomes increasingly technical, more and more people at all levels of planning and management make decisions about matters they are not sure about. This also applies increasingly to ordinary consumers, since we must choose between products it is claimed have special qualities which we cannot judge or confirm. In their advertising, competing manufacturers often assert that their product is the only one with the qualities claimed by each of them.

What are persons making important decisions concerning simulation, planning, and management to do in such situations? First and foremost, they must acknowledge the subjects which require special knowledge they do not possess. They must have the self-confidence to admit these limitations to themselves and to others engaged in the matter at hand. The decision makers must choose between accepting the report and conclusions of the specialist who prepared the material and presents it, or procuring a "second opinion" from another competent source. If decisions are made that are equivocal because of insufficient knowledge, it is best for all concerned that this is openly acknowledged, rather than unannounced and presumed by many people to be certain.

Confidence in the specialist is justified, but not assured, if he or she has a record of accurate reports and reliable conclusions in the past. The personality and deportment of the specialist may inspire confidence, but no one knows if this is justified until it is confirmed. The decision maker can ascertain by perceptive questions the specialist's record in his field and the particular subject matter under consideration, how confident he is that the information and conclusions he is reporting are reliable, and how willing he is to risk his professional reputation on their accuracy. Sometimes the material and findings are presented as positive and certain in order to produce a more effective report and presentation. Upon further inquiry, it turns out that they are subject to qualification, are not precise but within a range of accuracy, or incorporate other limitations. To what extent is the specialist willing to acknowledge uncertainties, to check with others and respect peer review? Is his performance comparable to that of others in the same speciality with established reputations and reliability? Has the specialized subject matter been fully explained to the decision makers in the simplest possible everyday language, rather than in the esoteric communication employed among specialists in the field but incomprehensible to the uninitiated?

A system of checks on the reliability of specialized information may be established within an organization. If someone within the organization is knowledgeable concerning technical material submitted by a consultant, he can be asked by top management for comment or an evaluation. A protective procedure may be needed to ensure that there are no constraints on supplementary opinions by knowledgeable employees, nor retribution for a difference of opinion by the consultant or others in top management. When a particular competence is needed frequently as a check but is not available within the organization, a panel of outside consultants or a research establishment can be maintained on call.

If the technical decision to be made is important enough, the Delphi technique can be employed. A group of recognized experts in the subject of immediate concern are brought together to give their respective opinions and if possible to develop a consensus by a structured process of questions, anonymous answers, and progressive feedback to expand and deepen their initial responses. Delphi groups provide executive managers and senior planning analysts with the special knowledge and collective conclusions they need to make certain critical decisions which they cannot provide themselves without this assistance.

These considerations and possible supplementary actions help decision makers to determine whether their initial reactions are correct, whether they should be modified, whether they accept the recommendations by specialists, or whether another technical opinion is needed. Ideally, questions which cannot be answered reliably and decisions which would be too uncertain should be avoided or postponed, if possible. But with the technical content of human affairs increasing, this can rarely be done. Decision makers are confronted with the fact that the individual cannot resolve by himself matters that require special knowledge he does not have. In these situations he must mediate as best he can the judgment of those with the requisite knowledge and his responsibility as the decision maker. There is no absolute answer to this managerial dilemma.

## VIDEOELECTRONIC

Rapid acceleration in the development and use of electronics since the early 1990s has brought into being new forms of simulation and greatly increased interactive communication. The most ubiquitous of these are the television sets and personal desktop computers which are a feature in more and more households around the world. These two instruments will be combined into telecomputers which will permit a host of interactive operations and simulate a wide variety of activities, events, situations, and subjects on the telecomputer screen. Linked together by networks with sources of information, knowledge, and interactive services around the world, telecomputers will comprise a vast human resource for the dissemination of information, education, entertainment, research and analysis, managerial decision and action.

With their speed and calculative flexibility, and because their logic and language are mathematical, telecomputers are the preferred means of analyzing matters that can be expressed mathematically. Computer programs will continue to be conceived and written to make full use of this analytical instrument which will be available almost everywhere in the world. Simulations will include whatever can be processed and displayed on the computer screen. Telecomputers will be an important part of comprehensive planning, depending on how much of the necessary information and analysis can be handled by the computer.

In considering videoelectronic simulations and their effect on and use in planning, it is important to bear in mind how universal telecomputers will be in the future. In time they will be found in almost every household in industrialized nations, and in most homes in developing countries. Most people want a television set now more than any other possession except the several they cannot do without. Telecomputers will be more common than the separate telephone, replacing it at least in part by facsimile and incorporating it as part of the interactive computer.

The advantages for all concerned to be attained by almost universal use of the telecomputer may make it cost-effective for government and private enterprise to subsidize personal acquisition of these instruments. Some cities have donated low-flush toilets to save water and avoid having to construct new water supply facilities for a growing population. Others have replaced refrigerators using chlorofluorocarbons (CFCs) which contribute to the destruction of the earth's ozone layer, increasing radiation harmful to humans at ground level. Widespread use of computers may reduce the cost of tax collection, banking transactions, marketing programs, dissemination of information, and other interactive operations sufficiently to warrant subsidization.

Of course, this will take time, but more and more people are acquiring computers, and more and more children are being introduced to computer keyboards and becoming computer literate at an early age. As the years pass, the number will increase at a compound rate as they become indispensable for certain activities, as computer prices are reduced, and they become "user friendly" for those with little education as well as for the well-educated. Conceivably, the keyboard may be eliminated eventually and replaced by voice activation. The educational level of all people could be gradually increased by instructional programs on telecomputer networks. Successful services provided on the interactive system should generate continued growth.

In addition to hundreds of millions of telecomputers in homes, most government agencies, business corporations, research establishments, professional offices, and smaller enterprises will be using telecomputers as they do ordinary computers today: for accounting, operations management, and special supportive services and contacts. As additional features and functions are added, telecomputers will become an integral part of daily life.

Many of our activities and affairs are monitored, controlled, or directed by images generated on computer screens. Hundreds of thousands of radar and computer screens are viewed continuously by air traffic controllers at hundreds of airports around the world. Radars are standard equipment on the bridges of most seagoing commercial ships and hundreds of thousands of recreational vessels. Every naval warship incorporates videos in its command control center, displaying vital operational information. Larger cities are installing traffic control centers. Computer screens are an essential element in the operations control centers of public utilities which have been functioning for many years. Railroads and package delivery service centers have many video screens for tracking the movement of objects throughout the system. In one such center, huge video screens cover an entire nineteen-state, 17,000–mile system. In another, two million packages are processed every day during the Christmas season. Small video screens are now being marketed which show the geographical location of the automobile on one of a series of map displays on the dashboard, enabling the driver to chart his way to his destination. Will these become options and then standard equipment in hundreds of millions of cars?

People around the world view the products of the moving picture industry in theaters, meeting rooms, and outdoor gathering places. Almost everyone views videotapes at home. Buildings, structures, and open spaces are monitored on video screens for security surveillance and operational purposes. In television broadcasting studios, stock exchanges, financial markets, and the trading rooms of large banks and brokerage offices, the information required for their operations is displayed on banks of computer screens. Recently developed medical imaging devices display their views of our bodies on video screens; arthroscopic and some brain surgery is performed by observing simulations on a video screen. Robots are guided by the images recorded on the controller's video screen of what the camera mounted on the robot perceives.

These examples indicate the enormous number of video screens which will be functioning worldwide in the future, for many purposes and as part of many interactive services. Billions of people will view some video screen every day. It will be, if it is not now, the most noticeable, single man-made object in the human scene. Altogether they will constitute the most powerful informational force created by man: a giant array of images representing just about every kind of information and activity. If they display the same information at the same time, the collective impact is immediate and overwhelming. There are no delays in delivery, no gradual filtering and absorption of the information over time.

This massive informational system in the making presents problems never before encountered. The particular information presented on television, radio, and other mass media of communication is what they select to broadcast, chosen from the almost limitless supply of information available. If the simulations do not depict the data or situation accurately, viewers who rely on them are reacting and acting on erroneous information. If misinformation is widely distributed, unintentionally or deliberately, the negative effects on individuals and on society are pervasive, profound, and compounded if it continues.

If the subject matter selected is a dramatic event or situation, its impact is magnified and it is fixed in the viewer's mind and memory. The "Rodney King" beating is an example recognized and remembered around the world. An ordinary item of information, outdated and no longer "news", assumes undue importance if it is treated emotionally and repeated often enough in order to increase "audience ratings" and advertising revenues, or to achieve greater political impact. "Sound bites" are based on this principle. Digitalized video images are easily altered. Slight modifications may produce a better image in the producer's or editor's opinion. Image-making involves many more people than generally realized: acting and voice coaches, makeup artists, hair stylists, dress designers, even specialists who prepare food to appear most delectable on camera. An unattractive image frequently repeated can by itself, without accompanying substantive content, depreciate a person or situation associated with the negative image. Witness the famous "revolving door" sound bite concerning recidivism by parolees, aimed at presidential candidate Michael Dukakis. The destructive effects of a false or degraded representation are never completely compensated by a retraction.

How the system of videoelectronic communication in the making will operate depends on the ownership and control of broadcasting stations more than anything else. Ownership does not necessarily mean control, if some other interest determines policy and directs operations. Several owners controlling video communications for an entire nation are more economically independent and politically powerful than a number of owners competing for a smaller percentage of the total population. If the broadcasting stations belong to the government, it is presumed that they serve a political purpose. If they belong to private enterprise, it is assumed that profit is the imperative objective. Revenues from the sale of broadcast time for commercial advertising and other purposes depends on "audience ratings" as the measure of the number and type of viewers. The personal political and socioeconomic power associated with owning a television station is also a consideration.

Were the interests and intentions of the two general categories of ownership carried out to the fullest extent, unrestricted in any way, what is the likely outcome for video and telecomputer viewers? In the case of government-owned stations, the position and policies of the controlling political power will be favored in the subject matter selected and reinforced by the programs presented. Different points of view and proposals are unlikely to receive more than incidental attention. The danger, of course, is the likelihood that a political monopoly is created. At best this discourages gradual innovation and improvement, constraining the forces for change which always exist and which, if totally suppressed, accumulate and produce political upheaval. Or at worst, political monopoly can lead to the completely controlled society imagined by George Orwell in his novel *1984*.

In the case of private ownership, efforts will be directed toward maximizing profits by giant conglomerates. Enough commercial, political, or personal advertising must be sold and broadcast to produce the desired income. Competitive audience ratings must be maintained or increased: achieved if viewers are attracted and held by intensifying the emotional content of programs with the most enticing, titillating, entertaining subject matter and format. This built-in dynamic of emotional enhancement emphasizes programs that appeal to our primitive preferences and inclinations, our innate predilections, which civilization seeks to sublimate. Television writers, producers, and directors incorporate more and more material in the script which they may describe as innovative, creative, or freely expressive, but others maintain is societally disruptive: violence, cruelty, gunplay, murder, crime, delinquency, explicit sex, aberrant behavior. Programs emphasizing virtues, positive actions, and constructive contributions are few and far between. In autocratic societies they are used to extol behavioral conformity, imputed contentment, and idealized achievement.

The subjects that can be simulated on children's comics, cartoons, and games are almost limitless. They are designed to intrigue, to stimulate, and entertain, rather than positively motivate and educate. They are criticized by some groups for incorporating too much aggressiveness, violence, gunplay, and aberrant behavior, and for popularizing fantasies among the very young before they have learned to differentiate between fact and fantasy or fiction. This can be psychologically and socially disturbing for some children. In general, the influence of video games is not constructive. They are popular because they are designed to be emotionally appealing, even addictive. They represent an enormous opportunity to contribute to childrens' healthy development, positive motivation, education, sound family and societal values, as well as to entertain.

The best interests of society are served by avoiding the extreme development of either public or private television and radio station ownership. Any limitations raise questions concerning the type and degree of regulation desirable: for some the specter of excessive constraints, for others societally responsible employment of the "freedom of speech" guaranteed under the first amendment of the U.S. Constitution. Most people would agree that video and radio broadcasts should not incite revolution or civil disorder; misinform or declare a false emergency to produce panic; induce criminal acts, assassination, injurious assault, genocide; or technically distort video images to deliberately misrepresent an individual, group, event, or situation. Inevitable questions concerning the exact meaning or interpretation of regulations would be decided by the courts as they are today.

In a democracy, prevailing political and economic power and predominant public opinion determine the system of videoelectronic communication which serves the public. The present dynamic of development in the

United States favors private ownership to the point where it may eliminate or diminish public television for some time to come.

Supply and demand operate more effectively for cable television and interactive telecomputer services. Banking by telecomputer is limited to a range of inquiries and responses if the financial transactions which are involved are to function efficiently. Requests of a reference service must produce specific and useful responses if it is to survive. An order for an item listed in a video catalog must provide the item promptly as mail-order catalogs must do today. If they can afford it, viewers will pay for and otherwise support interactive programs that produce results which satisfy them. Supply and demand comprise a societally constructive interrelationship except when interactive programs cater to the worst in man. Regulations comparable to those that are justified for network television are needed for cable, radio, and interactive telecommunication.

The societal significance of video communications, the opportunities and the problems they present are generally similar the world over. However, they differ markedly in their extent, form, and functioning in different countries at different stages of socioeconomic development, with different histories, languages, political systems, religions, mores, and culture. Some have sophisticated systems covering the entire country, others only radio communication and telephone in a few cities. It is reported that over one-half of the world's population lives more than two hours' travel time from the nearest telephone, but satellite transmission will rapidly close this gap in communication.

There is no international jurisdiction and organizational authority that could assume responsibility for maintaining video communication standards agreed upon by participating nations, and it is unlikely that there will be one for a very long time to come. Even a much strengthened United Nations would find it difficult or impossible to undertake such an operation in the future. Each nation will continue to have its own policies and practices with respect to video communications. Some of them will be completely controlled by the central government, some will have both public and private broadcasting stations, and the United States will probably continue with private enterprise dominating electronic communication more than in any other country.

The globalization of transportation, commerce and manufacturing, banking and finance, and communication has resulted in Internet, e-mail, and other networks linking people with personal computers around the world. More and more people want to communicate quickly and easily with relatives, friends, acquaintances, professional peers, and sources of information wherever they may be. Scientists, engineers, physicians, lawyers, specialists of many kinds, and people with particular interests want to contact and communicate with those who share their interests or engage in the same activities. They may discuss substantive matters, find out what others are doing, circulate ideas and research reports for review, gossip, or engage in some other interaction.

Such interaction is desirable and beneficial for all concerned, except for certain subjects and activities which most people believe should be discouraged or prohibited: child pornography, deviant sex, shared hate, ethnic animosity, civil disruption, fraudulent promotion, deliberate disregard or circumvention of laws; whatever a group wants to communicate and discuss regardless of its societal consequences. Personal animosities, unfounded allegations, challenges, threats, rumors, falsifications, and just about anything else can be circulated if there are no standards and prohibitions. The full range of human interests, attitudes, preoccupations, and behaviors—both good and bad—are involved.

Estimates of how many people used the Internet in 1995 vary from 20 to 40 million concentrated in the United States, Canada, Australia, and Western Europe, half of them outside the United States. Other networks interconnect additional millions. Rates of growth are high. As telecomputer costs are reduced, we can expect hundreds of millions and ultimately several billion people interconnected videoelectronically. They will reside in more than 180 nations, speaking several hundred languages and dialects. Eventually, the disposition of telecomputers throughout the world will approximate the distribution of population.

A universal code has been formulated which will enable computers to represent the letters and characters of almost all languages, and software is being developed which will automatically translate any language into any other. Reference resources and current information will be accessible to everyone; messages will be sent in one language and received immediately in another, automatically translated during transmission. With such advances, English may not be the world language of telecommunications, except perhaps for those technical specifications, processing standards, and other matters of common interest or concern to which most nations might subscribe.

Because of the basic differences between nations, subjects regarded one way in one or several countries may be regarded very differently in others. What is comprehensible or incomprehensible, right or wrong, moral or immoral, polite or impolite, desirable or undesirable varies among nations. Qualities of character, intuitive reactions, general attitudes, priorities, and other attributes of individual people reflect their particular society. Languages, dialects, and other linguistic characteristics differ.

International agreements concerning operating frequencies, and other technical matters which benefit everyone, can be established because they are expressed in the universal language of mathematics. Other agreements or guidelines involving content, which are as uniform and universal as those for technical operations, cannot be formulated because of substantive differences among nations. They cannot be articulated in the precise form required for implementation because of the difficulties of exact definition in many different languages. Words, concepts, and precepts in one language have a different meaning in another; subject matter is understood and interpreted differently. Statements intended to be consistent are not.

Electronic communication is effected by telephone lines, cables, radio, and microwave electromagnetic transmission in the air. Orbiting and geostationary satellites are becoming primary components in global communication systems. Satellite receiving dishes are small and may become smaller and almost undetectable. Electronic microwaves permeate the upper atmosphere encircling the earth, without regard for national borders and other territorial boundaries on the earth's surface. These transmissions are accessible to anyone with the necessary equipment. The nature and extent of coding to secure communications from unwanted or malicious intrusion is being discussed.

Even if international agreements concerning video content are formulated successfully, it is difficult to imagine how hundreds of millions of electromagnetic transmissions throughout the earth's atmosphere could be monitored. Even nations with centralized control of communications would find global surveillance operationally impractical or impossible, and there are always those who find ways of circumventing the established system. Certain groups will show that they cannot perform an important societal function without unregulated access to global intercommunications. Others will claim the same access as a special privilege to which they are entitled.

It appears that the nature and extent of international communications prevents any shaping of their content and operation in the general public interest. They will evolve in the marketplace of supply and demand, reflecting the full range of human characteristics and activities. The different forces involved will coalesce over time to form a common denominator of constructive and destructive human behavior as expressed in video intercommunication.

Videoelectronics have been treated at some length because they are the most extensive and impactful form of simulation. Hundreds of millions of video screens at hand will be continually or frequently observed by most people. They will have a greater impact on individual behavior and societal affairs than anything that has occurred in the past. If this vast array of simulation does not accurately represent what is actually happening and has happened in the past, people will be living and functioning in accordance with a mistaken or intentionally altered image of the existing environment and of history. To the extent that video images are inaccurate or deliberately manipulated, consequent human actions are based on unrealities. The actual world and the world simulated on video screens become progressively more different, with consequences difficult for any of us to project or imagine today. The subject matter presented or available on call on personal computers will determine the information absorbed by viewers from this primary source. It will affect our reactions, attitudes, conclusions, and at least to some extent our behavior with respect to many matters. When information is presented emotionally, its effects are magnified. If it is inaccurate and deliberately distorted, the consequences could be catastrophic. If it functions constructively, video communication can be the single most positive force for individual and societal advancement.

## MECHANICAL

With no moving parts, the hummingbird feeder is the simplest mechanical simulator imaginable. Drawn to it by the red color of the artificial nectar in its container base, the bird inserts its long thin beak into the small opening in a simulated flower and feeds as it would from a natural flower. A simple form of mechanized simulation is the "rocking horse" for children found at larger shopping centers. Its movement mimicking riding a horse or some other animal diverts and exhilarates youngsters accompanying their mothers on shopping trips. Enlarged to adult size, such machines with a real saddle and girth are programmed to reproduce the violent motions of a bucking horse or steer, used to train professional bull riders, and occasionally for entertainment after a few beers at night spots in the Wild West.

Skeet machines loft "clay pigeons" in different trajectories simulating birds in flight for trapshooting practice and competitions. Baseball pitching machines deliver fast and curve balls to professional players in regular batting practice, maintaining and improving their batting skills. Were it cost-effective, these machines could be built to deliver a sequence of fast, slow, curve, and knuckle balls, change-ups, and sliders over and missing home plate, selected at random or simulating the observed strategy of a particular pitcher. Ball machines are available that pass a football to wide receivers. Others drive or loft tennis balls in different directions at different speeds in quick or slow succession, when a coach or a willing partner is not available to perform the task during prolonged practice sessions.

The machine that tests whether aircraft jet engines at full throttle can withstand larger birds shot into them at speeds simulating actual flight has been mentioned previously in another connection. Another such machine hurls pieces of two-by-four lumber against laminated glass to test whether this strengthening of window glass in regions subject to hurricanes would reduce this major cause of injury and death during gale-force storms. Some 50 years ago the first ejection seats for fighter pilots were successfully tested on the ground, using an artificial human figure wearing a parachute and shoulder-strapped in his seat in the cockpit. Forcefully ejected through the powerful slipstream along the aircraft, he could safely bail out when this was the last resort. Today, automobiles with dummies inside simulating people are crashed against walls to determine the need for and effectiveness of safety features.

In one test facility, a hydraulic-controlled and gas-powered ram shoots out from a 100–ton block of concrete with such force that it accelerates a sled from a standstill to 30 miles per hour in one-sixteenth of a second, along tracks 120 feet long. Impact dummies on the sled are brightly lit and recorded continuously by high-speed video cameras along the tracks and several movie cameras on the sled. Inside each dummy are several dozen sensors recording continuously and simultaneously the forces exerted on different parts of the body. Special cosmetic makeup is applied to the heads of the figures to record external lacerations and abrasions. Laser beams are employed to place the figures in exactly the same position to ensure consistent results from successive tests.

"Biofidelic" dummies have been developed which mimic the human more precisely than earlier models; for example, with neck vertebrae and other parts of the body constructed of aluminum which has closely the same porosity as human bones, and plastic skin fabricated to show surface damage. Realistic dummies have been used by the military to gauge the damage done by gun shots, and to test whether armored flooring and different fender design of army trucks will reduce injuries and deaths from land mines exploding beneath the vehicle. The Federal Aviation Administration uses dummies to investigate the relationship between the design of seats in airliners and the injuries sustained by passengers in forced landings and other emergency situations. Some scientists believe it may be possible some day to simulate for injury test purposes the human body and its vital organs as a virtual realistic image on the computer.

Subsonic and supersonic wind tunnels are standard mechanisms simulating airflow and other aerodynamic conditions for basic and applied research purposes. For many years aircraft designers have relied on the wind tunnel to provide the data concerning airflow, turbulence, and other aerodynamic characteristics needed to design an airplane. Almost 100 years ago, the Wright brothers constructed a small wooden wind tunnel in their bicycle shop in Dayton, Ohio, to test the configuration of the wings they were designing for their airplane, which achieved the first manned motorized flight. As an example of the many uses for wind tunnels, professional bicycle racers pedal their bicycles against the airflow created in the tunnels to simulate racing conditions, in order to determine their posture and the best design of their racing cycle. The effects of airflow on models of buildings, other structures, and products are investigated. The present state of the aerodynamic art does not support construction of a hypersonic wind tunnel which could test the aerodynamic characteristics of rockets, missiles, and planetary probes travelling at more than five times the speed of sound.

Hydrodynamic water tanks serve the same basic research purposes with respect to water that wind tunnels do with respect to air. They can simulate tidal waves of different sizes, tsunamis, turbulence, and hydrodynamic chaos. The movement of both water and floating, submerged, and semi-submerged structures can be measured simultaneously as each wave strikes. Scale models of vessels and propellers are subjected to a controlled flow of water to determine the hydrodynamic efficiency of different designs. The formation of minute air bubbles which erode or "cavitate" the metallic surface of propellers can be studied. These bubbles reduce the efficiency of the propellers, require more frequent replacement, and by making them noisier present a serious problem for military submarines. The effects of different size waves on ships, mooring facilities, pier pilings, and sea walls in harbors can be simulated and measured with laser beams. At the Institute for Marine Dynamics in Newfoundland, models of ships, barges, bridges, and oil drilling platforms are tested under conditions which simulate complex wave actions, underwater currents, high winds, and potentially dangerous ice conditions.

Anechoic chambers create and simulate space devoid of the sounds that are reflected from any and all of the surrounding objects and other surfaces which are part of the natural environment. This is achieved by covering the walls, ceiling, and floor of the chamber with closely spaced foam spikes sticking out, which dissipate and absorb the sound waves that strike them. Whatever is to be tested acoustically, without having to take reflected sound waves into account, is placed on an open screen surface installed in the space between the solid floor and ceiling of the anechoic chamber.

Shaketables do what their name implies. They simulate by mechanical action the forces to which objects are subjected and the movements they make during ordinary use, while they are being transported or self-propelled, and under the most severe conditions. The packaging of products can be tested on the shaketable to make sure that they can withstand the buffeting which occurs during "shipping and handling" and normal use. With more and more products manufactured in one country and transported far and wide for sale in other lands, protective packaging which reduces damage to a practical minimum is an economic necessity.

Trash containers used by many households in the United States are subject to violent shaking to empty their contents into automated refuse collection trucks. Their covers would soon be torn off were the containers not designed and manufactured to withstand the shocks. Testing a prototype cannot be done manually because several strong men could not duplicate the violent mechanical shaking by the automated equipment on the refuse trucks. Children's toys must endure handling and uses which only children can dream up and execute, although manufacturing and marketing strategy suggests that early destruction of toys is expected if not arranged. Automobile seats, electronic products, and space vehicles are tested on shaketables. Small-scale models are used to determine which structural designs of buildings and structures will withstand different types and magnitudes of earthquake tremors and shocks.

A final example of simpler mechanical simulators is the centrifuge. It can produce limited acceleration, velocities, and G-forces that cannot be produced on shaketables. Man-made products travelling in near and outer space are subject to such forces, as are pilots in supersonic fighter planes during violent aerial maneuvers. Large centrifuges simulate these forces, but the rapid acceleration of rockets, missiles, and space vehicles during takeoff cannot be attained on existing mechanical centrifuges.

Flight simulators used to train, test, and maintain the skill of aircraft pilots represent an investment of hundreds of millions of dollars. Functional replicas of the complete cockpit of an operating airplane, mounted on a motorized base, simulate the full range of movements of aircraft in flight. On screens encircling the cockpit are pictures of what the pilot and co-pilot would see through the forward and side windows during the actual flight operation and situations which are being simulated: takeoffs, landings, in-flight conditions of all kinds, mishaps, and extreme emergencies. The sounds, vibrations, and smells associated with the situation portrayed are replicated within the cockpit. The mock-up and simulated experience are so realistic that the U.S. Federal Aviation Administration is considering certifying pilots of commercial aircraft according to their performance in flight simulators, rather than requiring a number of instructional and co-pilot flights in operating aircraft.

A duplicate Apollo space vehicle served as an unusual simulation during one or more of the space flights to the moon. Rather than only the cockpit section of a commercial airliner used in flight simulation, the Apollo vehicle on the ground was an exact duplicate in every respect. Any questions, problems, or malfunctions occurring in the vehicle in space, which could not be handled by the rows of specialists at their computers in the "trench" at mission control, might be investigated by examining, manipulating, or creating the same malfunction in the duplicate vehicle at hand.

Traffic control centers in cities simulate the primary highway network on special displays and computer screens. Electronic sensors in the roadbed and cameras overlooking critical locations in the system provide further information. In response to a traffic tie-up disclosed on the simulation, traffic lights may be adjusted, police advised, emergency vehicles dispatched, electronic road signs activated, traffic advisories broadcast on radio, and major accidents reported on television. As noted in another connection, public utilities maintain similar control centers simulating the electrical, telephone, gas, or water supply and distribution systems. A more extensive simulation control center is operated by the Union Pacific railroad. Every mile of track, switch, and signal light in the 17,000-mile system is represented on 172 television screens meshed together in a display 600 feet long. Day and night, 54 dispatchers watch four- by five-foot touchscreen computer terminals, monitoring 850 trains and controlling switches and signal lights throughout the entire system, in constant voice communication with train crews and other operating personnel.

For over 30 years, robots have simulated and substituted for human beings in intricate, repetitive, and potentially dangerous operations on manufacturing assembly lines. There were some 500,000 of these employed around the world in 1995. They are the only means of operating where and when it is impossible for humans to function. They have dug trenches in the ocean bottom for communication cables, explored active volcanos, completed salvage operations beneath the ocean as deep as 20,000 feet, and performed maintenance on oil production installations underwater such as drilling, cutting, bolting, and replacing gaskets.

Some scientists believe that robots will be able to perform more and more like human beings, with stereovision, mechanical movements, electronically sensitive tactile "feel", and voice recognition. They will be able to memorize a range of movements, position themselves precisely in space, follow certain behavioral rules, and anticipate certain situations and adjust their actions accordingly.

One of the most unusual examples of mechanical simulation was the Atmospheric Research Module, a joint project of Russia and Germany. In June 1995, from a Russian submarine in the Berents Sea near Murmansk, a modified, long-range guided missile was launched on a 3,000–mile flight over the former Soviet Union, landing on the Kamchatka Peninsula north of Japan. The thermal convection module was designed by the Germans to perform simulations, in weightless conditions, of complex atmospheric and surface currents of planets and other spherical bodies. In effect, this novel launch acted as an enormous centrifuge or catapult hurling the research module into weightlessness for twenty minutes, long enough to conduct the desired experiments.

Each of the above simulations relates to planning. Rocking horses are part of a shopping center's plan to attract customers. Birds shot into jet engines and car crashes carrying human dummies are part of air and auto safety planning. Research useful in planning and operations is conducted in wind tunnels and water tanks, anechoic chambers, shaketables, and centrifuges. Control centers are essential elements in the planning and operational management of an increasing number of activities and organizations.

They are not, however, the kind of simulation needed for comprehensive planning of socioeconomic organisms, as the process and these organisms are defined and discussed in this book. Mechanical simulations are basically single-purpose mechanisms. They take into account all the elements involved in performing the particular investigation or operation they are intended to resolve. They are categorized as mechanical because their primary operational components are physical in nature, with few indefinite, judgmental, economic, social, or societal elements. Within these parameters, mechanical simulations are comprehensive in that they cover what must be treated to fulfill their specific purpose. But they do not encompass all of the elements and aspects which must be considered in comprehensively planning a socioeconomic organism. Simulation for this most inclusive and complex planning is discussed in a later section of this book.

Because they are designed to represent a specific condition or situation, mechanical simulations are usually accurate and adequate for the planning purposes intended. The motion of the centrifuge can be measured precisely, and the effects of G-forces on humans are measured by body sensors and reflected in the facial expressions of the person riding the rotating boom, recorded by an on-board camera. The movements of a shaketable can be measured, and their effects determined by subsequent examination of what was tested. Do flight simulations replicate the actual experience of pilots in flight? They do, according to the reports of those who take the tests, and the recordings of their physical reactions by sensors during the test.

Some mechanical simulations are accurate and adequate enough to support useful conclusions. The results of others may depend on circumstances. The sensors on the dummies simulating humans in car crash tests record the physical forces exerted, but they are not the same as would be experienced by a living person, nor as injurious in their total impact. A five-year-old who has never ridden a horse assumes that the movement of the rocking horse in a shopping center is true to equestrian life, but we know better.


## LITERARY—WRITTEN WORD

Most people recognize the importance of the written word in describing and discussing events and situations, making personal statements, "putting on paper" matters in mind, and passing on experience and knowledge from generation to generation. Discovered some 15,000 years ago, written language is a recent addition to the human scene. The process of recording observations and thoughts progressed from word of mouth to clay and stone tablets, to papyrus rolls, medieval manuscripts, the printed page, and most recently to the computer with its calculative capabilities, video screen, memory, and means of permanent storage.

Most people, however, do not have reason to consider that all written communication is simulation. What has happened historically, and what is occurring currently in the "real" world "out there" today is simulated by a representative image within our minds, expressed outwardly as a spoken or written statement, or by our actions. Our mental images are personal. They occur within our minds as cognitive impressions. Collectively, they may comprise a consensus among a few persons, or combine as a common simulation in the minds of many people.

The written word is a means of expressing our feelings, attitudes, reactions, convictions, observations, and the wide range of emotions and thoughts which we experience. They can be expressed verbally and videotaped, but written statements are less expensive when sight and sound are not important and when there is much to be said. They are readily revised, extended, copied, distributed, and preserved. Many people articulate their thoughts by writing them out to clarify and confirm what was formless in their minds. Those who know the language of mathematics use it to formulate their intellectual concepts, but other thoughts and all emotions they cannot express in numbers and symbols are stated in written words.

All literary works are simulations. Novels are "fictitious prose tales of considerable length, in which character and actions professing to represent those in real life are portrayed in a plot". Even historical, biographical, and autobiographical works, which seek to be as accurate and true to life as possible, are also simulations. As are movie scripts, newspaper reports, and news broadcasts that are normally read verbatim from written statements on the teleprompter screen. Literature simulates the personal perceptions and interpretations of an author concerning what happened, or his speculative or imaginary formulation of events and human behavior. Consequently, no two literary works are the same. Another form of literary simulation, drama, employs its multiple means of expression to depict happenings and features of human behavior. And poetry, as "a literary imitation or creation, a representation, often the idealized representation of nature or history", employs its own vocabulary of words, sounds, symbols, and grammar in rhythmic or some other connective form.

Few informed people deny the far-reaching and long-lasting effects of literature, which constitutes the core of a religious or legal system: the Old and New Testaments, the Koran, the words of Gautoma Buddha, the Magna Carta, the U.S. Constitution and Bill of Rights. The attitudes and behavior of those who read books are influenced in some way to some extent by the literature which they choose to read from what is available, or which is part of their formal education. Usually, the most widely read and influential literary figures in a country are natives. They most successfully reflect the language, history, culture, and aspirations of a nation. Goethe in Germany, Dante in Italy, Borges in Argentina, Tolstoy in Russia, Tagore in India. Shakespeare is the most widely known and quoted literary figure worldwide as well as within his native land. Nowadays, the impact of authors is vastly increased when there are movie and videotape versions of their works, once available only in book form, which are seen far and wide by millions of people. Publication is big business.

Although *belles lettres*—"the literature of aesthetic as distinguished from informational or utilitarian value"—influence us individually and collectively, they play no direct part in the formulation of plans, operations management, or planning research. The form, language, and content of novels, plays, poetry, and other literature are not suited to planning purposes. The authors incorporate their own subjective interpretations, imaginary concepts, personal viewpoints, and expository purposes in their creative writing. Much of what they have to say is expressed indirectly, often subtly. It is neither their intention nor their capability to formulate written material which treats subjects as objectively, accurately, precisely, and adequately as possible for informational and analytical purposes. Others can interpret, evaluate, and use this material for analysis, reaching conclusions, making decisions, and taking action. And it provides a reliable operational and historical record and reference. These qualities are rarely found in *belles lettres*, but they are essential in successful planning.

Journalistic literature—the written words in newspapers, periodicals, and the text read by newscasters on television—have an overwhelming and far-reaching impact. They are the main means of conveying current information and developing knowledge to the 5.5 billion people on earth in 1995. They influence how people react to the subjects covered, feel about them, and reach certain conclusions, more than any other source of information including the family, friends, acquaintances, the church, and state.

Journalistic literature is produced not only by professional newswriters, but by authors of best-selling books, scriptwriters, scientists, and others expressing their opinions, describing their works, or disseminating knowledge through the mass media which reach most people. Their written words not only report the event or discuss the subject, but the particular expression affects the attitudes of most readers toward the events and subjects treated and their conclusions concerning them. These reader reactions may persist for a long time, regardless of subsequent events or circumstances which suggest modification.

For years, the view of the American Civil War in the South was drawn from *Gone With The Wind*. How to raise infants and youngsters was explained by *Baby and Child Care*. *Everything You Wanted to Know About Sex* provided in written form what most families were unwilling to explain verbally. *Shogun* established in the minds of millions of readers and movie audiences an image of Japan during the earliest days of Western influence after centuries of national isolation. The group of *Godfather, Rocky, Karate Kid,* and other such movies have carried images of acceptable violence far and wide.

### Written Word

It is generally recognized that information must be accurate to be useful, and to avoid the damage that can be caused by wrong conclusions based on erroneous information. We know that our checkbooks and bank accounts must each be correct and in agreement to avoid bounced checks and credit problems. Financial transactions of all sorts, manufacturing schedules, or marketing strategies depend on accurate numbers. An important decision based on a wrong number can make a significant, even a catastrophic difference. As noted earlier in another connection, different people may understand and react to information differently, depending on their age, sex, education, experience, religion, and consequent attitudes and convictions. But all of us, for example, are irritated when we are given wrong directions to reach our destination, or confusing instructions on how to install or use a household appliance. We depend on the accuracy of the written word from the morning newspaper, during our activities throughout the day, until we turn out the light at night.

Since written information is a substantial part of the simulative substance of planning, its treatment is a critical consideration. There are certain facts, cautions, and procedures with respect to collecting, evaluating, and using information which must be considered if communication and simulation in planning are to be accurate and reliable. Law, engineering, and the physical sciences have their particular vocabularies and informational requirements. Planning does not, although it is an activity inherent in human affairs, formally established in government, business, and the military services and incorporated as a functional part of most fields of knowledge and most professions. Each of these three major applications of planning has selected its own descriptive terms. In business, there are corporate and lower-level organizational plans, and plans for different functional elements such as production, sales and distribution, finance, personnel. The military services prepare strategic, operational, tactical, logistic, and contingent plans. There are master, community, specific, and project plans in urban and regional planning by governments. Similar statistical, mathematical, and other techniques are employed by all of them. But there has been no synthesis of comparable terms, no amalgamation of similar substantive requirements, procedures, analytical techniques, and decision-making methods.

Planning is not yet recognized and established as a distinctive process and intellectual discipline, an area of special knowledge, professional competence, a way of managing and operating, the system underlying the endeavors of different organisms to select and attain designated goals and objectives. Its informational requirements have not yet been propounded and incorporated in existing graduate educational programs concerned with urban, regional, corporate, or project planning. At the present time, none of these programs offer or require a course devoted specifically to the collection, evaluation, and use of information from sources that are multiplying in number and diversity, including "remote sensing", which provides by far the largest amount and the greatest variety of information that can be gathered by any one method. Military intelligence and national security are subject areas which emphasize the operational importance of the written word. The accuracy, adequacy, clarity, unambiguity, timeliness, and comprehensibility of information can be a matter of life and death for individuals, victory or defeat for a nation or society. University courses in literature and creative writing treat the written word with respect to the subject matter and purpose which are their concern, not with information as such.

Information is of the essence in all human activity, including planning. And *accuracy* is the most important requirement for reliable information that does not mislead. Are the facts accurately identified and reported, the written statements correctly descriptive? Unless a person is so inclined by temperament and experience, accuracy requires a continuing awareness of its importance and deliberate efforts to achieve it. This means intentionally careful rather than casual or careless observations, double-checking one's observations, and carefully rereading written materials several times when this is possible, with brief intervals between each review. Computers make checking much easier.

Words and phrases are selected that have the same meaning for most people. Unfamiliar terms and complicated phrases are avoided in favor of the simplest synonyms and equivalent statements. What is said and written must favor correct and consistent understanding or interpretation. References are complete. First names or initials identify individuals with the same last name; spelling out the full name of organizations commonly referred to by acronyms makes for easier understanding and fewer mistakes. Descriptive words require further specification if they are interpreted differently by different people. What is the precise meaning of such words as large, many, widespread, soon, successful, good? Proper choice and use of words in planning are essential because written statements simulating situations, events, and actions constitute most of the substantive content of planning.

Substantive understanding is improved when comparable entities and concepts expressed in different words are identified. In the United States, inches, feet, and statute and nautical miles are not readily transferred, in most peoples' minds, into centimeters, meters, and kilometers, which are the units of measurement in Europe and other parts of the world. The same entities expressed differently are most readily and correctly understood when they are stated in the terms most familiar to those who will make the most use of them. Everyone benefits when the common aspects of the customs, mores, beliefs, and attitudes of different cultures are noted as well as those that are fundamentally antithetical.

Writing style affects accuracy. For example, the different elements and aspects in an informational statement are more likely to be separately identified and clearly comprehended when they are expressed in short sentences, rather than in long sentences incorporated in long paragraphs. Of course, they should not be so abbreviated that description and explanation are incomplete or unclear. The simplest words, prose, and direct statements avoid the different interpretations which can result from expressive embellishment. Writing emphasizing the informational quality of its content may be somewhat stilted at times, but since written words are most of the substantive content of planning, their effectiveness for this purpose is the critical requirement.

It is not enough to be accurate according to the dictionary definition of the word. A naval air intelligence report, for example, is incomplete if it correctly identifies a hostile cruiser but does not note its class or type, and two accompanying destroyers. Businesses want to know as much as time and cost permit concerning their chief competitors. An item of information noted but not included may turn out to be very important. Physicians and dentists want as much background information concerning the current health and medical history of their patients as the records reveal. This may lead in time to a system which enables people to maintain their personal health records on a tiny computer chip on a card carried in the handbag or wallet. It would eliminate trying to remember and write out on a form facts, figures, and dates covering years of medical history every time one visits a doctor or dentist for the first time. There are always limits to how much information can be collected and reported in the time available and at an acceptable cost. An awareness of the importance of *adequate* as well as accurate information is characteristic of those trained or experienced in gathering and transmitting information. People with this mind-set consider adequacy part of accuracy.

*Clarity* and unambiguity are two sides of the same informational coin. If we have not had occasion to test ourselves in this respect, we assume that we communicate clearly. To doubt this capability is self-deprecatory. One way of testing our communication capability is to compose an informational statement and see if a set of readers understand it in the same way. Or more practical and likely, we can note the occasions and explain to ourselves why we are misunderstood. Except for a few gifted people, maximum clarity requires conscious effort. This includes using words meaning the same thing to most people; spelling out rather than abbreviating or cutting short; organizing information into categories or groups of closely related content; reiterating important items of information to ensure that they are comprehended and recalled.

All this can come to naught when there is *ambiguity*. Words which can be understood in several ways impair the accuracy of information. Poorly written legislation, regulations, and procedures are examples. They may invite different interpretations which must be resolved, often at great cost, or they may contain deliberate loopholes or ambiguities which can be exploited. Some words have so many different meanings that their use without further specification may be confusing unless the context reveals the intended meaning. Thumbing through the dictionary reveals many such words. The following are examples of familiar words frequently employed, with the number of different meanings in parenthesis: carry (16), discharge (10), free (11), hard (17), sweep (11), time (20), world (13).

It is generally recognized that the *timeliness* of information is an important consideration. In military affairs, intelligence after the fact is useless for operational purposes. It can only be used for postmortem review or historical study. It was the timeliness of remote sensing information, revealing the installation of intercontinental ballistic missiles (ICBMs) in Cuba by the Soviet Union in 1962, which prevented nuclear war between the USSR and the United States. In business, important marketing information is of no immediate use if the products involved have already been distributed and cannot be redirected or recalled. The belated information may or may not apply to some future distribution. Preelection propaganda is useless after the polls close, at least until the next election. The availability of accurate information when needed yields the highest return, even if it cannot be complete. A blanket assumption that it is always best to produce information as soon as possible runs counter to the usual operating requirements and experience which do not call for such a rush. There is always the choice between the immediate availability, the accuracy, and the adequacy of information.

There are other generalizations which can be made concerning the most effective written information. Some information is best presented by words alone, some by numbers, some in graphical or other visual form, some by mathematical statement. In general, the more briefly the same substantive content can be stated, the better. If drawn out without increasing the informational content, there is that much more for users to absorb, and recall. Excessive compaction of messages to speed up their transmittal by eliminating grammatical elements that do not affect the content, results in a "shorthand" format which is more difficult for most people to understand.

Written information is the main means of expression, consideration, and conclusion in almost all forms of planning. As noted at the beginning of this section on literature, *belles lettres* may affect some planning indirectly. Literature as written material comprising information is of the essence because it constitutes most of the substantive content of planning.

## MUSICAL—SOUND

Music in the form of bird songs and other musical sounds in the animal world predated its use by humans by millions of years. There was no human ear and brain to declare these animal sounds musical, but they served their evolutionary purpose. Musical sounds by humans probably began as primitive statements of inner feelings and as a means of evoking a response by others. Together with bodily gestures, oral sounds, and spoken words, music was a way of communicating before a written language added another means of communication. It evolved as a universal expression of personal emotions: pleasure, pain, joy, grief, the full range of human feelings. In song, dance, music, hymns, dirges, and other forms, music provides collective enjoyment, entertainment, or other fulfillment for small and large groups of people. Music symbolizes meaningful personal experiences, and it is a vital element in the culture of a society reflecting its pleasures, beliefs, aspirations, and history.

Some music is specifically simulative. *The Sorcerer's Apprentice* by Paul Dukas depicts an imaginary humorous event. In *Afternoon of a Faun,* Claude Debussy expresses the relaxed meandering of this human creature in a sylvan setting. Johann Sebastian Bach memorializes a religious experience in the *Saint Matthew Passion;* Dmitri Shostakovich the heroic defense of Leningrad during World War II in his *Symphony No. 7.* Maurice Ravel simulates the quintessence and rhythmic sense of a particular dance form in *La Valse* without the constraints of the repetitive beat and regularity of an actual dance. In *Götterdämmerung,* Richard Wagner fictionalizes mythical heroic figures and events. Most of the music of these composers and of Mozart, Beethoven, Brahms, Chopin, or Sibelius is "pure" music in that its purpose is not descriptive or specifically suggestive beyond what its emotional and cognitive content imply.

Music has been called the "loftiest of the arts" because it is the most direct and intense expression of our feelings and imagination, without the conscious, deliberative, and cognitive content of literature and of the visual arts to a lesser extent. It simulates needs and desires within us, fulfills us in ways depending on the memories it evokes or the circumstances with which it is associated. It entertains us, sets our feet to dancing, our spirits soaring. It can stir our patriotic feelings. It is part of musical drama, theatrical dance, public ceremonies, and many of our other activities.

The child listens entranced, his developing body and mind absorbing the music. The juvenile carries his "boom box", enjoying the beat and continuous musical distraction. The adult finds entertainment, satisfaction, stimulus, diversion, inspiration, or other inner effects. The elderly find solace, comfort, remembrance, vestigial hope. A soothing background of music purportedly keeps us happy while we wait for a delayed appointment or a human response on an 800–number telephone line.

In such ways, music in itself and as part of our cultural heritage relates to planning indirectly, because it affects us in many ways. It affects our emotional sensitivity, our cultural attitudes and aesthetic values, our personal characteristics, and sometimes our substantive conclusions. Since people are involved in all planning, whatever affects us personally relates indirectly to planning, at least in some remote way.

Music involves planning by the composer. Rarely does a new musical work "spring full-blown" into the mind of a composer, needing only to be transformed into the notation of music. A musical form must be selected to best express what the composer has in mind or what may be required by circumstances. A musical structure must be adopted or developed for the composition. There must be a beginning and an end. The use of different musical instruments separately and in combination has to be worked out. Such decisions are not normally made in the preconscious mind of a composer, but are part of his or her cognitive planning.

The gifted composer, however, can conceive, hear, and develop a complete musical composition within his mind. He does not need to have the work performed to experience it. He can "hear" it in his head as precisely as if he had listened to it played by live musicians in an auditorium. Similarly, master chess players can remember hundreds of openings and other situations on the chessboard. Tartakower, one of the foremost chess players in the world during the 1920s, claimed he could recall every game he ever played. Many grandmasters can visualize and plan entire competitive games in their minds, without the actual chessmen and board at hand. Likewise, some composers do not need a piano and music score sheets to compose. Both conceive, organize, and plan their respective formulations within their preconscious minds.

The performance of music requires organized forethought, including preparatory rehearsals. For orchestral works, musicians, conductor, performers, stagehands, concert manager, and others must come together at the scheduled time ready and able to make their individual and combined contributions. They must transform the musical score, which simulates what the composer has in mind, into the sounds it represents. Chamber music involves few people but comparable planning. Most operas require a librettist working with the composer. In addition to members and supporting staff of the orchestra, an opera performance includes principal singers, prompter, chorus, stage and costume designers; and most recently, someone to translate into written form on a screen, which the audience can see and understand, the verbal content of an opera sung in a foreign language.

Music is part of planning when it is a business: companies producing musical instruments and manufacturing electronic equipment involving acoustics, artist agencies, and other organizations related to music; when music is a cultural concern of a community and an element in its budget; and when music is carefully selected in sound movies to stimulate an emotional reaction in the viewer which reinforces what he sees displayed on the screen. The background music is absorbed by our senses while we watch the movie, without our being aware that it is affecting us emotionally. Music can enhance the impact of public spectacles and events planned to stimulate, impress, inspire, intimidate, or arouse emotional reactions, attitudes, and consequent actions by masses of people.

As discussed in a previous section, the written words that comprise the language of literature are understood by most people; few people understand the graphical notation of music. Both are simulations. Written words represent the substantive matters described; music represents the structure of sounds conceived by the composer. These sounds constitute an additional simulation since the composer seeks to evoke in the listener the emotional-cognitive construct which he or she conceived and expressed in musical notation. Musical language has its own particular terms describing different considerations, such as harmony, homophony, counterpoint, leitmotif, modulation, timbre, semiquaver, speccato, triad, and many more.

## Sound

Sounds which are not music in the usual meaning of the word play a vital role in animal life: human and non-human. Some animals identify their offspring by sound, an identification essential in evolution. The Quelea birds in East Africa can locate, identify, and feed their chicks among literally hundreds of the young birds perched side by side on the branches of a small bush, refusing to pay attention to any others. What makes possible this identification by simulative sound in a massive swarm of hundreds of thousands or millions of Quelea birds remains a mystery. Many species of birds signal activities relating to mating, warning of an approaching predator, or territorial claims by sound or song. Some animals depend on another species sharing their habitat to provide the warning of danger which they cannot provide. Elephants have developed a language of low-frequency rumbles, and whales higher-frequency sounds, which enable them to communicate messages over long distances. Evolution has acted to select the different sound frequencies most suited to sound transmission through the air and through water. Many insects are also sound sensitive. In each of these examples among thousands, sounds simulate some condition or situation relating to successful survival.

Together with sight and smell, sounds alerted our hominid ancestors to the presence of game in dense vegetative growth, warning them of danger from other animals, alerting them to natural hazards, and providing rudimentary communication. The development of verbal language by Homo sapiens not so long ago introduced a new form of simulation with vast cognitive and cultural consequences. The special languages of different professions noted in various connections in this book have come about as scientific and technological advances produce new terms. In addition to the simulative sounds incorporated in movies, sign language simulates the unspoken language within the deaf person's mind. Lipreading simulates the language of the speaker by the movements of the mouth. Both the internalized language expressed by signs and the spoken language read by lips also simulate the actual conditions, situations, events, activities, and whatever else they depict.

The mechanism of human hearing involves two simulative systems. Special cells in our brains detect, locate, and also encode sounds coming from any direction in the 360 degrees of space around us. These encoded sound signals comprise part of the internal "maps" or representations of space we have within our minds. Our visual, auditory, olfactory, and tactile sensory systems combine to create a composite which is constantly altered and recreated as we react to the external world around us.

The Industrial Revolution brought about new sounds in the workplace and in the environment. Research has revealed that man-made noise can be disturbing and damaging. Prolonged exposure to loud noise which we hear, and to sounds of such high frequency that we do not consciously hear them, can cause damage and permanent loss of hearing before we are aware it is occurring. Invention and development of instruments simulating the effects of sound have made such research possible. Instruments recording the impact of different sounds at different intensities on the inner ear and hearing, and the effects of noise on the emotional-mental system measured by neural sensors, have produced medical information indicating the organic damage and psychological disturbance caused by loud noise.

For example, many people show increased aggressiveness and annoyance when exposed to noise. The person bothered by noise is more likely to oversimplify social relations or to act impulsively. Investigation of an unusually large number of collisions between emergency vehicles and private cars revealed that the sirens of ambulances, fire engines, and police cars were not heard by many people in air-conditioned cars with the windows closed, the radio turned on, and particularly when the driver is one of the many persons with some loss of hearing. Research indicates that emergency sirens are most likely to be heard in time to avoid collisions when their sound is high frequency, discordant rather than melodic, varying in intensity, interrupted rather than continuous. Such developments employing simulation could not have occurred without planning, and they affect planning by individuals and organizations.

Noise has become a recognized environmental concern and a matter of public policy and product design by private enterprise. Noise-level meters monitor excessive noise in many workplaces and in the outdoor environment. Eliminating sources of disruptive or damaging noise is the desirable solution when this is feasible. Shielding or redesigning noisy machinery, sound insulation, or workers wearing ear plugs or muffs may be required. Under public nuisance law, except in emergency situations or under exceptional circumstances, noisy construction activities are limited to those hours of the day when most people are not sleeping. Materials meeting certain sound insulation requirements are incorporated in many local building codes. Acoustical walls or earthen berms may be required as buffers between single-family residential subdivisions and the roar of traffic from an adjacent highway. Noise at urban airports has resulted in prescribed flight patterns which reduce the very loud noise and sonic vibration produced by jet aircraft taking off over adjacent residential areas. The sonic boom produced by supersonic aircraft is not yet an issue of public policy. The Concorde is the only such aircraft and its flight plans are drawn to reduce the effects of such booms on inhabited areas.

Private enterprise has produced effective sound insulation materials, protective ear plugs and muffs, double-pane windows with the air space in between reducing sound transmission. Small machines have been produced to emit sounds simulating the soothing sounds of the sea to lull insomniacs into peaceful sleep. Aircraft jet engine manufacturers redesigned engines so that they produce less noise without loss of power. Automobile manufacturers advertise low sound levels within their cars, making conversation among passengers and on the car phone easier and listening to the radio or playing music more pleasurable. Manufacturers of gasoline-powered leaf-blowers, lawnmowers, and other noisy machines are under pressure to reduce the disturbing sounds they make. In all of these activities the simulation of sound is involved.

In art and nature alike our knowledge is based primarily on observation of existing phenomena . . . first comes creation; then, second in sequence, comes theory trying to describe and explain.

Ernst Toch, *The Shaping Forces of Music*, 1958, p. iii

# Chapter 4

# Applications

## MEDICINE

Perhaps the most intensive and diverse use of simulation occurs in medicine as it is practiced in industrially developed nations. Since survival is an innate drive within us, we are deeply concerned with our physical well-being. In the United States, we spend over a trillion dollars annually on medical examinations, treatment, and surgery; hospital and home care; research, education, and advertising; health programs and insurance; exercise equipment and health clubs; and personal medication.

In "destructive" testing an object is subjected to an increasing intensity and diversity of physical shocks until it is damaged, breaks, or is completely destroyed. This is the most direct and convincing test of the durability of an object to external forces. As noted in the section of this book on mechanical simulation, the shaketable simulates the effects of rough handling and damage during transportation, earthquake tremors and shocks, or the "wear and tear" of operating conditions. Similarly, small-scale models of aircraft and other objects in model form or full size are subjected to dynamic tests in a wind tunnel which simulate the aerodynamic forces encountered in ordinary flight and under unusual conditions. Models of ships, marine propellers, and shore installations are placed in a hydrodynamic water tank to extrapolate the effects of hydraulic actions on them in the real world. A mathematical equation which accurately symbolizes the interactions between external forces and the physical condition of an object can replicate model tests on the computer and produce the results on its video screen.

Although destructive testing of people is morally and legally forbidden in reputable medicine, the Nazis performed such experimentation on victims of the Holocaust and prisoners of war during the Hitler regime. And in the United States during World War II, blind tests were conducted on patients deliberately exposed to high levels of nuclear radiation. Prison inmates and terminally ill people volunteer to test drugs, but experimentation with animals is the most common method of medical testing. So that useful deductions can be made, animals are selected for tests which most closely simulate humans in the medical matter under study.

Technological advances in recent years have expanded medical simulation. This is exemplified dramatically by the simulative instruments connected with sensors attached on and inside a patient in intensive care following surgery in a well-equipped hospital. They continuously monitor heartbeat, blood pressure, urine output, fluid balance, blood oxygen, and sugar content if the patient is diabetic. Each instrument is simulative, since amplification or some other modification of the initial input is incorporated in the measuring mechanism to produce an accurate recording of the condition. The instruments concentrated in intensive care are, of course, employed separately in medical practice outside the hospital. Cheaper versions of such instruments are available from mail-order catalogs for personal use in the home, such as thermometers, finger and electronic blood pressure monitors, blood glucose testers, and computerized devices recording the percentage of fat in the body. Professional blood analysis has been extended from examining its cellular composition and chemical characteristics relating to diabetes, infections, and other diseases to include prostatic specific antigens (PSA) and other components.

Instruments for medical purposes have been under development for a long time. The binaural stethoscope and the ophthalmoscope were invented about 150 years ago; x-rays were discovered 100 years ago. Today, four imaging mechanisms simulate internal conditions within the body, providing precise information for diagnosis, treatment, and the specific procedure required when surgery is called for by what the imaging reveals. Imaging has advanced to the point that exploratory surgery is rarely required these days.

Fluoroscopy records images on a fluorescent screen produced by x-rays transmitted through the body. Inserting a dye or another "marker" within certain systems or organs within the body highlights them for detailed examination. In optical imaging a minute lens attached to a fiberoptic filament is inserted in the body, enabling the diagnostician or surgeon to view through an eyepiece the area inside the body surrounding the light-emitting lens. It is used to explore and to operate on parts of the body: for example, the colon (colonoscopy), intestine (enteroscopy), abdomen (laparoscopy), and rectum (proctoscopy).

At first thought, optical imaging may seem to be direct viewing rather than simulation. It is a lens, however, and not human eyes which produces the initial image of the part within the body under examination. And the light rays from this man-made device are transmitted through a fiberglass filament into a man-made eyepiece or video screen. The natural optical mechanism of the eye receives the image and records it on the photoreceptors of the retina. This image is transmitted by the optic nerve to the brain for reconstitution into conscious awareness and emotional-cognitive consideration. And as noted earlier in this book, how we "see" and interpret this final, internalized mental image relates to our physiological and psychological state. Even prescription eyeglasses correct deficiencies in our natural eyesight to simulate what we consider a more accurate rendition of the object or scene in the "real world". With optical imaging there are five interventions between what is being viewed and its rendition in the conscious mind. With prescription eyeglasses there are three.

There is yet another simulation in connection with optical imaging which is involved in laparoscopy: surgery which allows instruments and a camera to travel into the body through small incisions. A "boot camp" has been established by the director of endolaparoscopic surgery at a foremost school of medicine to improve the necessary skills of such surgeons by a set of specially devised exercises simulating the visual and manually manipulative skills required with *both* hands while watching the video screen. As of late 1995, 400 "trainees" had attended the camp.

X-rays image the internal components and certain conditions within the body (computer-assisted tomography: CATSCAN), and also disclose areas of internal metabolic activity (positron emission tomography: PETSCAN). Ultrasonic machines produce simulations of the structure and activity of internal organs such as the heart, liver, or prostate, and tumorous growths. Magnetic resonance imaging (MRI) produces a detailed simulation of the internal composition and condition of the body. Hyperpolarized gas magnetic resonance imaging (HGMRI) shows lung and brain functioning, and blood vessels in the heart better than ordinary MRI.

High-resolution MRI can also be employed to produce a remarkably detailed digital, computerized, virtual view of the body along its entire length, as if it were sliced vertically millimeter by millimeter with a super-sharp precision knife, through the brain, heart, lungs, bones, liver, whatever is cut along the millimetric slice from head to toe. This computerized simulation is better for anatomical study than the traditional dissection of cadavers. Derived from an actual human body as a computer program, it can be viewed on a personal computer as often as desired along any one of the superthin slices, rather than only once in an ordinary dissection. The only thing missing in the computer version is tactile feel, odor, and the psychological effects of directly handling a human body. Within several months after its introduction in 1995, this computerized anatomical simulation was being used in 300 locations in 23 countries.

Surrogate intelligence is another form of simulation which is being applied slowly and tentatively in medical practice. Several such programs employed by attending physicians have supported more accurate diagnosis of a few illnesses than were made by physicians without the assistance of collective experience. The knowledge accumulated by foremost physicians during years of practice can be incorporated in a computer program. When not absolutely certain of a particular diagnosis, a physician can input the symptoms observed into a surrogate intelligence program and have called to his or her attention additional questions which might further clarify the condition described, or a more complete list of diagnostic possibilities than most physicians can recall. Computer programs can be updated regularly far more readily than reference books in looseleaf form.

Few people would suggest that a diagnosis be made by surrogate intelligence rather than the attending physician or a specialist called upon for an expert opinion. But few would support a physician who fails because of false pride or unjustified self-confidence to use information which is available, affordable, and could increase the assurance of correct diagnosis.

Computers are also employed in medicine for business and operational purposes as they are in most human activities in many countries. Patient records, billing, and other office activities are conducted on computers. There are few physicians' offices in the United States that do not contain one or more computers. And almost every activity in hospitals and health maintenance organizations (HMOs) is simulated on computers: admissions; patient and personnel records; administration, equipment, and supplies; marketing; cost accounting; tax, insurance, and financial affairs.

Simulation in psychiatric medicine dealing with the mind and emotional system is very different from the informational displays on video screens, instruments, and laboratory tests used in organic medicine. Simulations in psychiatry representing different psychological states and mental-emotional dynamics are terms expressing concepts, rather than visual images and scientific tests. Psychiatry is rooted in descriptive terms simulating basic realities of mental-emotional life, such as id, ego, superego, conscious, preconscious, unconscious, repression, obsession, delusion, affect, attachment, narcissism, transference. Each such term represents a psychological condition or dynamic force in the mental-emotional life or psyche of a human being. Because the terms are very general reflecting the present state of psychiatric knowledge, they subsume a wide range of definition, interpretation, diagnosis, and treatment by different psychiatrists. More specific simulations are not yet possible because the mental-emotional components of our being and our personal and societal behavior are much less understood than the physical system of our body, its functioning, and organic diseases affecting society at large.

Pharmaceutical advances are producing drugs which ameliorate certain psychological disorders, such as lithium for manic-depression, and prozac for mild depression, and risperidone to reduce the effects of schizophrenia. It is estimated that in the mid-1990s, three-quarters of psychiatric patients are taking a therapeutic drug. Imaging mechanisms revealing physical and emotional interrelationships within the brain are establishing definitive links between physical and psychological systems in man. For the most part, these have been considered and treated separately in the past. Advances in neural knowledge are made possible by such fast imaging methods as positron emission tomography which allow researchers to take snapshots of interactions between parts of the brain in action, receiving and processing various internal thoughts, reactions, and external stimuli.

Scientific research is confirming the significance of the unconscious mind in responding to meaning, forming emotional responses, and guiding most of our actions without our conscious awareness. Our brains are arranged so that key aspects of emotional life, such as primitive fears, operate largely independent of thought. Powerful emotions within us may override careful rational thought, without our realizing that this is occurring. Interrelationships between the psychological and physiological aspects of dreams are being explained by scientific experiments in sleep laboratories.

The function of that part of the mind just below conscious awareness and immediate recall as a precursor of deliberate thought is being confirmed by experiment. The preconscious recovers relevant information from unconscious memory, organizes it, and performs preliminary analysis involved in the thought emerging into consciousness. This appears to have been the experience of Thomas Edison, history's most prolific inventor, with 1,000 patents and 3,500 notebooks depicting the process of his creative thinking. The fact that "he wrote literally to find out what he was thinking" suggests that his preconscious mind was the critical element in his creative thought.

Behavioral research reveals our innate tendencies toward self-deception and wishful thinking. They are so strong that the individual needs to counter their internalized influence on his or her attitudes and thinking, with a keen awareness of the realities of the external world and a willingness to accept them. Collectively, people must seek or at least respect the truth, and there must be a means of identifying it throughout a society. Highly emotional people are attuned to emotional appeals, "low-intensity" people are more influenced by rational arguments. The more amiable the interpersonal relationships among members of a policy-making group, the more likely independent critical thought is replaced by "groupthink", the lowest common denominator of agreement. The significance of such human predilections and behavior for comprehensive planning is obvious.

This brief discussion of medical simulation also illustrates the difficulties posed for comprehensive planning when different intellectual disciplines and different professions employ special terms and their own operational language. Within the specialties, acronyms are often necessary as additional operational simulations, to eliminate the practical inefficiencies of using tongue-twisting, space-consuming, and memory-challenging terms. A number of these have been used in previous paragraphs; for example, MRI for magnetic resonance imaging, and PSA for prostatic specific antigen. This problem of understanding and communication is referred to in several previous sections of this book. No one person can comprehend and keep current with more than several disciplines and different operations. Incorporating them into comprehensive planning requires particular procedures, superior analysis, and extra managerial effort.

## MILITARY

Military histories do not treat simulation separately, as it is defined and discussed in this book. It seems reasonable to assume that some representation of how fighting forces might be deployed in different situations was developed once a ground or naval force was big enough to be divided into separate units which could be disposed differently on the battlefield or on the ocean. The manufacture of miniature "toy" soldiers was probably instigated to simulate tactical situations before they became playthings for children. To this day, small, non-professional armed forces in developing countries use objects in a sandbox or marks on bare ground to represent soldiers and military equipment, to study and explain their deployment in battle. This has probably been done throughout human history. Historians and military analysts employ similar graphical symbols to portray military engagements: the geographical situation, the disposition and movement of troops, artillery and missile emplacements and direction of fire, the location of important terrain features and installations.

During the past century or so, the use of simulation by the military services has vastly expanded as science and technology have advanced at a remarkable rate. Many of the mechanical and electronic simulations referred to throughout this book originated in the military services. Remote sensing, discussed in a previous section, was initiated and developed by the military into the most extensive and diverse simulative source of information concerning the earth and human activities for intelligence and operational purposes. Sound simulation devices and acoustical detection systems have been subjects for research by the U.S. Navy for many years, in connection with antisubmarine warfare, target identification, and silencing submarine movements. The U.S. Air Force was the first to build large centrifuges subjecting a person to up to ten times the force of gravity (Gs), to determine the effects of such pressures on fighter pilots during "dogfights" and violent defensive maneuvers to avoid hostile ground-to-air missiles.

The strategic decision has been made that U.S. military forces will emphasize high-technology weapons systems in the future. The intent is to first support, then supplement, and ultimately replace the soldier on the battlefield. War will be fought in large part by "smart weapons" with devastating accuracy and destructive force. This will require a high order of simulation because these advanced weapons systems will be controlled by military personnel at video screens located several hundred or even thousands of miles from the target area, or by automated directive systems incorporated in the weapons systems themselves.

As in medicine, the military cannot conduct "destructive testing" by matching two friendly forces against each other in an actual firefight resulting in the injury or death of some participants, in order to simulate as realistically as possible military operations against a potential enemy. The U.S. Army arranges large-scale mock battles covering several hundred square miles and lasting several days, between one regular army unit and another acting as a hostile force with actual or closely comparable "enemy" equipment. To train and test emergency procedures and crews, the U.S. Navy simulates as closely as possible the destruction caused by an enemy missile on a naval vessel, including feigned dead and wounded members of the crew covered with "blood". In the civilian sector, comparable disaster drills at airports and other public and private installations simulate emergency situations to test and improve the responses of emergency crews, equipment, vehicles, and procedures.

The video screens in military command centers serve a purpose with respect to military operations similar to the imaging machines in the intensive care units of well-equipped hospitals monitoring the condition of the patient, and the control and distribution centers of utility companies. Such command centers exist in every naval combat vessel, at the headquarters of every major army unit, at the operational headquarters of the strategic air defense system and the intercontinental ballistic force located inside mountains to provide protection against air attack. One type of command center, the U.S. Air Force Aircraft Warning and Air Command (AWAC), operates for fifteen hours on patrol at high altitudes overlooking a large ground area, protected by a squadron of fighter aircraft. At any one time, half of the crew of 24 specialists are looking at video screens recording aircraft movements for several hundred miles in all directions, identifying them as friendly or hostile when this can be done. Also, receiving information from various sources concerning what is happening in the airspace under surveillance, and transmiting what is revealed to those who decide what if any action to take, or acting on its own if the situation requires immediate response.

In each of these examples information is processed and analyzed, conclusions are reached, and decisions are made by observing and manipulating images formulated by computers and displayed on their video screens.

Human senses cannot see or absorb what must be detected within a large airspace to serve the purposes of a military command center. The situation outside the command center is simulated completely within an enclosed space without windows, which is electronically in close, continuous, and immediate contact with the exterior space it surveys.

Simulations are the brains of "smart" weapons. They substitute for the human senses when and where these cannot function effectively, and when surrogate intelligence can operate faster and more accurately than the human mind. The handheld antiaircraft "stinger" missile, an early version of a smart weapon now available around the world, is guided to its target by an infrared radiation heat-seeking device in its nose. Handheld rifles with infrared "sniperscope" telescopic sights are used at night; the human target is not visible to the unaided eye, but is seen as an image of a person produced by the heat emitted from the animate body. Air-to-ground missiles may be laser-directed or radar-guided. Smart torpedoes are acoustically guided. Targets appear as a "blip" or distinctive discontinuity in the continuous track of the radar or acoustical image on the electronic "retina" of these simulative devices guiding the missile or torpedo; as a "hot spot" or blurred profile in heat sensors; or as a "dark mass" different from its immediate surroundings for television. The geodetic information required to direct a ballistic missile to its target is programmed in its inertial guidance system; its programmed path cannot be altered in flight.

Direct visual control of missiles is relinquished to a simulative device from launch to impact on a target miles away. When the four air-to-air missiles clustered in a single AMRAM weapons system are fired from a fighter aircraft, their radar-directed sensor takes over. An electronic computer in each of the four missiles directed at one of the four hostile aircraft seen on the fighter pilot's radar screen in the cockpit plots a course which will intercept the moving targets out of sight but within range of the missiles, even when the radar-jamming mechanisms in the enemy aircraft are working. This disassociation of the pilot from hands-on guidance of missiles has progressed to the point that an experimental helmet is available which enables a pilot to direct a missile by movements of his head.

The missile has replaced long-range artillery and may in time replace the handheld automatic rifle. The Big Bertha siege gun developed by the Germans during World War I to reach Paris 76 miles away, and 16-inch battleship guns firing huge projectiles 20 miles over the horizon, are a thing of the past. They have been replaced by cruise missiles which can fly hundreds of miles over "hill and dale", guided by terrain maps implanted in their electronic brains. They make the necessary flight adjustments caused by wind and weather as they follow the course programmed to match the terrain below, flying low to escape radar detection close to the terrain features incorporated in the guidance system.

Such targeting was not possible until after World War II. The geographical coordinates associated with many places on earth were not accurate enough to serve as precise aiming points for intercontinental ballistic missiles directed at targets thousands of miles away. Errors in ground survey and the slightly oblate shape of the earth had to be taken into account for pinpoint accuracy. It was remote sensing from orbiting satellites and aircraft which produced more accurate maps and exact geographical coordinates for possible targets. The simulation represented by remote sensing contributed to the guidance of cruise missiles by electronic systems simulating human pilots.

Years ago, small, unmanned airplanes or "drones" were used in testing antiaircraft guns. They are used today for special reconnaissance and surveillance missions. Simulative guidance systems which automatically pilot, navigate, and geographically position an aircraft have been available for years. An airplane can be flown from takeoff to landing thousands of miles away without human hands touching the controls. U.S. military planners project that there will come a time when battles involving a considerable geographical area are won not by air strikes and forces on the ground, but by unmanned "aerocraft" positioned over the target area.

Such a weapon, guided and controlled by simulative devices, would be directed like a cruise missile to the target area. It would survey the area, comparing what it sees and senses with the map of the area in its computer "brain". It would confirm matches between the man-made facilities and installations it sees and those shown on its internalized "mental map", and identify features not recorded on the map. Its surrogate intelligence would analyze the situation, determine priorities among known and new targets, and launch its multiple smart weapons accordingly. All this could be done in seconds, or the unmanned aerocraft could transmit what it sees on the ground and its surrogate analysis to the command center far away, where live analysts and the commanding officer would decide what offensive and defensive actions the aerocraft should take. This decision involving several people would take longer than an automated response preprogrammed into the surrogate mind of the unmanned aerocraft. Such a machine might even return after executing its mission to its base or to an alternate site and be used again.

A large terrain model simulating such a scenario, with mechanical positioning arms and electronic detection devices, has been built in Orlando, Florida, to investigate unmanned, automated warfare. Such research is not only required to develop new weapons systems. It is just as essential to decide when existing weapons systems should be replaced by new ones which can be maintained in operational condition by military personnel, and withstand manhandling, environmental damage, and rough use in actual military operations.

There are innate limitations to how much operational complexity a human can manage. The most advanced air-combat systems impose rigorous requirements for successful pilot performance. As a single example, the pilot of an F-15 fighter aircraft faces 310 switches and 75 displays in the cockpit, 11 of them on the control stick, 9 on the throttle. The left hemisphere of the human brain administers, receives and records information, and establishes priorities. The right side flies the airplane. The two hemispheres must constantly communicate and cross-check. When this does not occur fast enough because of "informational overload" and mentally overwhelming complexity, this "biological barrier" can impair pilot performance. It may have been the cause of half of the fatalities of fighter pilots since World War II, flying hi-tech supersonic aircraft on training and other peacetime missions.

The U.S. Navy Triton-class, nuclear-powered submarine, carrying 24 intercontinental ballistic missiles each with 8 nuclear warheads, is in effect a several billion dollar simulation: 560 feet long, 4 stories high, displacing 18,000 tons. For its crew of 165 specially selected people to exist and perform within its titanium hull for 80 or more days submerged, the air inside must be constantly monitored, purified, and recirculated to approximate the earth's atmosphere. Water, food, and light must be provided; waste disposed. The underwater living and working environment is so different, with its routine of six hours on duty and twelve hours off, that there is no environmental awareness of day and night other than that suggested by the difference between the food served at breakfast, lunch, and dinner. Most of the lights are on all the time, with no nighttime darkness. Except for eight short messages from their families during the more than two and a half months submerged, which they cannot answer because it might reveal the sub's location, there is no personal communication between the crew and the outside world.

During its patrol the submarine must remain completely hidden from everyone except its command control center: capable of launching 192 nuclear warheads on its 24 ballistic missiles at 192 different targets up to 4,000 miles away, when ordered to do so by the president of the United States. Operating and weapons systems incorporate an array of simulative mechanisms relating to acoustics, communication, diving and ballast tank adjustments, speed, navigation and geographical position, nuclear propulsion, and every other specific operating system aboard. On a much smaller scale, high-flying aircraft and space vehicles also simulate normal living space, in an atmospheric environment fatal to human life unless it is enclosed within a protective structure and provided with the air its crew needs to survive.

The military services in the United States account for a large share of national expenditures. They involve several million people directly, and many more indirectly in connection with their ongoing operations and the procurement of supplies, equipment, and weapons. An order form for all the material things and human services the military forces require would be longer and more completely representative of everything our society produces than the order form for any other societal activity. To the extent they can, the military services utilize, encourage, and financially support scientific research and advanced technological developments which could serve a military purpose. Many mechanisms, planning procedures, and organizational arrangements initiated by the military are employed in the civil sector. Today, the military services have the confidence of the populace more than any other major segment of society, including civil government.

They engage in more intensive, extensive, and continuous planning than any other comparable category of human affairs. They employ more forms of simulation than anyone else. Planning is not only the essence of military operations; the military establishment itself is organized as an operational hierarchy of planning and control. The chain of authority and command necessary in the armed services makes it much easier to require the formulation and implementation of plans than it is in civil society, where individual choices are greater and refusal to comply is an option. Command headquarters are an integral part of military planning and operations, more so than the corporate planning staffs of some large corporations and the operations control rooms of utility companies, petroleum processing plants, and some manufacturers with automated production.

During peacetime the military services devote themselves to training; improving existing procedures, equipment, and weapons systems; developing new weapons; and preparing contingent plans for situations which could occur. Once military actions are imminent or war is declared, there is no time to prepare new plans. Efforts are concentrated on successfully carrying out those which have been formulated in case of the need. Plans can be revised or abandoned when necessary, but it takes time and usually requires revised logistics, altered tactics, and possibly changes in longer range strategy. While revisions are underway, military capabilities are temporarily reduced. All of these plans are simulations of presumed situations.

Disregarding the possibility of weapons more destructive than those that now exist, a half dozen nations have the means of delivering atomic bombs, deadly viruses and other destructive diseases, fatal nerve gases, radioactive and chemical poisoning. We can exterminate ourselves as a species. Recognizing this fact, for 30 years heads of state have assumed that those with such destructive capabilities will not use them because of "mutually assured destruction". If this presumed state of human affairs is incorrect or impermanent, the human race must expect a possible Armageddon and act accordingly.

If the presumption continues to be accurate and prevents nuclear and biological catastrophe, will people avoid self-destruction by waging war with unmanned automated weapons? Human societies have done something similar in the past, choosing champions to do battle and decide the issue. Dominant males in certain groups of animals engage in conflicts which establish territorial and reproductive rights, but rarely result in serious injury. Perhaps in a desperately dangerous future a chess match—a game which may have originated to study military strategy—or some other non-lethal contest or game of chance could decide political and tribal differences instead of war. In the meantime, in the early 1990s there are 140 USSR and 33 U.S. ballistic missile submarines, and 200 USSR and 88 U.S. hunter-killer submarines. At any one time at least one-third of these are on patrol beneath the surface of the seven seas, unseen and capable of delivering nuclear destruction many times the total firepower unleashed during both world wars.

## ENGINEERING—ARCHITECTURE

Engineers have to do with more human activities than any other profession. They are a key component of industrialized societies, keeping them functioning mechanically, and together with scientists directing their technological advancement. They do not, however, receive the public recognition they deserve for resolving technical questions and problems, and transforming all kinds of proposals and plans into finished products and completed projects. These accomplishments are not connected with engineers in the public mind because they are associated with the organizations, officials, entrepreneurs, and individuals other than engineers who instigate, promote, or underwrite most products and projects. And the people who use them are unaware of the role of the engineers, or take their crucial contribution for granted. As a consequence, engineers operate "in between" producers and consumers, largely unappreciated by the public at large.

As long ago as the ninth or tenth century B.C., "engineers" designed and directed the catapults used in war. And for many centuries thereafter they were concerned mainly with military matters and civil projects for heads of state and princes of the church. The Industrial Revolution led to the definition of engineering as the "art of managing machines". Since then the field has expanded enormously as science and technology have mechanized the world. The dictionary definition of engineering is now almost all-inclusive:

Applied science concerned with utilizing inorganic products of earth, properties of matter, sources of power in nature, and physical forces for supplying human needs in the form of structures, machines, manufactured products, precision instruments, industrial organizations, the means of lighting, heating, refrigeration, communication, transportation, sanitation, and public safety, and other productive work.[1]

The open-ended last phrase of this dictionary definition and the almost unlimited scope of engineering today are borne out by the continuing addition of new specializations within the field: automatic weapons systems, nuclear fission and fusion devices, medical instruments and prosthetics, computer design and production, information processing, aerospace vehicles and space stations, robotics, microsystems, genetic production and utilization. There appear to be as many different specializations in engineering, denoted by accompanying adjectives, as there are particular needs which provide enough demand to justify concentration in practice and engineering education.

This universality comes about because of the unique role of engineers in industrialized society. They are the middlemen and middlewomen who transform technical ideas, scientific concepts, proposed and approved projects of all kinds into operating mechanisms and physical structures in the real world. They resolve problems which occur continually in the technical systems that enable modern societies to function. As societies become more complex, maintaining the technical infrastructure becomes ever more crucial.

Almost all of the "necessities of life" in the United States today, which primitive people derived directly from nature, are now provided after intermediate processing of some kind. Other than sunlight, moonlight, lightning, and fire, we generate the lumens we live by from fossil fuels, wind, water, and radioactive matter. More and more of the water we drink is processed by treatment plants or produced as bottled water. As we continue to pollute surface sources and underground aquifers, drinking water must be processed to avoid a health hazard. Almost all the food we eat is altered in some artificial way: by spraying for different purposes; by the addition or subtraction of chemical components for dietary, preservative, or aesthetic reasons; and most recently, by genetic manipulation to improve the disease resistance, nutritious quality, production rate, or marketing of foodstuffs. The air we breathe is often conditioned in the workplace, home, and our cars to be hotter or colder than the natural atmosphere. The disposal of our bodily and production wastes involves treatment facilities of various kinds to avoid different forms of pollution harmful to our health or sensibilities. Even our entertainment is for the most part electronically produced or processed, rather than experienced directly in person.

This widespread intervention between the natural world and man's activities and products is characteristic of technologically advanced societies. The process of producing sound concepts and useful things involves a sequence of interrelated human efforts. It begins with investigating a tentative concept, intention, proposal, or commitment. At the end are the results of intermediate testing and development which confirm the instigating purpose and result in completing the planned project. Or the investigation reveals that the original idea is not feasible or its realization requires revision because of technical difficulties, cost, production problems, or some other demonstrable difficulty. It is this intermediate phase in the sequence of examination and realization which is the domain of the engineer.

As societal functions become more complex, technical, and scientific in nature, engineering expands its scope and depth of knowledge to perform its investigative and developmental functions. This has led to the increasing numbers of specializations referred to above. Some projects require so many of these that an overall or coordinating engineer is needed to make sure that the different components worked out by different specialists fit together. No one person or organization can encompass them all. The difference in knowledge which once existed between the engineer and the applied scientist and applied mathematician is disappearing as the scientific content and mathematical analysis of human activities increases. Engineers must know more science and more mathematics.

Simulation is crucial in the process of determining whether a concept is valid or the physical entity in mind works and can be used for the purposes intended. The concept cannot be verified or the proposed product confirmed until the research and development process is completed. Some form of simulation of the end objective is required which can be modified as the R&D process proceeds. It may be a drawing on paper or a visualization on the computer screen which can be transformed into a three-dimensional or perspective view, and shown as it would appear from different viewpoints. Many kinds of physical models are fabricated to simulate what is being investigated. As mathematical analysis advances, an increasing number of entities, conditions, situations, and events can be expressed mathematically and by engineering analysis performed on the computer with the results displayed on the computer screen. For example, automobile and aircraft design which used to require mock-up models and several years of progressive refinement and checking, can now be accomplished on computers in less time, using mathematical and graphical simulation. Any of the many simulations noted throughout this book can be used by engineers if they are relevant to the task at hand.

Crude sketches were probably the first form of simulation in "engineering" a few thousand years ago. Excellent drawings were the main means of representation by the two foremost engineers in history: Leonardo da Vinci and Thomas Alva Edison. They typified for their respective times the combination of engineering skill, inventiveness, and applied scientific knowledge which will be required increasingly in the future as technology progresses. Leonardo is known to more people as the painter of the Mona Lisa in the Louvre Museum in Paris and The Last Supper in a convent church in Milan than as the chief engineer, at different times, for two powerful dukes and a king. His famous Codex notebooks were filled with drawings and notes written in mirror image which simulated his many engineering devices and projects, his anatomical explorations, and his inventive and scientific ideas. More than 400 years later, Edison also simulated his over 1,000 inventions by drawings and explanatory statements in 3,500 notebooks, including the first electric light bulb, phonograph, motion picture camera, printing machine, and electric meter. Each simulation was drawn and described so clearly that an experimental or working model could be constructed by his laboratory assistants without further information.

Both engineering and the simulation it employs have developed so rapidly and so radically since Edison's death 65 years ago, he would be hard put to catch up today. Leonardo would require years of indoctrination before he could begin to comprehend so different a state of scientific and technical affairs as exists today. The high level of engineering sophistication is demonstrated in the nuclear-powered and nuclear-armed missile submarine referred to previously in connection with military applications of simulation. Another outstanding example is the complex engineering and extensive simulation required in space exploration and travel.

Space vehicles are conceived, designed, constructed, and sent on their missions: ranging from communication, photo reconnaissance, and other special-purpose, earth-orbiting satellites, to space vehicles carrying people to the moon, around the earth for weeks, and in space stations for years. Besides the usual engineering considerations concerning material selection, strength, weight, operational features, feasibility, cost, and reliability involved in designing and building any structure, space vehicles pose an additional set of requirements. What materials will best withstand the subzero temperatures and other environmental conditions in orbital and outer space? How can cellular panels for solar power, antennas for communication, and other appendages be tightly packaged so that they are small enough to be launched or carried into space, and then extended to function as intended? How is movement of the installation in space to be effected and controlled? How is information concerning the performance of the space vehicle itself, and the information gathered by its sensors collecting research data, to be recorded, stored, and relayed back to earth from hundreds, thousands, or millions of miles away as the vehicle speeds at thousands of miles per hour? How much of a "safety factor" should be built into component parts to forestall their failure, and how much "redundancy" by providing "back-up" systems to take over if the primary system fails?

An entirely new kind of living environment for a few people was devised, designed, and constructed: with its own self-contained atmosphere; special features required by weightlessness; provision for artificial power and light, food and drink, waste disposal, physical exercise, and relief from the psychological stress of living under most abnormal conditions. Within these confined quarters there is also the equipment required to control the movements of the vehicle in space, to communicate with the earth below, and to make the observations and conduct the research called for during the mission. As if these accomplishments were not enough of an achievement, a microenvironment is created within individual space suits, with the life support system as a backpack, allowing astronauts to move about in outer space and perform work while in earth orbit and to walk on the surface of the moon.

Within the natural environments simulated in the nuclear missile submarine and space vehicles, instruments continuously monitor internal and external conditions or events which could cause catastrophe. As many as 30 operators at the NASA Operations Control Center monitor the space vehicle: watching the simulations on their computer screens of different operational systems within the vehicle; wall displays of certain functions; and a large screen showing the exact position of the vehicle in space and its past and projected flight paths. They listen to and record the information transmitted from the space vehicle concerning its current condition, as a vital part of monitoring its performance; directing its operation when required; and detecting, diagnosing, and helping to correct problems. Sometimes ground controllers may use a full-size replica of the space vehicle on the ground to simulate a problem which has developed in its twin hurtling through space. In the case of Apollo 13, the lives of three astronauts depended on these simulations which enabled ground controllers to bring the severely damaged vehicle back from outer space, through the earth's atmosphere without burning up, and parachute-land it safely in the Pacific Ocean within close range of the waiting aircraft carrier.

Altogether, space operations represent the most inventive, diverse, complex, rigorous, and successful engineering in human history, and the most intensive use of simulation for many purposes.

## Architecture

Architecture shares with engineering the need to visualize the ultimate entity as the design process proceeds: as an internalized visual concept within the mind, a descriptive drawing, computer simulation, small-scale model, or some other form of representation. Until recent years, preliminary and working drawings prepared on a drafting board and written specifications simulated the completed structure accurately and in sufficient detail to guide its construction. This method dates back at least to Roman times when full-size architectural plans were inscribed on flat pavements alongside or near the Tiber River, and used by workmen to cut large blocks of marble transported to the site into pieces of marble of the exact size and shape required to construct the building. The pavement served as a drawing board with the designs for the building "drawn" full-size on its surface. "Blueprints" of this kind are reported to have been used for the Pantheon in Rome and the Temple of Apollo in Didyma, now in modern Turkey. They demonstrate precise calculations and considerable engineering skill.

The computer is replacing manual drafting. A structure can be represented visually on the computer screen in three dimensions and virtual reality, rather than depicted by a two-dimensional, isometric, or perspective drawing. The computer simulation can be modified in form, viewed from different angles and perspectives, measured, and annotated on the computer screen. The final design developed on the computer and recorded on a computer disk can be enlarged and printed out on paper or viewed on a video screen by those who finance the structure, review the simulation for necessary approvals, use it to direct construction, and plan the optimum utilization of the structure after it is completed and certified for human occupancy or use. Specifications can be expressed in the computer in as much detail, as many ramifications, and with as much supplementary information as desired.

Along with everything else, structures are becoming architecturally more complicated. Most buildings involve geological, climatic, and local environmental considerations; structural requirements; plumbing, electrical, heating and air-conditioning, telephone, cable television, and often additional systems. Each of these requires engineering know-how which few architects possess. No one architect or engineer can handle them all except, perhaps, for a deliberately simplified structure. Normally, the architect calls upon different engineers to meet technical requirements and to design the utility systems. There are other specialists who may be called on to design a high-volume cafeteria, auditoriums and meeting rooms with excellent architectural acoustics, or a building refitted structurally to meet seismic safety requirements.

The architect must obtain and coordinate the work of a number of engineers in the design process. His unique contribution is the "organization of space": determining the function, number, size, arrangement, interrelationships, and general characteristics of the different spaces that comprise the structure. In the design of the structure for the purposes intended, the architect is usually more sensitive than the engineer to the needs, characteristics, behavior, and desires of people. The engineer is usually more knowledgeable concerning technical subjects and mathematical analysis.

The architect is also responsible for the aesthetic quality of the structure. In both his spatial and aesthetic conclusions, he must make a conscious choice between the client's wishes and his own convictions if they conflict, as these usually do in some respect. Ordinarily, this results in a compromise between what the client prefers functionally and aesthetically and what the architect considers a superior design. Sometimes architects are willing to put aside practical requirements or important aesthetic preferences of the client in favor of what they consider better and more pleasing design. Most people find this hard to believe or difficult to detect, but it happens.

A residential architect was so enamored of the aesthetic quality of an uninterrupted straight-line facade with floor-to-ceiling doors and windows, he wanted the client to endure an undersized kitchen with the dual kitchen sinks—the most used fixture and the busiest spot in the home—installed up against a blank wall instead of facing a window smaller than the architect preferred, with a pleasant view. As another example, studies of the spatial requirements for a research and development center called for a four-story executive office building, containing enough space for the principal executives who needed to be near each other. The architectural firm wanted a taller building which would purportedly provide a more visible and aesthetically pleasing "vertical accent" in the complex of five two-story buildings. They persuaded the company president to approve adding two floors. This opened up the first two floors to intense maneuvering by middle managers wanting offices next to top management, producing the divisive personnel and operational problems associated with such scrambling for opportunistic proximity and reflected status.

Most people are confronted with alternative choices. Artists must decide whether to paint or to sculp what they want to express in the manner they prefer, or what they know current taste requires if they are to sell any of their works. Cézanne, for example, is reputed to have been "far more interested in his own patient search for beauty than in pleasing the public". Authors and publishers know that certain subjects and styles of writing will have few readers. At the present time, there are few if any poets in the United States who can make a living writing poetry. In the musical world, the late works of Beethoven were criticized at the time because of "obscurity, exaggeration", and "unintelligibility". Some of his concerti were called "unplayable". More recently, Igor Stravinsky's *The Rite of Spring* produced riotous reaction at its premiere. The works of living "modern" composers are often derided by audiences when first performed. Even in mathematics, there are works which attract very few people. A proffered proof of Fermat's Last Theorem could be validated 328 years after his death by only a dozen or so people in the world who comprehended the content of the proposed proof. In our daily lives, all of us are faced with situations where we must decide whether to do what we want regardless, what is more appropriate or considerate, or what is to our personal advantage.

For the engineer and architect, choosing between different partisan claims and firm beliefs concerning design is assisted by simulating them in small-scale models, or on computers showing them from different viewpoints or as experienced in "virtual reality". In the previous examples, the working drawings simulating the completed residence revealed the architect's intention, and the validity of the architectural firm's aesthetic reason for adding two stories to the executive office building in the R&D Center could have been visualized in a small-scale model.

## LAW—USE OF WORDS

Law is the most crucial element of democratic society. As the "authoritative regulator of social relations", law provides the cohesion and stability required for a society to function and develop. It cannot be so unalterable that change is impossible or so absolute it cannot be improved, nor so unrestrictive or unenforceable that it breeds increasing social turmoil and eventual disintegration of the existing society.

Law is the hallmark of civilization. It indicates the extent to which people want, or are willing, to sublimate primitive drives and self-interests to the "rule of law". It provides social order and gradual advancement of individual welfare. Law is the societal matrix which represents the form of government: democratic, royal, religious, military, tribal, or dictatorial. It expresses the political prerogatives of the regime and the general objective, type, and conduct of the planning which must take place in all societies if they are to function. Individual forethought is severely constrained if the society is in such turmoil that only the most primitive reactions and self-centered actions by its citizenry can be expected. And no constructive planning can be effected by groups of people if there is not enough "law and order" to ensure coherent interactions among different elements and activities of the society. Even the most restrictive legalities do not preclude planning, since it is inherent in some form in peoples' motivation and activities directed toward surviving individually and evolving as a species.

Primitive precepts of societal behavior were outgrowths of evolutionary instincts becoming established customs: concerning the care and protection of the immediate family, maintaining extended family ties, prohibiting incest, propitiating supernatural forces, collective action in the face of danger. As human intelligence and social awareness progressed, customs were extended as rules of behavior and societal organization: covering more aspects of individual activities, collective responsibilities, personal and property rights, civil and religious affairs, settlement of disputes, accumulation and transmission of knowledge, community guidance, and other matters important for the survival of the society. Handed down from generation to generation by word of mouth, such rules simulated a larger and larger body of acceptable behavior and desirable organization as the society developed internally, and external circumstances required new or revised prescriptions. It represented what the community decided through instinct, reasoning, and experience was necessary for societal success and survival.

With the development of writing, an era of more precise statement was ushered in. The first such statement known to us today, Hammurabi's law code for use in the courts of the Babylonian Empire, was formulated in cuneiform writing a mere 4,000 years ago. We are at the earliest stage of societal systems of law as we view them today, hopefully, with hundreds of thousands, perhaps millions, of years in the future for improvements by Homo sapiens.

The simulative situations were different before and after the advent of the written word. Regulation was by word of mouth. Although a verbal code of behavior might be altered to reflect drastic change, it could not incorporate and reliably transmit the continuous modifications and changes required as a society develops and changes progressively over time. There are too many different people recollecting what they were told and recounting it to others. The nature of spoken language precludes its use as a precise reference. It is the most imprecise form of communication: subject to the different vocabularies of different individuals; particular emphases, intonations, and other variations in delivery among speakers; and diverse understanding and interpretation by listeners. Not to mention that what listeners hear varies with auditory impairment, the acoustical situation, the circumstances under which precepts are recited, and the mental modification of what is heard, depending on the state of mind of the listener at the time.

Verbal regulations cannot be formulated accurately enough or enunciated consistently enough to *direct* individual behavior and societal actions. Only written laws can be precise enough to do this, although we know that they are subject to differences of interpretation. Written laws create reciprocal simulations. In one, written laws and regulations represent the realities of societal custom, experience, and tolerance. At the same time, in the other, they signify and enunciate how people must behave and act.

In democratic societies there is constant interaction between the two simulations: on the one hand, there are laws which codify people's customary behavior and stated preferences, and on the other, laws that are formulated by elected representatives empowered to enact regulations in the general public interest. For example, with respect to the first of the two simulations, customary driving habits must be taken into account if traffic regulations which call for different behavior behind the wheel are not to be ignored. And laws enacted by our elected representatives in the second category requiring us to use seat belts are supported by statistics indicating that they significantly reduce personal injury in automobile accidents.

Prohibition of alcoholic beverages in the United States is probably the supreme example of well-meaning legislation requiring unacceptable change in human behavior. Even dictators are limited in their regulation of society by what the populace will tolerate, although it may be a long time before unbearable living conditions bring about change. The time required for such change would be prolonged, perhaps delayed for a very long time, were the manipulations by the mass media hypothesized in George Orwell's *1984* to be realized. These would include deliberate misrepresentation of reality; reconstruction of history to suit current political purposes; manufactured events that never occurred to affect public attitudes and conclusions; ersatz entertainment and enjoyments portrayed on video screens rather than experienced directly.

The legal system symbolizes the political form and the operational characteristics of a society, which determine in general what is possible in planning, how plans are conceived, programmed, and effectuated. Because it is a process inherent in human affairs, planning is occurring all the time in all societies. But the purposes, specific objectives, and methodology are different in different regimes, at different stages in the socioeconomic and technological development of the society, and depending on circumstances within and outside the society. Objectives may be modest or ambitious. They may have to do with shorter range operations or longer range strategic intentions. The means and methods of planning may be coercive, persuasive, collegial, or consensual; centralized or decentralized; formally organized or casually conducted. Decisions may be made at different managerial levels or with the advice and consent of the majority of those involved. Planning functions differently in different economic systems. The existing situation and decisions concerning such considerations determine the type of planning required, and what it can and cannot accomplish in a particular society at a given time under existing conditions.

The United States is organized and functions under the "rule of law" more completely than any other nation in the world today. Since its inception only 220 years ago, it has introduced, considered, and enacted more laws at its three levels of government—and engaged in more actions in its courts—than any other nation in history. With 50 states, over 3,000 counties, and many times as many municipalities, each empowered to enact laws, the flood of legislation is overwhelming. With federal and state supreme and appellate courts, district and chancery courts, municipal courts, and private judiciaries, the United States is by far the most litigious nation in the world. There are more lawyers per capita, more public and private money spent on litigation, and a higher percentage of the population in prison than any other country in the world.

The first thought of those concerned with a serious social situation or a major problem involving the populace is usually to pass another law. Reform by statute has remained the primary characteristic of American government and law. Several times the number of laws enacted are introduced into the "hopper" every year by legislators, to impress their constituents or for other purely political purposes, knowing full well that the proposed laws will not be formally considered much less enacted. Legislators are also aware that the rules and regulations required to implement many statutes, worked out after their passage, determine what the law really means for those affected by its specific provisions. Knowledgeable special interests focus their persuasive attention on this final stage of the legislative process. Unpublicized "riders", amendments, and surreptitious insertions in laws by legislative committees—often unrelated to the subject matter at hand—are used for partisan purposes or to reward political supporters.

Legislative excesses and the eagerness or willingness of many lawyers to take any legal action which promises to be profitable has produced a situation bordering on legislative and judicial deadlock. The average citizen has learned to stay as far away as he can from lawyers and the attendant costs, unless the legal case or concern is so strong that he or she is willing to undertake the prolonged, stressful, distressing, and costly procedure. In some areas of the law, patchwork legislation has produced complication and confusion beyond legal understanding. As a single example, federal tax law in the United States has reached a point where it is actually incomprehensible, even to tax lawyers in private practice and those employed within the Internal Revenue Service. In 1913, the entire tax law, plus explanations and other related material, fit into a single 400-page volume. In 1995, it had expanded into 22 volumes totalling 40,500 pages. Many outdated laws remain on the books until unusual circumstances or a resourceful lawyer resurrects them for a purpose usually different than originally intended. Such unique uses of outdated laws often create a new set of legal considerations added to the overabundance of complications already existing.

With social changes, industrialization, and advances in science and technology, law has been broken up into as many specializations as have other subjects and professions. For example:

| | | |
|---|---|---|
| antitrust | entertainment | patent |
| civil | equity | personal injury |
| common | genetics | private |
| constitutional | international | probate |
| contract | land use | real estate |
| copyright | liability | securities |
| criminal | libel | space |
| divorce | malpractice | sports |
| ecclesiastical | maritime | tax |
| environmental | martial | tort |

Within these specializations there are existing subclassifications or concentrations, and new ones are created from time to time. As an example, "tortious interference" was known to only a few lawyers until it was employed in late 1995, in a widely publicized challenge by a tobacco company to a proposed program on CBS's *60 Minutes*.

Like other substantive fields and professions, law has its own specialized vocabulary leaving casual spectators in the dark as lawyers and justices carry on in a language of their own: mandamus, certiorari, writ, habeas corpus, amicus curiae, and a host of terms unfamiliar to the ordinary citizen. Because of their historical origin, many of these are expressed in Latin, a language which is understood by fewer and fewer Americans. Many legal expressions in ordinary English cannot be understood without special knowledge and familiarity with their use in law: mitigation obligation, redeeming social importance, advocacy of abstract doctrine, true statement of facts, eminent domain, and many others. Only those who have studied law understand its substantive language and the specific ways it is effectuated in society. Can a process, incomprehensible to most people, serve successfully as the directive basis for constructive individual and collective behavior in a democracy? Could it become a body of precepts and ritual enforcement which is accepted on faith as sacrosanct by the populace, with lawyers as its priestly practitioners?

The purpose of the above observations is not to pass judgment on the law as presently practiced in the United States, but to illustrate the simulative framework of law and societal behavior within which planning must function. The nature of planning and its success, on the one hand, and the legal system which determines the conduct of human affairs, on the other, are two inseparable aspects of the same existential reality. The aspects of human behavior and the organization of human activities that are similar for all people are incorporated in the laws of almost all countries. Except for these commonalities, the legal simulation which directs individual and societal behavior is different in different countries, reflecting their history, culture, economy, form of government, and the aspirations of the people.

Throughout history, royal, religious, and secular authorities have controlled human affairs in different countries at different times. They have shared certain features of law directed toward maintaining a peaceable, productive, and morally observant society. The methods of analysis and projection employed by the different regimes to prepare and implement plans are comparable. But those who make the decisions, their objectives, the means and methods of achieving them, and the criteria of success are different.

Religious law is considered by believers to be divinely inspired. The word of God is infallible or subject to reinterpretation only by religious authorities. But what is meant by the divine pronouncements, how they are to be interpreted, and what they allow and forbid is subject to debate and different conclusion by religious scholars of each faith. Religious regimes are by no means as benign as might be hoped or even expected. Under canon law, at times they have morally and legally justified the torture and death of people with different religious beliefs and those accused of being influenced by the Devil. Assassination of those regarded as disrespectful, blasphemous, or actively pursuing contrary aims is condoned by some religions. Compliant behavior is rewarded in the afterlife.

Secular law, as it has evolved in the United States, also simulates ethically and societally permissible individual and collective behavior. It prescribes penalties and punishment for transgressions, including the death sentence in many states, and provides inducements for proper conduct. Imprisonment for offenses against the civil code of law has tripled in the United States during the past twenty years. The costs of incarceration have become a major item in governmental budgets, increasing from $6.8 to $30 billion in the past 25 years. In mid-1995, more than 1.5 million adults were incarcerated in the United States. Atrocities have been committed as lawful acts under secular law. Accused "witches" were prosecuted and executed in Salem, Massachusetts, only 300 years ago.

Religious and secular law change as conditions and prevailing attitudes change, but both maintain the basic objective of a safe and politically stable society, progressively more productive and more civilized. Except in relatively few matters concerning which there is strong or even violent disagreement, religious and secular law share many of the same moral values and standards of good and bad behavior. The most significant difference between the two is whether religious authorities formulate and implement the law according to divine revelations and religious precepts, or whether it is conceived and implemented by civilian officials representing the populace and public concurrence. From a professional point of view, planners can work effectively under either religious or secular rules of law, provided their personal morality and societal convictions are not compromised to the point that the planner is uncomfortable or less effective in his or her work.

As scientific knowledge advances, more and more is revealed concerning our evolutionary past extending back several million years as hominids; concerning the earth's place in our galaxy, and our galaxy within the enormous expanse of the universe. Belief that human origin and religions relating to an anthropomorphic being or spirit existing several thousand years ago must be reconciled with our much earlier evolutionary beginning and the awesome force which created the earth and universe billions of years ago. Rather than a legal code of conduct based on divine precepts as they are conceived by many today, an equally ethical and more universally acceptable code of deportment and law can be based on our individual and collective behavior as human beings, required if we are to survive and prosper as a species.

### Use of Words

Law and literature are two simulations formulated and employed with written words. Law is a special part of the total preserved writings belonging to a given language or people. It is not that part which is notable for literary form or expression: belles-lettres. But because it fulfills the most essential requirement for any society to function, it transcends in its significance all other literature. Written words are "of the essence". Theoretically, but all too often not in practice, they are intended to indicate precisely what the law decrees. But there is the difficulty or impossibility in some instances of exact expression. Language is an imperfect means of transmitting information. It is subject to misunderstanding and different interpretations. As noted earlier in the section on the written word under "Literature", a single word in the English language may have as many as ten or more distinct dictionary definitions and uses.

An example of the legal difficulties that can arise concerning the meaning of a single word involves the everyday verb "use". A federal law imposes a mandatory five-year prison sentence on anyone who "uses or carries" a gun in connection with a drug offense. Is a gun "used" when it is hidden under several piles of old clothes in the trunk of an automobile carrying drugs under the front seat? Or when one is found unloaded and locked in a box in an apartment where drugs are sold? These questions worked their way up from two U.S. Court of Appeals decisions to the U.S. Supreme Court, which concluded unanimously that

"use" must connote more than mere possession of a gun. . . . The government must show that the defendant actively employed the firearm during and in relation to the [actual] crime. This "certainly includes brandishing, displaying, bartering, striking with and, most obviously, firing or attempting to fire, a firearm". Also included is verbally referring to a gun.[2]

The Supreme Court sent the matter back to the Appeals Court to consider whether the defendant might have "carried" a gun, also in violation of the same law but not considered by the Appeals Court. Hundreds of prison inmates may now seek to shorten their prison terms, and hundreds of people will have wasted much time and public money because of careless use of a word.

The matter is not yet clarified. The dictionary definition of "gun" and "firearm" are different. In view of the development of new weapons, including missiles and deadly or paralyzing sprays, should the definitions of gun and firearm include "any weapon which propels a bullet or other object or material which can cause injury or death to a human being"? As words are added to form more completely descriptive phrases or sentences, the possibility of different interpretations may be decreased or increased, depending on whether the added words make the statement clearer, more specific, and less subject to different interpretations. Or are the added words subject themselves to a new set of questions or interpretations to be settled in the courts.

It is often impossible to write with more precision than is done in statutes in common law. Rather than risk the harm that can develop from the use of unduly exact terms in situations where they do not apply, most laws are written in very general form, whether derived from legislative enactment or judicial decisions. Case law accumulates to clarify the meaning and application of laws. They cannot be composed so exactly that all valid questions that may arise and unanticipated situations requiring review are accounted for in advance. Progressive development brought about by appeals to the courts provide for constructive change in laws to meet changing conditions, public consensus, and needed improvements in the law itself. But this should not be necessary because of careless thinking and ambiguous wording in formulating laws.

There are no laws so universally conceived and written for all time that they will always be applicable under all circumstances. The ongoing arguments concerning what the U.S. Constitution simulates in the way of individual and collective deportment do not claim that the original documents, written over 200 years ago, indicate precisely what they require and prohibit in the way of human conduct throughout the United States today. The arguments are really about which of several subsequent interpretations of the original language should prevail, each of which can be logically argued on the basis of very different but reasonable assumptions. The actual controlling constitution is in large part the constitutional law that the courts have made in the name of the written instrument.

There are numerous terms employed in legal practice which require and receive progressive clarification as new situations and circumstances arise. For example: administrative relief, beyond a reasonable doubt, clear and present danger, diminished mental capacity, good faith support, indecent programming, social value, obscene material, sexual harassment, sovereign immunity. The likelihood of most laws being progressively clarified or modified over time does not lessen the importance of their careful formulation in the first place. All too often, not enough time, effort, and thought are devoted to devising the original legislation. Careless writing can complicate and prolong implementing the law because of litigation that need never to have occurred. "Loopholes" left in the law will surely be exploited, cause needless complications and costs, and the adverse consequences of actions which the legislation sought to prevent. Some of the requirements of composing information in written form, which can be transmitted without ambiguity among different people, are noted in the section of this book on literature as simulation.

One group of laws is conceived, written, and enacted to simulate what is considered necessary, acceptable, or desirable societal behavior with respect to human affairs. They represent political and philosophical conclusions concerning the desirable functioning of society, and constitute the main means of achieving particular behavioral and operational objectives. Another group of laws, probably larger in size, is manipulative rather than straightforward. There are two, three, or more purposes incorporated in the law, an extraneous addition, a hidden or disguised provision, a tactical partisan purpose below and beyond the basic behavioral objective.

There are laws that are carelessly written because legislators and their supporting staffs do not take the time and expend the effort justified for so potentially significant an effort. The legal competence required is not obtained or the legislation is not seriously considered in the first place. Some laws are written without regard to whether they can be enforced without extensive changes in regulatory or inspection procedures, or whether their enactment will impose additional costs on a community struggling to make ends meet, and on those affected by the legislation. Some jurisdictions require cost estimates accompanying proposed legislation, but these are often overoptimistic, inaccurate, or insufficient. Some laws, especially those concerning governmental budgets, are presented to the legislature in such complex form that they are incomprehensible without extensive study, which few legislators undertake. They focus on the items most important to them politically, often without understanding the full import of what they are enacting. Budget bills and other complex legislation can be formulated and presented in a form which alerts the ordinary person to their provisions and significant implications.

As noted previously, there are laws introduced by legislators to convince their constituents or a particular special interest that they have their concerns in mind, although they know that the law may not be taken up or will not be approved by the legislative committee which reviews it and recommends consideration by the full legislative body. The bogus bill can be publicized in the lawmaker's electoral district as a responsive and valiant attempt against the odds to satisfy their wishes, without any indication that the entire effort is concocted. There is the infamous "rider" attached to legislation with which it may have no logical connection, enacted unnoticed except by those who study the law carefully. Fellow legislators may decide not to call attention to it because they may want to use the tactic themselves some time in the future. Without any attempt to conceal it or make it inconspicuous, the rider may be attached to legislation which is so popular or so necessary, fiscally crucial, or the product of so much "blood, sweat, and tears", that its perpetrators hope it will pass despite everyone's awareness that the rider would not be enacted on its own. There are laws enunciating a constructive public purpose desired by most of the electorate, but so written that the rules and regulations required for their implementation after their much publicized enactment permit special interests or political supporters to be singled out and favored, or other objectives to be attained that bear little or no relation to the stated intent of the legislation. There is "blackmail" legislation carefully crafted to incorporate provisions which would not be enacted separately, but may be accepted nonetheless because of the dire consequences of rejecting the law as a whole.

There is almost no limit to the legislative manipulations attempted to achieve political purposes different from or in addition to those initially intended or outwardly professed. And there has developed throughout the United States an attitude that ignoring, misinterpreting, taking advantage of any and all inadvertent loopholes in a law, or difficulties of enforcement, is not only morally permissible but accepted as a sign of initiative and ingenuity. This is one of the reasons why the United States has more lawyers per capita and is the most litigious nation on earth.

Addressing the valid questions inherent in our legal system and answering them in the courts has brought about progressive clarification and gradual improvement of the system as a primary instrument of individual and collective justice and behavior. It has gradually changed to meet the changes which occur in us individually and in our society. None of this advancement can be credited to the manipulative maneuvers practiced by our legislatures. In this regard they denigrate rather than uphold legal morality.

It is within the matrix of federal, state, and local laws, regulations, and penalties that planning occurs. The legal system, as conceived, written, and practiced, shapes every aspect of planning: what it can attempt, how it must be conducted, and what it can achieve. The sounder and more astute the planning, the more likely that positive results can be achieved within the existing legal framework.

## NOTES

1. *Webster's New Collegiate Dictionary* (Springfield, MA: Merriam, 1951), p. 273.

2. Linda Greenhouse, "Justices Narrow Definition of 'Using a Gun', Wording in Drug Law Led to Widely Different Interpretations", *New York Times,* 7 December 1995, p. A12z.

# Chapter 5

# Institutions

---

## RELIGION

Religion is an important consideration in planning. Together with secular authority, it is a primary determinant of the form and functioning of many societies. This is most evident in countries outside the United States. Almost nine-tenths of the world population of more than 5.5 billion people, but less than two-thirds of the U.S. population, are reported as members of an organized religion.

Religion is a term encompassing the supernatural, a supreme being, the divine, God, belief, worship, rites, faith, devotion, and observance. All of these terms are found in the brief definition of religion in a collegiate dictionary. To these can be added many additional considerations: divinely bestowed infallibility, ecclesiastical authority, the nature and conditions of afterlife, Satan and the Devil, morality and behavior, church and state, the cross and the sword, priests and prophets, psychology and religious beliefs. The single word religion involves a host of considerations concerning people individually, their activities, and society as a whole.

The roots of religion extend back eons in geological and evolutionary time when our earliest ancestors became mentally as well as inwardly and emotionally aware of their surroundings. All animals are sensitive to environmental conditions which affect their survival: food and water, weather, climate, territory, predators, procreation, and potential dangers. Animals do not appear to be emotionally disturbed during storms, floods, and fires which occur frequently in parts of the world, or even with earth-shaking events which occur less often nowadays than they did millions of years ago. They position and arrange themselves physically to withstand the onslaught as best they can, seek temporary shelter, or return to the den. When potentially life-threatening events become "a clear and present danger", animals flee. To escape predators, they do so with every means nature has provided, or fight back as best they can.

Our earliest ancestors walking on the ground were physically and emotionally aware, through experience, of the potentially catastrophic natural events occurring at the time. When their minds developed to the point where they could consciously conceive of their surroundings as a material fact, they must have been awestruck by the overwhelming power of supernatural forces: violent storms, floods, landslides, earthquakes, severe droughts, fires, and volcanos spewing ashes, gases, and lava flows. They must have been frightened and aware that they were a small group of creatures in what seemed to be endless space. And they must have felt helpless in the face of threatening conditions and overwhelming events. They could not comprehend, much less understand as we believe we can today, what causes these events beyond perhaps associating some of them with the seasons and with each other: rains and resulting floods, lightning and grassland and forest fires.

At this stage of development, it was natural for early man to regard the primary forces of nature as enormously powerful, unpredictable for the most part, incomprehensible, and crucially related to his survival. The only way he might change the situation in his favor was to reduce the frequency and severity of these earthly events, and increase the occurrence of beneficial conditions. And the only way this might be achieved was to entice whatever caused them to act more propitiously with respect to him personally, his family, and the small group of which he was a part. The only means he could conceive were ceremonies acknowledging the power of supernatural powers and designed to propitiate them. As his mind and self-awareness evolved into the prototype of ours today, he began to view natural forces as something akin to himself. His innate psychological tendency was to project something of his own newly recognized self-image into the inanimate powers. They became gods.

As time passed, early humans evolved gradually into primitive people. With their increased mental awareness of themselves as distinct individuals and as humans different from other animals, they viewed external forces as spirits, supreme beings, or gods. Supernatural relationships they could not understand developed into firm, proto-religious beliefs, and propitiatory ceremonies became religious rituals. They were individually satisfying and a cohesive activity in society. It would be discouraging and self-defeating to conclude that appeal to the gods did no good. There were few opportunities to compare rituals to placate the gods and reciprocal actions by the gods. Religious ceremonies became established custom. As occurs with most operational elements of a society, rituals became more complicated as additional ceremonial aspects were devised to meet the presumed wishes of the gods and obtain their favorable action.

As human populations increased, so too did the interactions among people at a compound rate. Individual members of larger groups were more diverse in their physical features, personal backgrounds, emotional and mental characteristics. The similar beliefs, customs, habits, and ways of thinking and acting found among members of the same family were less likely among the many members of a larger community. More interactions among more people produced different attitudes, reactions, individual and collective actions. Many more behavioral questions arose. There were more personalities and more interests to be taken into account. The functioning of the community became more complicated and fewer and fewer activities could be left entirely to happenstance.

During this prolonged period of a hundred or so thousand years of population growth, new societal considerations emerged. In larger settlements, people's lives were no longer bound to the immediate family. Social interaction and certain responsibilities included the extended family, distant relatives, and the community at large. Individual and collective behavior had to change accordingly: what was permitted and encouraged by tradition, and what was prohibited by taboo or custom. Rather than each family providing all its own food and water, the application of special skills and collective efforts in supplementary hunting, gathering, and later growing foodstuffs, benefitted everyone, as did a division of labor for some productive activities. Methods were devised to resolve disputes which could not be settled within the immediate family, involved different families, or the entire community. Ownership and inheritance of property became more complicated. New ways of organizing and directing settlements as they grew were needed: chieftains, councils of elders, communal meetings, or some other arrangement. The role of a more organized religion with full-time priests or shamans in the governance of the community and in the individual and common affairs of its members was determined. Religion was always an important element, often predominant.

Ethical principles are rooted in the sanctity of tribal custom. Early versions of the spiritual, moral, and, behavioral precepts of religion were formulated during the above period. A god takes on new qualities and aspects in response to the needs and desires of worshippers. These precepts were expressed in scriptures or synthesized in codes of conduct by prophets, priests, and other religious figures concerned with the divine will and human behavior. Particular places were designated exclusively for worship. Rituals were expanded to include parochial concepts as well as divine commitments. The foundations of religion as we know it today were established:

service and adoration of God or as a god expressed in terms of worship, in obedience to divine commands, especially as found in sacred writings or as declared by recognized teachings and in pursuit of a way of life regarded as incumbent on true believers.[1]

Moral laws rank as divine commands, ethical duty as a religious obligation.

The relationship between humans and supernatural forces in early evolutionary times has continued as a predisposition toward religion. As noted at the beginning of this section, four out of five people in the world associate themselves with one of the many religious faiths. Religion can provide many personal satisfactions: the opportunity to believe in and be associated indirectly with a recognized divinity, to participate in the ceremonies of worship, and to subscribe to the tenets of the religion. We may enjoy or need this regular communion with others of like mind. At loose ends in a wide world of complication, unexpected events, and never-ending decisions to be made, we may welcome the leadership, rules, and code of conduct required by a religion. We may seek solace from the trials and tribulations of everyday life, redemption from our transgressions, assurance that there is an afterlife. For some people the ethical standards of the faith may be the attraction. We may have been introduced to a religion at an early age, accompanied our family in religious ceremonies for years without personal conviction and commitment, and never considered doing otherwise.

There are those who cherish the aesthetic aspects of religion: the rituals, liturgical music, sacred and associated art and architecture. A substantial portion of painting, sculpture, graphic arts, and architecture in the past has been dedicated to the simulation of sacred subjects or was commissioned by a religious personage or institution. The art of faiths which prohibit the portrayal of their religious icons is abstract and stylized. Every individual has his or her very personal reasons, conscious and unconscious, for a particular religion or faith—or none at all.

Many different forms of religious expression and faith have existed during human history. Some have long since disappeared, a few have existed for many centuries, and new religions and modified versions of existing faiths have been created. At first small in size, since there were only a million people all told scattered in the populated portions of the globe in 10,000 B.C., the major religions have mushroomed in size to accommodate more than 5,000 times as many people today. The half dozen religious categories with the largest memberships account for 95 percent of the religious population in the world. Within these general categories are subcategories, and within many of these various sects.

There are a host of particular religious faiths with small memberships and limited facilities. Deities have included supernatural powers, supernatural beings, gods and goddesses, heavenly bodies, amorphous spirits, many different animals, combinations of animals and humans, ancestors, priest-kings, exalted individuals, prophets themselves and as interpreters of a divinity. Religious rituals have incorporated incantation, prostration, drums, dance, costumes, music, song, sacramental simulation, trance, flagellation, animal and human sacrifice, sacred symbols, processions, and gymnastics. Ecclesiastical officers have multiplied correspondingly in number: popes, cardinals, archbishops, bishops, priests, priestesses, acolytes; clergymen, ministers, deacons, subdeacons, churchwardens; caliphs, imans, mu-adhdhins, and nuns; shamans, witch doctors, and holy men. The range of diversity of religious observance and practice can only be suggested here.

Religions manifest themselves in two contradictory ways. On the one hand, they are a powerful force affecting their membership and society in general, evoking a divine being which will enable people to achieve personal fulfillment, ethical and constructive behavior, peace and goodwill on earth, and a happier afterlife. On the other hand, religions have condoned and directly practiced relentless intimidation, exile, torture, death by bloody sacrifice and burning at the stake, assassination, execution as punishment, murder as prerequisite for membership, and religious warfare. This contradiction in religion is a societal manifestation of opposing societal forces within all of us: our continuing struggle between the aggressiveness and potential violence latent in our emotional instincts, and our rational efforts toward more civilized behavior.

Throughout human history, ecclesiastical and civil powers have vied for the directive control of nations and societies. During the Crusades the church became an all-controlling power, establishing its own law courts, tax collectors, and prisons in nearly every European country. A century and a half of continuous religious wars in Europe ended only about 300 years ago. And today, religion is still a critical element in wars and civil hostilities occurring somewhere in the world. A religious belief or a "religious right" is an active proponent in the contest for political predominance endemic in some countries. Religions have to do with almost all aspects of our existence, practical as well as spiritual, such as financing, constructing, and managing various properties; arranging religious services; organizing religious education and special programs for adults.

Religions as a constructive force in society pose a moral dilemma. The precepts of many religions call for understanding, tolerance, forgiveness, and the peaceful resolution of differences, under divine encouragement and guidance. Some religions consider their interpretation of divine guidance as infallible or the only valid and permissible basis for behavior and action. Some believe that those who do not share their beliefs can be shunned, persecuted, or killed without compunction. Assassination of political opponents and those who are irreverent toward anything regarded as sacred, terrorism by voluntary martyrs, "ethnic cleansing", and active obstruction of the affairs of others may be condoned, advocated, or formally blessed.

A religious end justifies any means of attainment. War on behalf of a religious faith is a justifiable war. Many religions reflect this basic moral dilemma in contradictory statements in their own scriptures concerning peaceful persuasion and forceful action, compassion or sanctioned cruelty, religious morality, and control or civil ethics and authority.

Collectively, modern religions are the most revealing of human activities. They reflect our most deeply seated instincts, emotions, and beliefs. They have to do with almost all aspects of existence. Religious services represent our conclusions concerning the extraterrestrial forces behind the creation of the earth, animate life, and the human saga. They symbolize the extent to which we are spiritually, emotionally, and intellectually self-sufficient: what we need or welcome as divine support. In their teachings and occasional actions, religions reveal the state of man along the long path from primitive times and purely instinctive reaction to thoughtful response and civilized behavior based on ethical and legal rules of conduct. They present a choice between his desire for a religious experience, the individual and societal behavior the religion requires or proposes, and the contradictory acts it commits and condones at times.

Religions are also an important indication and a determinant of what comprehensive public planning—as discussed in the section on government—can and cannot achieve within a religious sphere of influence at any given time, and how it must be conducted if it is to succeed at all. Planning for our collective welfare signifies the combination of religious belief and scientific thought we want or are willing to accept in different situations and under different conditions. To what extent should planning in the general public interest respond positively and actively to religious purposes and objectives? Since it is an element of society, it must be considered in comprehensive public plans, and taken into account in their effectuation. In countries where religion dominates, comprehensive planning by the religion for its purposes may be the realistic course of action in the general public interest.


## BUSINESS

Simulation is essential in business because it involves more risks than any other usual human activity. The reality of these risks is evidenced in large layoffs by corporations, extended periods of unprofitability, or abandonment of an unsuccessful product, as reported in financial newspapers and newsletters. About one-half of small businesses in the United States fail within two years after their inception. The risk of failure is reduced by simulating the current situation and prospects of the business enterprise. This analysis discloses the nature and extent of specific risks, how they could affect the business, and what precautions might be taken.

Corporations are themselves a legal construct which simulates the organizational conditions needed to conduct large-scale business activities:

[A]n association of persons. . . . which has the rights and duties of its own which are not the rights of its individual members. . . . The rights and duties descend to successive members. . . . A legal person distinct from the sum of its members and in that the members can escape personal liability.[2]

Financial markets comprised of stocks, bonds, mutual funds, and other instruments of investment, expressed in numbers, words, and symbols, are simulations involving millions of items, hundreds of millions of people, and billions of transactions worldwide. There is no exchange of tangible goods or services as there is in food, flower, and "pick-up labor" markets where buyer and seller meet face-to-face. In financial markets, a printed certificate in hand or a "book entry" elsewhere represent the buyer's share or interest in the ownership of a company, partnership, or other entity.

There has been a trend in recent years to eliminate the considerable costs of printing, distributing, storing, replacing, and exchanging stock, bond, and other "ledger book entries" recording ownership. The United States Treasury has not issued "paper proof" for every one of its enormous number of transactions for some years, and some cities are following its example with their municipal bonds. Great increases in the size of financial markets, in the diversity of the financial instruments traded, and their electronic integration into one giant global conglomeration favor increased use of computers. In a single lifetime, stock market information has progressed from postings with a piece of chalk on a blackboard by a telegrapher to a flood of computerized data in daily newspapers, on television, and on computer screens.

With more and more people and organizations using computers, and a generation coming along which will have grown up with one or more computers in the home and as part of their education, paper certificates of ownership will be foregone and replaced entirely by "book entries". Financial markets will be totally computerized, ownership and transactions will exist only as simulations in computer memories and storage, physically distinct from the tangible objects they represent.

Accounting statements, a mainstay of business operations, are simulations which are required to successfully conduct a business. Four of them, for example, represent a small business sufficiently for management purposes: balance sheet, operating and profit-and-loss statements, and cash flow projection. They portray the principal elements of the enterprise and their interrelationships. They indicate when revenues are not meeting expenditures, when there will not be enough cash or credit to meet the payroll or debt charges, how much capital is needed to conduct the business, and information concerning other aspects of the enterprise. These four statements are enough to manage a small business, and they underlie the more complete simulations used for complex and larger enterprises. A chief executive cannot carry this information in his or her head and manage by the "seat of the pants". Some important information, such as net return on investment, requires a graphical display for many managers to understand the different accounting elements involved and their arithmetical interrelationships.

Accounting simulations indicate the past performance and present condition of a corporation, and provide information useful in estimating its future prospects. They are used in quarterly and annual corporate reports as the best way of indicating performance for the ordinary person. And together with other material, they serve individual investors and fund managers in making investment selections. They do not provide direct information concerning important considerations which cannot be expressed in numbers, such as the general competence of management, the quality of research and development, the legal situation with respect to suits and patents, or the level of satisfaction of customers.

The representation of the corporation as a whole, which provides an analytical basis for operational management and planning in well-run companies, simulates the primary components of the enterprise and their interaction. It permits an evaluation of current activities and projecting them into future time according to different assumptions concerning coming events and conditions, and different corporate objectives. An analytical instrument for national governmental planning, comparable to a corporate simulation, is described at the end of the following section on government.

There are many specific simulations within the overall representation that serves to direct the corporation's present and future. For example, personnel and the office space they require must be kept in balance. A growing enterprise is building or leasing new space. A company shrinking in size must sell, lease, or abandon excess office space. Capital requirements must be kept in feasible relation to debt. Inventories must be controlled. To reduce the cost of storing a large supply of parts in inventory, Japanese manufacturers developed the "in-time" system. Independent suppliers schedule the manufacture and shipment of parts so that they arrive precisely when needed in the primary production process. Such components of the overall corporate representation are important simulations in themselves.

The operational centers maintained by utility, transportation, and communication enterprises are another form of simulation having to do with the primary function of companies that provide vital public services—such as electric power, natural gas, and water—which, if interrupted, would cause widespread hardship. These specially designed rooms with large wall surfaces contain graphical displays and electrical signals depicting the supply and distribution system around the clock. If an interruption in the public service occurs, engineers at computerized control desks locate the problem, bypass the trouble spot, or arrange for alternative supply. These centers are concerned with the uninterrupted functioning of the operating system, not the wide range of considerations which must be taken into account in planning the corporation as a whole. Their planning is limited to improving the normal operations of the supply and distribution system, and devising the best way of handling emergencies. Violent storms, floods, and other natural hazards account for most of the interruptions of service, but a squirrel gnawing at the insulation on a wire can knock out a telephone or electric power system.

Local and regional producers of electric power are tied into a national network or grid, which can provide power to an area with an overload or emergency blackout, from a generating plant in another section of the country in a different time zone. Government-operated air control centers are linked together passing on control of aircraft from one to another.

In these and other simulative control and planning centers, and in almost all corporate operations, computers are used extensively. They lend themselves to the numerical and mathematical analysis which is especially effective in business management and planning. The principal elements in a corporate simulation can be expressed in numbers which represent the effects on company operations of unexpected internal events, or external situations which require prompt decision and action. The complex interrelationships between the elements change accordingly. Computers can perform these calculations rapidly, and simulate the consequences of various assumptions for the company. All sorts of "what if" scenarios can be examined in this way. And the results of a wide range of managerial decisions affecting the company's present and future can be tested by computer simulation.

The use of simulation to evaluate risk is illustrated by an analysis of the fire damage to be expected in a major earthquake in San Francisco. An insurance company needed this information to decide whether it would continue to offer earthquake coverage in the area, with premiums people would be willing to pay that were high enough to cover the risk. Such a decision can make the difference between an underwriting profit or loss in the area.

Employing geographic information systems, maps of the street system and various installations in San Francisco are portrayed on the computer screen. The seismic conditions and destructive consequences of the 1966 earthquake are superimposed on the city maps of today. Factored into the analysis are specifics affecting the outcome: the location of gas lines, other potentially explosive installations, fire stations, the speed of fire engines on streets strewn with rubble, natural and man-made firebreaks, the types and construction of buildings, soil types, and ground conditions. Computer programs correlate the interrelationships between such factors, seismic events, damage control efforts, and the passage of time. A simulated seven hours later, when the fires have burned out or been controlled, fire damage and claim costs are estimated for the insurance company.

This form of simulation is referred to as risk analysis, assessment, or management. Along with cost-benefit analysis, it has been passed in the U.S. House of Representatives and proposed in the Senate as a requirement before any new federal governmental regulations are imposed. Whether or not this comes to pass, insurance companies must continually assess, by the best simulations they can devise, their risks and premium rates with respect to covering natural and man-made hazards. Insurance as such would be impossible without successful simulation of the risks involved, based on accumulated data and skillful analysis.

Possibly the most complex simulation organized and operated collectively by business interests is the reservation and ticketing subsystem of the worldwide commercial air transportation system. Its continuous operations involve hundreds of thousands of scheduled flights night and day. In the New York–New Jersey metropolitan area alone, there are 3,000 flights in and out of its three airports every day. Thousands of aircraft and airports, millions of people, and some 180 nations are involved. The millions of interconnections among these myriad elements defy ordinary description. Without high performance computers with enormous memories and information storage capacities, and provisions against the loss of stored information in the event of a power failure, catastrophic interruption, or malicious interference, the air transportation reservation system as we know it today could not exist. All of its parts together constitute a reality beyond the comprehension of any individual mind or the collective minds of a group of people. The computer record is the only manifestation of the reality.

An inkling of the complexity of one aspect of the simulative system is suggested when we consider what is involved when we purchase an airline ticket and reserve a seat. Our request for a non-stop flight between places we have selected, at a particular time of the day or night on a date of our choice, must be correlated with scheduled flights which most closely meet these requirements. Also to be correlated with what is available is our choice between coach, business, and first-class sections of the aircraft if it is so divided; between a window, aisle, or bulkhead seat if such assignment is available; between smoking and non-smoking when this choice exists. Are meals served?

If mileage credits, advance ticket purchase, group travel discount, or other special arrangements are involved, they must be factored in when only a limited number of seats are available for specially priced fares. Special diets for health or religious reasons, children's safety seats, or provisions for the disabled on the airplane and at the airports may be required. As if all of the above correlations were not enough, a history of "no-shows" on certain flights, consequent "overbooking", and possible penalties may have to be taken into account. Special instructions for passengers may also be needed.

The ticketing-reservation system must be sufficiently flexible to provide for frequent changes. Weather conditions or traffic control problems can shut down portions of the system. Routes and schedules are changed. Aircraft are unexpectedly taken out of service and replaced with different equipment. The simulative system must be able to make such changes immediately, along with the related adjustments in the service available and interconnection among airlines.

Simulation has always been part of product and project design. An informal sketch of what the designer visualizes in his mind on a scrap of paper may be enough sometimes, or preliminary drawings or a small-scale model may be needed. For many years automobile companies constructed full-size "mock-ups" which could be molded by designers to demonstrate different exterior forms for the proposed vehicle. Aircraft manufacturers built full-size models at great cost because designers could not visualize completely and accurately in three dimensions forms subtly shaped to meet aerodynamic requirements, nor the maze of interior ducts, cables, piping, and wires comprising the flight control system. The "lead-time" for a new model automobile was five years or more, for a new aircraft close to ten. During this period of accumulating expenditures for design, engineering, and preparation for manufacture, developments which could not be anticipated could adversely affect the sale of the car and aircraft five and ten years later.

Computers have completely changed the design process and the time required. Both automobiles and aircraft can now be simulated on computer screens: inside and out, from different viewpoints, at small or large scale. Conflicts and inconsistencies between parts are identified and highlighted by the computer program, and the design modified directly on the computer simulation to correct the problem. New cars can now be designed and manufactured in two years or less. And the Boeing 777, a radically different aircraft—with its "fly-by-wire" rather than hydraulic control system, and two engines instead of four for an airplane its size—was designed in a year employing six mainframe computers, without a mock-up model.

Vastly less complicated simulations are the market and public opinion surveys and focus groups which are part of much business planning. The latter groups, composed of carefully selected individuals, concentrate on a specific topic such as a food taste comparison, a choice among package designs, reactions and comments concerning proposed products or services, anything influencing an important business decision which can be discovered or explained by questioning such a group. One might be composed of homemakers familiar with household appliances and products; another of users of a particular product, whose reaction to a proposed change is needed. Or a group of people are selected who have accumulated wealth and can comment on their preferences among proposed investments. Mock juries are used by lawyers to determine their strategy and tactics in the actual trial.

Market surveys are structured to identify rational and intuitive preferences, attitudes, and tastes that relate to sales and various business decisions. Since scientific sample surveys require questioning only several thousand people representing the public at large, they are a very cost-effective means of closely simulating the response of the population as a whole, or parts of it. Elected politicians rely on them to disclose opinions and characteristics of their constituencies which affect their legislative actions and their reelection.

All of the mechanical simulations noted in previous sections are used by business. Shaketables test whether products or packaging can withstand rough handling. A computer-operated shaking machine subjects the automobile seats to the bumps and bangs encountered on a test track. Seat belts and automobile bumpers are tested in crash simulators. Wind tunnels with smoke generators reveal aerodynamic turbulence and drag in the flow of air over an automobile or scale models of airplane wings and other components. Flight simulators replicate different emergencies that have occurred in flight operations, so that pilots can experience their effects and learn what action to take. Robots are performing more and more manufacturing tasks previously performed by workers on the assembly line. And electronic "black boxes" in cars react to certain operating and driving conditions faster than the average driver. For years "automatic pilots" have been relieving their human counterparts on portions of long airplane flights.

The use of simulation by business has kept pace with administrative and technical developments. Professional accounting ushered in a more disciplined method of conducting business. Mathematical developments expanded quantitative analysis and calculative concepts. As science moved forward rapidly after the Industrial Revolution in England, new means of testing materials and simulating production processes became available. It is the last century and a half of intellectual and scientific advances that have brought about the widespread use and successful application of many forms of simulation. There appears to be a natural correlation between these advances and the need for simulation. These advances and the need for simulation appear to coincide.

## GOVERNMENT

Government emerged and developed to perform those directorial or supervisorial activities which enable a society to function and survive. Research reveals that the simian species from which we evolved engaged in aggressive behavior, infanticide, and murder, but maintained a system of collective behavior which favored their survival. For the community to survive, some system of collective action was required in the first tiny human settlements to supplement the water, food, clothing, and shelter produced by separate families. Conflictive actions by individuals or among families would prevent the community from functioning as a societal entity. Co-operative actions became established customs, passed on by example and later by word of mouth from generation to generation.

As communities grew in size and complexity, established customs were formalized as precepts of rudimentary governments. As societies gradually changed in character during tens of thousands of years of material, technical, and cultural advancements, the functions of government expanded to encompass new considerations and interactions among more people. The changes in societies brought about by the industrial and scientific revolutions over the past several centuries have vastly complicated the functioning and overall management of technologically advanced societies. Present trends will not only continue, but are almost certain to accelerate.

The historical evolution of government throughout the ages and throughout the world has included at one time or another almost every form of supreme authority imaginable; every degree of individual participation in and exclusion from the governmental decision-making process; freedom and restriction of personal expression; maintenance of "law and order" by custom, codes of law, canons of religious behavior, military might, and police power; different economic systems and means of production; wide variations in property rights and inheritance. But all of these different forms of government have had to perform certain essential functions, depending on the stage of development and circumstance of the society at the time. At a minimum, some form of collective oversight must have existed in the earliest human settlements to ensure that the essentials for survival were provided. These most fundamental provisions for societal survival are still a primary governmental concern. In industrialized countries they have expanded and become increasingly complex. Government must perform in ways few people anticipated not long ago. Its essential role will increase rather than decrease in the years ahead, despite any public or political wishes to the contrary.

### Existence

First and foremost, the ruling authority or government must exist in such form that it has an operational life expectancy and is not so transitory that little or nothing can be undertaken and accomplished. The forms vary. In the world today, these include democracies, constitutional and absolute monarchies, religious autocracies, military and civil dictatorships, and tribal councils. An operational life expectancy requires sufficient stability to enable the primary or national government to function, without such constant turmoil, civil resistance, terrorism, insurrection, or revolutionary attacks that little can be accomplished beyond bare existence.

Taxation is an essential element of government. Unless there is a source of external income from the sale of natural resources or some other national asset to another country, taxes are required to meet the costs of the functions, facilities, services, and public improvements which are part of an operating government. Taxes provide most of the income side of the national budget. Their disbursement requires that the monetary system permit the productive interchange of goods and services throughout the nation.

Some form of national taxation is accepted by most people as clearly necessary, and desirable provided that the use of the taxes is disclosed, they produce visible results, are not onerous or confiscatory, and are not preempted by rulers, politicians, government officials, or others in their own personal interest rather than the public welfare. Avoiding or minimizing such a situation varies, of course, with the nature of the ruling regime and the methods of collection. In many countries, there is little or no recourse for complaint. Taxation which is not uniform can and usually does incorporate a wide range of special provisions for political, economic, business, or social purposes—unknown to most people unless called to their attention. Applied ruthlessly, the power to tax is the power to destroy.

Military defense of the realm is a responsibility of government. It alone can marshal the total national effort that may be required to repel hostile attack, or "to protect vital national interests" which may be located far beyond national borders. And it has self-preservation as a motivation to do so, because it is the governmental entity an enemy must overthrow to achieve victory. Throughout human history, military forces have involved collective response by a community as a whole; a single champion chosen to do battle with an opponent designated by the enemy; warriors selected for their marshal skills; citizen soldiers impressed or drafted, paid or otherwise rewarded for their military service; volunteer armies, or hired armies of paid professional soldiers. The history of man is also the history of offensive and defensive war; of human capacity for violence; the continuous invention of more destructive weapons, accelerated in recent years by scientific and technical advances; and the dissemination of ever more lethal devices throughout the world. Military preparedness is an integral element of human existence, a major societal effort consuming a large portion of national budgets.

By definition and in fact, foreign affairs must be conducted by national governments, since they represent the purposes and activities of an entire nation with respect to other countries. Foreign policy is part of national defense, since it may avoid, discourage, encourage, or precipitate conflicts and wars. It also expresses the interests and objectives of a nation with relation to legal, financial, and commercial interrelationships with other countries, and initiates actions to these ends. Foreign policy is increasingly vital as continents, regions, and nations are interconnected by treaties, agreements, and laws; monetary exchanges; international financial investments and productive operations; rapid transportation of people, goods, and services far and wide; immediate global transmission of information; widespread reconnaissance intelligence; and worldwide military operations.

## Stability

In order to function, a government must maintain enough "law and order" to enable the essential productive activities of the society to operate. This does not mean, of course, that there can be no progress or rapid change. It does mean that the society cannot be so unstable and transitory that it does not exist long enough to operate effectively, and is replaced shortly by another government. Societies can endure only so much turmoil and turnover until a form of government develops or is accepted which provides the stability and the time required for productive recuperation.

Throughout history there have been many means of maintaining law and order. Custom, tradition, and communal concurrence served the purpose in the primitive community. A code of laws, skillful administrative practices, and a network of paved roads permitting the rapid deployment of Roman legions to threatened areas controlled an empire which was the largest in the world at the time. Religious precepts, canons of behavior, excommunication, courts of inquiry and punishment, prisons, tithes and taxes, and supportive military might served papal purposes. Kings and queens ruled by royal authority and taxation imposed upon or accepted by the populace. Hitler and Stalin ruled by absolute military and police power, and nationalization of all assets.

Democracies and constitutional monarchies live by the law, relying on the family and on education to inculcate in the young the moral values, ethical behavior, and knowledge needed to perform as societally responsible citizens. The range and effectiveness of different consequences for violations of the law, and the feasibility of rewarding good behavior and rehabilitating transgressors are debated, as is the allocation of funds for law and order between prevention, enforcement, punishment, and rehabilitation.

Juridical organization is a vital element in the governmental regulatory system. In all countries, the principles, rules, and practices of detention, arrest, trial, appeal, and decision in the civil, religious, royal, or military courts of the land indicate whether the ordinary citizen can test, clarify, or challenge existing methods of maintaining law and order. In constitutional governments such as the United States, federal, state, and local courts apply and interpret the content and intent of the constitution in the light of new conditions and unanticipated situations. The confidence of the electorate in the basic precepts of democratic government is supported by allowing for their gradual adjustment to changing conditions. This flexibility counters the contention of some people that societal progress requires arbitrary and radial change in the existing political system.

A single monetary and financial system is required. An impossible economic situation is created, which cannot last long, if different parts of an industrialized country employ different currencies, assign different value to a national currency, or rely on random barter. Without a well-ordered monetary system, deposits cannot be made at different locations, retained for future use, or transmitted among individuals, institutions, and enterprises for investment in productive activities.

Each of these basic governmental functions requires people, organizations, and facilities to carry them out. Whatever the form of government, there must be a group of people or a staff of some kind to conduct the activities directly supporting the supreme authority in its position of power and leadership. Taxation requires a treasury and government officials to receive, record, safeguard, and disperse tax revenues procured by tax collectors. National defense necessitates units for command and control, military installations, equipment, weapons, and military personnel. Foreign affairs needs a headquarters facility and offices abroad for regular contact with other nations and to receive their dignitaries. Maintaining law and order takes people, structures, and equipment for a police force, jails, prisons, and courts. Governments require people, professional skills of many kinds, and numerous facilities to simply exist and function.

The role of government beyond basic requirements varies with the size and population of the country, its industrialization, and its use of advanced technology. The differences between nations can be extreme. Saint Kits and Nevis, the smallest of the United Nations located in the eastern Caribbean Sea, has a population of about 40,000 in an area of a little more than 100 square miles, with one telephone for every 7,000 people. The People's Republic of China has about 1,200,000,000 people in an area of 3,700,000 square miles, with one telephone for every 178 people.

The United States is the supreme example of governmental responsibilities and problems in a highly industrialized nation which develops and employs the most sophisticated technologies. It indicates what must be addressed in the future by developing nations with comparable forms of government. Nations with very different governmental systems must cope with the same inherent problems in their own way. The system of administration in the United States maximizes all the difficulties of law-making. It does not work as a whole. The executive branch is a group of persons, each individually dependent on or answerable to the president, but with no joint policy or collective responsibility. The whole includes: a national constitution and amendments; the legislative, executive, and judicial branches of the federal government; independent federal agencies; and comparable bodies in 50 states with their own constitutions, rights, privileges, and responsibilities as defined in the U.S. Constitution and Supreme Court decisions and interpretations.

Differences of opinion concerning federal and states' rights have presented problems since they were articulated in the Constitution in order to obtain agreement among the founding fathers and form a new nation. Considerable differences in the actions and activities among states in the earlier years of the country presented no major impediment to territorial expansion and the gradual development of a federal government. The American Civil War demonstrated what can occur when there are irreconcilable economic, ideological, and political differences between regions in the country. It was the supreme test that: "If a house be divided against itself, that house cannot stand". There are those today who advocate almost complete independence of action by individual states. The dissolution of political and corporate entities into one or more parts is a constant consideration by those with different opinions concerning how they should be conducted, a particular strategic or operational dissent, or self-interest.

The United States is, of course, a far different entity today than it was two lifetimes ago. The population is almost eight times larger and more diverse. The nation is tied together by a national system of highways, railroads, and airways, which was inconceivable at the time of the Civil War. There is intense and constant movement of people and material around the country. Communications interconnect individuals and organizations as never before. International trade, foreign investment, offshore manufacturing, and global services are important activities affecting all parts of the nation. Scientific and technological advances impact everyone. And human affairs in general require greater uniformity and consistency as they become technically more complicated and interrelated. In time of war, civil emergency, natural catastrophe, and economic crisis, everyone is affected directly or indirectly and federal action is necessary. More rather than less enlightened leadership and action by the national government is required in the self-interest of most individuals and the public interest at large.

Historical, economic, cultural, and religious differences certainly exist between regions and between individual states. They tend to diminish with time as the need for and benefits of consistency in human affairs increases with more interaction and participation among people. Differences may increase in some parts of the country because of immigration, local economic distress, or other causes. In today's and tomorrow's world, needless discrepancies in basic laws, regulations, and operating practices bring procedural difficulties, superfluous litigation, and unnecessary costs. And they reduce the likelihood of accomplishing projects and activities involving several or many states, those that are nationwide in scope, or are in the broad public interest.

Uniformity is not a desirable objective in and of itself, since it tends to reduce individual creativity inspired by differences. But there are many uniformities needed for technical compatibility, legal clarity and consistency, and operational efficiency. The application of broad policies and federal legislation can be modified at the state and local level to accommodate ethnic, cultural, religious, and other differences. Those that cannot be modified and still fulfill their basic purpose should not be changed.

The belief that nationwide programs—such as those relating to the health, welfare, and education of people throughout the country—are best formulated and carried out independently by separate states is an operational delusion. More likely, such a transfer of authority by the federal government would be to escape political responsibility for poor performance. The inevitable differences among 50 states in the implementation of a nationwide program would produce indefensible inequities; economic, migratory, and legal problems; and poor results overall. If the federal government fails in its function of national leadership and constructive action, its performance must be improved rather than its role and responsibility abrogated. Congress must shed its operational infirmities and structure itself so it can conduct its affairs wisely and well.

The organizational problems of governance are made more difficult by the fact that the United States is the most polyglot of all nations, having officially welcomed waves of immigrants during its relatively short history, and allowed a large number of illegal immigrants to enter the country. Private enterprise must cooperate in many governmental endeavors, since it performs more of the essential elements of the economy than is the case in any other nation. Together with its organizational diversity, other characteristics of the country make it harder for a democratic, constitutional, and federal form of government to function effectively.

### Transportation

Every nation requires a system of transportation throughout the country which enables it to function as an economy. Even in small nations with few people in a few thousand square miles of area, the movement of people on foot, by bicycle, on horseback, or by other means provides the interaction among the population and the interchange of goods and services required for an active economy. The national highway, railroad, and major waterway systems in the United States serve this essential economic purpose for surface transport, and constitute critical interconnected networks of circulation in case of national emergencies. Highways in the sky, designated and traffic-controlled by the federal government, serve the same purposes for this newer form of transportation which began and became the incredible system it is today in less than 100 years: one long lifetime. The postal service network delivered 180 *billion* pieces of mail in 1995, some 700 items for every man, woman, and child in the United States.

None of these systems would work if individual states imposed requirements or restrictions which prevented or significantly impaired their functioning. Operational and technical developments require a national
integration and standard procedures which only the federal government can
provide. All the more as the population and domestic travel increase with
faster aircraft, hydrofoil vessels, high-speed "bullet" trains, and probably
rockets in the future.

## Communication

Communication has been, and is today, the most crucial element of human activities since their beginning several millions of years ago: initially
between the first animate organisms and their environment, later in the
interaction among our simian ancestors, more recently among primitive
human beings, and now as spoken and written communication among people as they are today. It has, as we know, been enormously expanded during the past 150 years by the invention and development of the printing
press, telegraph, telephone, typewriter, radio, microwave transmission, sonar, television, facsimile, interactive computers, satellite relays, the emergence of English as the international lingua franca, and the beginnings of
the automatic translation of languages.

We live in a world of instant and constant communication. Events occurring almost anywhere on earth are reported within minutes to the rest
of the world. National leaders, politicians, businessmen, academicians, and
everybody else with access to modern communications can contact one
another with little delay. Governmental, monetary, financial, commercial,
scientific, and other transactions occur continuously around the world day
and night. Reportive facts and figures, information and analyses of all kinds
and descriptions, are disseminated regularly. Vast repositories of accumulated knowledge and documentary material from the past, stored in libraries, universities, museums, and other institutions, are or will soon be
available over international computer networks.

This is the beginning of what no one knows may develop in the future.
With communication equipment becoming smaller and smaller, portable,
and less expensive, all of us may be "wired in" at all times to everybody
else. Perhaps a superminiaturized communication device will be implanted
in a convenient but inconspicuous location on the body of every infant,
with its social security number inscribed on its forehead in invisible and
indelible ink. Purchases at the supermarket and other stores will be paid
for by pressing the forehead with the identifying social security number
against a television-like screen, with immediate automatic deduction of the
purchase price and tax at the bank as is done now with direct deposit credit
cards.

Science fiction as this may be, it seems certain that communication will become more than ever the critical element in highly developed societies. With most of us in the United States getting our news and depending daily on information disseminated by the mass media of communication, the reliability of the information is crucial. A society cannot function constructively and could deteriorate if inaccurate or confusing information was widely circulated.

Compared with not so long ago, an enormous quantity of public information is generated and distributed each and every day throughout the United States. It determines what we are aware of beyond our personal observation and experience. Our initial reaction and the decisions we make on many matters depend on what we read in newspapers, reports, periodicals, books, and other printed materials; what we hear on the radio; see on our computer screen, and see and hear on television. It is from these sources that we learn what is "going on", something about the specific events and situations that are reported, some of the considerations to be taken into account. What information is reported and how it is presented influences and may determine the conclusions we reach.

It is certainly impossible to monitor the flood of public information and ensure its accuracy, nor is this needed. To a large extent, the "information market" is self-regulating although, as will be discussed later, this is changing because of television and interactive telecomputing. Statistical data regularly reported are checked automatically if the calculations used in their formulation produce figures that are very different from what they were previously, or from what would be expected for other reasons. They are then double-checked for accuracy. Scientific research is evaluated by a system of peer review, and after publication by the critical examination of fellow scientists who use or read the research. In the competitive world of scientific investigation, inaccuracies are quickly noted and corrected. Ultimately, confirming experiment or related research establishes whether the work is valid.

The many professional people who refer regularly to the reams of economic and financial data and analyses published daily in major newspapers are so familiar with the conditions they represent that conspicuous discrepancies are questioned. In order to detect fraudulent invasion early on, banks may call the attention of those with sizable accounts to transactions that are markedly different from the usual pattern. The members of every field of special knowledge or activity will note and make known major discrepancies. There are usually, if not always, those with different opinions on every subject who are happy to point out any errors by those with whom they disagree. Some information is admittedly or obviously partisan, personal, or promoting a special interest. The receiver is on notice to decide for himself the reliability of the source, supporting data, and reasoning. Many exhibit healthy skepticism. Unfortunately, many do not, particularly if the information confirms what they want to believe. Since most literary works portray or express events, situations, stories, or behavior which are not objectively or scientifically verifiable, their validity or meaningfulness must also be judged by personal experience or subjective evaluation.

The source of information may indicate its probable reliability. With few exceptions, most notably the tabloids, American newspapers have a record of presenting "all the news that is fit to print" as accurately as circumstances permit. Their dependence on advertising for income has not significantly compromised this reliability. In general, they have fulfilled their responsibility of "investigative reporting", calling to public attention misdeeds and gross inefficiencies of both government and private enterprise. Deliberate misinformation is rare.

In sharp contrast, "scandal sheets" are known to exaggerate, to circulate rumor, allegations and innuendo, to overemphasize those aspects of information which attract readers emotionally rather than treat the matter in a balanced manner. Nonetheless, many people retain a residue of the misinformation or exaggeration despite their recognizing it as such. Deliberately fraudulent "pitches" concerning investment opportunities are made by telephone from "bucket shops", in newspaper advertisements, and by direct mail solicitation. They are spotted by those who are cautious or skeptical, particularly by those who take seriously the well-known admonition "if it seems to be too good to be true, it probably is"; but not by those who are incapacitated, gullible, or unrealistically optimistic. We are all subject to some publicly disseminated misinformation.

The public information provided by the mass media of communication has been a positive force in American life, but they have developed to the point that we live in a media era in which television, radio, movies, and print have a more immediate and pervasive influence than any other institutions in our society. Television has become the most powerful of the mass media. American families view it an average of some seven hours every day. The 42 television broadcasts which attracted the largest audiences before 1995 averaged over 34 million viewers. One of these was watched by more than 50 million people. During the preceding decade, the most popular seasonal "shows" were seen on the average in over 91 million households.

Television is the chief source of news, entertainment, and other information for most Americans. It affects viewers' reactions to what is portrayed, their attitudes toward the subject in general, their substantive values, and often their consequent actions, more than the government, educational institutions, the church, and even the family. It determines who is known and widely recognized, who achieves or retains "star status", who is regarded favorably in the public arena, and therefore who is most likely to be successful among those who require or cherish frequent and positive exposure.

Few public officials stand a chance of election or reelection without personal appearances on television and other public exposure designed by expert media consultants to generate favorable viewer reactions. Larger and larger portions of larger and larger campaign funds collected by aspiring politicians are spent on television, which more than anything else determines who will be the next president of the United States, the next senator or member of the House of Representatives, the next governor of a state, and other public officials who represent an electorate and shape the nation.

By selecting which of the myriad events or situations that occur every day to broadcast or print as news, the mass media determine what we are aware of beyond our direct experience. What goes on in the world is what we see on television, hear on the radio, and read in print. O.J. Simpson was the most widely known person in the United States, and possibly in the world, for a year, and little noted thereafter because he was no longer "newsworthy". When events are repeated over and over again on television, they are etched in our minds. The Rodney King beating by Los Angeles police officers has been shown more often on television than any other single event in history. It is not only fixed in the mind and memory of hundreds of millions of people in the United States and around the world, but it has had a trenchant impact on race relations and police practices. It may be more than historical coincidence that television coverage of these two trials emanated from Los Angeles, the mass media capital of the United States. Television has the power to affect us deeply and permanently.

Another form of repetition or collective emphasis by the mass media is occurring. More and more reports and articles first published in scientific and professional journals are rewritten for newspaper and television coverage. This may represent a healthy broadening of subject matter covered by the media, or the fact that rewriting is a less expensive way of producing a news report or a story than *in situ* reporting. To avoid the high cost of television coverage in far-off places, most television stations rely on a single agency to record newsworthy events abroad. The mass media are communicating in an increasingly powerful voice because it is increasingly uniform.

Reenactment or simulation of historical personages and events is a third kind of repetition. Motion pictures shown on television and programs written specifically for television present the author's or producer's view of a life, situation, or period in history. Two movies released in the mid-1990s reenact portions of the lives of two presidents of the United States. Historians maintain that there are significant factual and interpretative errors in both. Whether or not this is the case, it raises the question whether history is being "rewritten" to provide dramatization and emotional content which attracts viewers and increases ticket sales and advertising revenues. When does the "artistic license" and freedom of individualistic interpretation and expression of a writer or television producer become historical distortion or falsification?

This question applies also to literature, including the textbook selections debated by local school boards and state legislatures. There are almost always a number of books on important historical subjects, with different viewpoints or emphases which together present as accurate a composite simulation or reenactment of the historical reality as we can achieve. Movies and television programs are different from books because they cost so much more that multiple copies are not available for comparison and synthesis. But by combining visual, verbal, and aural expression, their mental and emotional impact is much greater. Television audiences may be hundreds of millions of people, rather than hundreds of thousands for a best-seller book. The concept of the South after the Civil War ingrained worldwide by *Gone With the Wind* is the product of the movie far more than the best-seller book.

Related to what is selected for broadcast and how often it is repeated is the built-in dynamic of television toward emotional content. Commercial television income depends on advertising revenue, which depends on audience ratings, which depend on how many viewers are attracted to a particular broadcast. The larger the audience, the higher the rating, and the more profitable the program. The instincts we inherit from our animal ancestors, which were crucial to our survival in the past, predispose us toward emotional material. Only recently in our evolutionary history have we developed rational capabilities to support the progress of civilization. Television advertisers, station owners, producers, directors, scriptwriters, actors, and everyone else involved are aware of our emotional predilections. And they know "which side their bread is buttered on". Hence the increasingly violent content, prurient material, explicit sex, and aberrant behavior we have witnessed on television in recent years, which certainly do not contribute to civilized deportment. In the intense competition among local newscasts for high audience ratings, crime and emotionally charged events are selected as the main fare, as if they were the only newsworthy happenings of the day. There are those who maintain that television news is the most devastating example of the degrading of the medium in the race for ratings; "if it bleeds, it leads". Even the vocal overtones of most news announcers, when reading from the teleprompter screens, are intentionally emotional rather than "cool, calm, and collected". To a much lesser extent, this dynamic also occurs in newspapers and radio broadcasts.

The built-in tendency to attract, exaggerate, and intensify content has affected "entertainment" on television. For example, sports are being transformed to enhance television coverage. Not long ago, the interesting features, excitement, tactics, and strategy of sports were contained within the football and soccer field, court, rink, diamond, or other area of action. When first televised, there was a single announcer with little to say beyond descriptive necessities. The viewer's attention was directed exclusively to the game itself and his or her analysis and appreciation of what was occurring. Today, there are two or three announcers or guests in the broadcast booth, often a roving reporter on the field to interview players or spectators during the game.

In professional football, the palaver of announcers may take up more time than the action on the field. The scores of other games and statistical information may be superposed on the television screen. Players gesticulate or engage in antics directed to stadium and television spectators not only after touchdowns, but whenever they want to call attention to something they have done. With helmets, face masks, armor pads on their shoulders and other parts of the body, exhibitionistic behavior, and increasing injuries, football players become more and more like the gladiators fighting to the death in the Coliseum in Ancient Rome. This has occurred mainly in professional football because it involves the largest athletic investments, operating costs, and profits. It increases broadcast costs and pressure to attain higher audience ratings. With present policies, it is only a matter of time before other sports are transformed into "shows" more than real sports events. In fact, they are now usually referred to as shows. This is beginning to occur in professional golf and tennis. Induced dramatization is likely to be applied to any television program if it increases its audience rating.

Television is a powerful directive force in society. It affects people through the dissemination of news, the human episodes and behavior it depicts, and the response of viewers to the claims and causes advanced on television by special interests purchasing broadcast time. The claim that what is shown on television only reflects what people want and are really like is refuted by research which shows that television influences people. Issues, events, and behavior portrayed on television correlate with reactions, attitudes, conclusions, and actions by viewers. Television is a directive force as well as a responsive fulfillment. Surely not less than the generally acknowledged influence of newspapers, radio, journals, and other sources of information on how people react and what they think.

If television is only a mirror of human wants and characteristics which already exist, why do advertisers pay premium prices for exposure on television? Is it only to remind people of their wants, to whet existing appetites, or to create desires and induce needs? Many television programs do indeed mirror certain human traits. But some of them are designed to appeal to emotional instincts which need to be constrained rather than encouraged if civilization is to progress: thoughtless overreaction, senseless aggression, unjustified prejudice, arrogant disdain, violence and cruelty, self-satisfying hate.

Television has an especially formative impact on those of our population who are economically, educationally, and otherwise societally disadvantaged, living for the most part in run-down sections of our larger cities. They include: the 40 or so million Americans whose income is below the poverty level as defined by the federal government; most of the 30 percent of high school students who do not graduate; the several million permanently unemployed; and many of the 90 million people who have "weak reading skills". It is the group with the highest percentage of people on welfare, unmarried mothers, single-parent families, broken homes, drug traffic and addiction, crime and gangs, and the lowest average educational level.

Many are disheartened, unmotivated, and fatalistic in their outlook and actions. Television is a respite, a babysitter or distraction for children, the source of news about events outside the neighborhood, entertainment, and "education". What is seen on television is most likely accepted at face value, and the behavior and ethical values represented in entertainment are apt to be adopted in everyday life. The "role models" are those characters who are most impressive on the television screen. What is portrayed on television newscasts, talk shows, and soap operas represents current affairs and the existing social situation for disadvantaged viewers. Living at the brink of active disillusionment and despair, some of them can be provoked into violence, civil disturbance, rioting, and looting in the sections of our large cities that are societal minefields.

Television cannot be considered in general apart from computing. The two are converging into a single mechanism which combines the pictures and programs presented on television, and the capability of computers to store, structure, and manipulate information, provide network access and interaction, and perform many kinds of analyses.

The rapid growth in the use of computers is indicated by a few "facts and figures". Sales of computers have tripled during the past decade. By 1996 more than one-half of U.S. households contained computers; over 10 percent of these were advanced instruments (CD-ROMs). More than a third of adults aged eighteen years and over used computers in 1993, twice the percentage ten years earlier. We can expect accelerated growth as the 59 percent of children three to seventeen years of age who used computers in 1993 continue to employ them as adults and encourage early use by their children and grandchildren.

## Natural Resources

It is not surprising that our predecessors in early America could delude themselves for so long that natural resources were unlimited. Settlers along the eastern seaboard saw a seemingly bountiful and boundless geographical expanse to the west. As the country was explored and settled, as a nation was formed and populated, it was impossible to imagine that a time would come when there would not be unlimited pure water, fertile land, virgin forests, and wildlife. The great expanse of the sky above arched over a vast cornucopia of natural resources. Man was a tiny element in a limitless earth.

In a little more than one-half of our national existence, we have contaminated much of our surface water; overdrawn and diminished our underground aquifers; polluted and overfished our coastal waters; allowed erosion to strip as much as five tons of topsoil per acre per year from a million square miles of land; despoiled large areas of land by overgrazing, strip-mining, dumping of toxic wastes, destructive chemical emissions, and irradiation; destroyed animal populations, including all but a few token herds of bison; polluted the air we breathe over many of our metropolitan urban areas.

We have populated and industrialized our country to the point where we threaten our long-range future, unless we assume that we can change our behavior, that science will supply alternatives for depleted or exhausted natural resources, and a new ecology will evolve which favors our continued survival. This sketch of American experience with respect to our environment may seem to some overdrawn, almost apocalyptic. But it is a fact.

Man's relation to his environment appears to have varied greatly in the past. In earliest times when his senses, conscious awareness of his surroundings, and his accumulated knowledge were rudimentary, he husbanded the resources on which his life and future depended. This is still true for nomads living in sparse desert regions. At a later stage, when man had learned more and was tending agricultural plots, he could abandon a location when its fertility declined because of overuse, and proceed to slash, burn, and plant in another place nearby. After he had removed the readily available firewood from one area, he could move to another. Today, firewood is the only fuel for cooking available to millions of people in Africa and other parts of the world. Animal dung may not be a feasible alternative and kerosene is too expensive. Accordingly, large acres of land are stripped of every stick of wood, accelerating the erosion of topsoil and altering the local ecology and microclimate.

Traditional customs and official policies based on self-preservation conserved the natural resources of many countries during recorded history. The Industrial Revolution, a rapidly increasing world population, global transportation, and financial interconnections have internationalized and created new demands on natural resources. They can no longer be considered and implemented within national borders, without regard to the rest of the world. One country may sell its forests to another nation to obtain foreign currency. Nations once self-sufficient import food from other countries, depleting their natural resources. Acid rain, radioactive fallout, and other atmospheric pollution are not contained within national borders. Diseases and infections affecting human and natural resources, once limited to certain regions, can now be disseminated inadvertently or intentionally at any port or airport in the world, despite the best protective practices. Our greatest natural resource, the ocean, covers three-quarters of the earth's surface. Its pollution and depleting its marine life by overfishing affects everyone in the world sooner or later.

As populations increase there are more mouths to feed. Unless new foodstuffs are found or created synthetically, existing foods enhanced or their production increased, existing resources will be depleted until they are exhausted. Industrial, technological, and scientific advances may add to the intrinsic quality or value of a natural resource, or increase the quantity available. Many years of genetic research on rice has increased the food value, regional adaptability, and resistance to disease of this staple consumed by hundreds of millions of people in the Far East. And the development of hybrid corn and wheat has benefitted the West. Oil has been discovered by making possible deeper exploratory drilling, offshore drilling platforms, and pressurized methods of extracting most of the oil from existing pools. New discoveries and improved extraction augment the current reserve, but the total amount formed in the earth's crust eons ago has not changed and will be exhausted in time.

Technological developments are causing the exploitation and exhaustion of vital natural resources, affecting geographical and environmental features around the world. Remote sensing from the air, discussed earlier in this book, and sonar echo-location detect concentrations of fish in the open ocean. New types of trawl nets a mile long scoop up great quantities of marine life. Floating factory ships specifically designed for the purpose roam the high seas hunting fish, which are being harvested at such a high rate that entire species are at risk and some have been almost eradicated. In another form of harvesting, machines are available which fell and dismember a tree in much less time than with the usual logging methods. Like every other large moving machine, this logging apparatus damages or destroys the microecology at and just below the surface of the ground beneath its treads as it moves about.

The tragedy of many such operations is that they are also wasteful. The haul from large commercial fishing nets usually includes many fish besides those targeted. The unwanted fish are dumped back dead into the ocean. Attempts are being made to reduce the inadvertent trapping and destruction of dolphins, sea turtles, and other marine resources along with the species sought for commercial purposes. Human tastes for particular food, the lure of profit, and television are part of the picture. The willingness of large population groups to pay premium prices for what they consider a delectable delicacy finances and ensures the profits and return on investment derived from highly mechanized commercial fishing. Production efficiency and ecological disregard preclude preserving the unwanted portion of the catch.

Worldwide television whets people's appetites and creates desires for products other people enjoy but many television viewers do not. Television advertisements promote profitable products, and export tastes by sales pitches and the choice of paraphernalia shown on television programs. The world sees and judges the United States by the movies it exports and the television broadcasts shown abroad more than any other contact or interaction.

For the world at large, extensive destruction of basic natural resources is the supreme example of the "tragedy of the commons" which occurred in England during the Middle Ages. This unfenced open land was available for pasturage to members of a community. Each member had the "common" right to pasture a number of livestock in proportion to the arable land he was entitled to farm. When too many animals grazed in the commons, they denuded the land. Their number had to be reduced to the "carrying capacity" of the land, so that the grass would grow again and support a limited number of livestock.

Whose animals would be removed? Should there be a limit to the number of animals one person could pasture on the commons? Self-interest and competition among members produced inequitable use and the gradual abandonment of these collective pastures. Individual interests were "enclosed" (fenced) for private use on separate land: a consequence of the fact that "share and share alike" becomes more difficult as the number of people increase and life becomes more technically complicated. Today, the oceans and forests of the world are "commons" crucial to the geographical, biological, and atmospheric well-being of all people on earth. Will overfishing, overcutting, misuse, and pollution produce an earthly tragedy of these commons?

Environmental concerns have always involved individual attitudes and considerations relating to the use of one's time, employment, and economics. Early man moved his rudimentary farming when the yield from the plot he was cultivating declined from continuous use. There was plenty of virgin land available nearby. If he lived near the sea, a large lake, or river, primitive man could fish to his heart's content since the supply far exceeded his needs. Early American pioneers could clear-cut as much timberland as they chose since there was plenty more nearby or not far away. Until the Industrial Revolution, pollution was not a serious concern. The population explosion had not begun.

Public concern and legislative restraints with respect to the environment have come about during the past 25 years. Information concerning the supply and use of natural resources, and scientific knowledge concerning our relationship with the environment accumulated, and was brought to the attention of the American people by the mass media and a wide range of publications. Perhaps our attention was diverted previously from this critical subject by our commitment to use any and all resources required

to win World War II. Our environmental mistakes were unnoted and ignored except by those directly affected until the postwar attention of the
media and research revealed the effects of human activities, polluting practices, injurious industrial operations, and excessive depletion of natural resources. As a consequence, we are confronted today with environmental
and resource problems which call for concerted remedial actions we are
not yet prepared to take. Prevention is costly. It will eliminate some jobs.
Clean-up is expensive.

The American people are not yet ready to act decisively with respect to
the longer-range prospects of our society. Satisfying immediate needs and
preserving current operations receives almost exclusive attention. For example, overfishing and overlogging continue because cutting back would
mean loss of jobs for those producing the questionable increment of production. There are few well-run, effective programs supported by business
and government to train people who have been laid off to qualify for different jobs or self-employment. Nor is there intensive scientific research to
find substitute materials to reduce our enormous consumption of paper,
wood products, and other substances depleting our natural resources.

Opponents of conservation point out that unless there are international
agreements, cutting back our overfishing and overlogging enables other
countries to reap the profits we forego if we adopt environmentally sound
schedules of production. They believe that science will surely find feasible
substitutes which will be adopted to reduce our gargantuan use of news-
print, bags, cartons, containers, and other paper products before all of our
forests are gone. Tree farms will provide us with all the wood we need for
articles that must be made of this material. New foods will be discovered
or produced synthetically which will be nutritious, tasty, odoriferously appealing, and visually attractive. And their disposal after use will require no
more landfills or be no more difficult to recycle than present substances
and products.

It is clear from only these several examples that a single action cannot
resolve a significant environmental problem or any other matter of societal
consequence. By their nature such problems involve several or many aspects
of a society, and their resolution requires actions in concert by the different
elements concerned. This is what comprehensive planning is all about.

All of the elements noted in this section are essential for a functioning
government, but natural resources are especially noteworthy. They are the
features of the world that are most critical to human survival. They constitute the most complex component because they include the physical
world, animate life, biological and chemical mechanisms, and evolutionary
processes. They are the most difficult element to comprehend for these reasons and because of our limited knowledge concerning the interactions of
the many forces involved.

## Human Resources

When we talk about natural resources we focus almost exclusively on physical, geographical entities. We tend to forget human resources, although it is people we are most concerned about. We are not only vitally affected by our surroundings, but we affect and can destroy the environment as a habitat for human beings. It is we, the people, who will act or fail to act with respect to our society and its future.

We are a human entity of about 250 million people in the United States, which can be counted, evaluated, improved, or worsened over time. In the early 1990s there were fewer younger people and many more older people than there were previously. The population is more racially and ethnically diverse than ever before, posing problems of compatibility and integration. Black and Hispanic minorities, 13 and 10 percent, respectively, of the population, seek better treatment and political power. Almost 9 percent of our population is foreign born. People of Spanish origin have more than doubled during the past decade. Spanish is spoken at home by one-half of the 13 percent of children over four years old who do not speak English in the home. For those who cannot or do not communicate in the common and official language of the land, participation is more difficult.

The basic unit of our society, the family and household, is changing. There are now three-fifths as many non-family as family households. Only 63 percent of men and 59 percent of women are married nowadays. It looks as if there will be as many unmarried as married men and women before long. Only three-quarters of children live in homes with two live-in parents. Almost three-fifths of women sixteen years of age and older are employed. Families with employed mothers and preschool children spend 7 percent of their incomes for child care.

With respect to education, about one-fifth of our population over 24 years of age never completed high school. Four out of five of us have had no higher education. Many of those lacking the minimum education needed for most employment opportunities in the 1990s are among the 15 percent of our population below the poverty line as defined by the federal government. With respect to unlawful behavior, millions use illicit drugs excessively. Every year, those so inclined commit about fourteen million criminal acts, which landed more than a million people in jail.

These data suggest the hundreds of millions of personal problems and decisions people face en masse each day. They also define major categories of necessary accomplishment. The different racial groups in the United States will not interact constructively nor integrate successfully without policies and programs formulated and implemented to this end. Otherwise, we can look forward to divisive social confrontation and conflict. With free-flowing communication a key requirement in technologically advanced societies, citizens need at least to be able to understand, read, and write the official common language of the land, if the body politic is to function effectively and democracy is to prevail. This will require special educational incentives and linguistic programs. Those without a high school education will find it difficult or impossible to find employment in an increasingly technologically complicated world. Advanced education or special training will be needed for more and more ordinary activities. Great advances in public and "self-service" education are required.

The traditional "family unit" must be revitalized, if indeed this is possible with failed marriages, single-parent homes, neglected and abandoned children, and other deterioration in the marital and household situation. Or another "building block" must be found or created to inculcate in children the positive attitude and the ethical, social, and educational values needed for individual and collective progress. This should contribute to reducing delinquent and illegal behavior, and disregard for the rule of law and representative government. In all of these attainments, the mass media must exert a positive influence.

To achieve these improvements, human resources must be treated as a system of interrelated parts. Ethnic attitudes, literacy and educational requirements, the job market, the family, personal and societal behavior, and constructive citizenship are interrelated. When treating forest resources wisely and well, we take into account the principal components of the system as an entity: existing woodlands, depletion, biotics, ecology, weather and climate, logging practices, commercial and recreational use, related employment, preservation, and forests as an element in the local, regional, and national economy.

For too long we have deluded ourselves that there was a simple and easy way to resolve multifaceted societal problems by taking sporadic actions concerning one element, without considering and acting on dependent factors. Advancement in the quality, capability, and collective performance of a population requires overall policies and simultaneous actions with respect to interdependent elements.

For some time to come maintaining and creating new jobs for growing populations will be the primary concern of developing nations seeking to improve their economy by rapid industrialization, avoiding the civil unrest and societal disintegration which could result from a slower development or restrictions on the use of natural resources. No society can tolerate a substantial proportion of its population unemployed, with minimal income, and disaffected. Under such circumstances, most environmental protection and conservation of resources must await a more fully developed economy.

## Standards

The United States, with a federal government, 50 states, and its territories and possessions, could not function without certain national standards.

Communication, transportation, postal service, monetary and financial systems could not operate effectively or at all if there were inconsistent requirements imposed by each state. Procedures for safe flying and air traffic control cannot change at successive state lines for aircraft travelling at speeds of hundreds of miles an hour, or for radio and television frequencies transmitting electromagnetic impulses at close to the speed of light. Different postage rates or special charges among states would lengthen delivery times and increase costs. Different monetary exchange rates would make a national financial system impossible.

If information collected by different states for regional and national surveys is not consistent, it cannot be aggregated into the weather forecasts, financial data, and other reports covering these larger areas that are used by individuals and organizations throughout the land. The more rules, regulations, requirements, and procedures that can be made consistent or the same among the states, the more efficient and less costly the operations involved and the less exasperating the conduct of human affairs. Of course, such standardization is impossible, impractical, or undesirable for certain activities. For example, geographical, geological, and climatic differences among states call for variations in regulations and requirements with the same purpose and much the same content. The strength required in local building codes for buildings to meet minimum standards for public safety is greater in states with heavy winter snows than in those where snow is rarely seen. No special structural strengthening is required where there is little or no seismic activity and none expected, based on historical experience and geological knowledge.

Large states with few people and long distances between populated places favor higher speed limits than small states packed with people and experiencing traffic congestion. Historical and cultural traditions regarding family formation, educational imperatives, or religious convictions in different states relate to acceptable behavior, which in turn affects certain laws and regulations. Although there are such modifications, most of the content of comparable laws in different states is similar or the same for all intents and purposes. It saves time, effort, and money if these principal provisions are uniform. Sometimes states copy verbatim laws that have been applied successfully elsewhere, to discover later that certain details are inappropriate or conflict with existing provisions in the state adopting the law.

Federal laws apply to all states. They are concerned with activities which by their nature require national action, benefit everyone equally, or "make sense" by preventing the confusion, conflict, and additional costs which arise when states set different standards. Requirements relating to air and ground transportation and communication systems illustrate the first category. Laws establishing standards for the production, handling, and safe consumption of food and use of drugs to protect the public from contamination, poisoning, disease, or injury belong to the second group. A federal law requiring that motorists wear seat-belts makes sense because accident data indicate that they save lives and reduce injuries. People comply because they agree with the law. Most regulations cannot be enforced completely and continually because the surveillance required is impractical, impossible, or far too costly.

Less publicized, but essential in science and engineering, are governmental standards defining and applying exact units of measurement and comparison. It would be operationally impossible if different states used different units of distance, temperature, pressure, electric current, seismic movement, and other indicators used to compare different measurements of many kinds. Science, engineering, and industry employ many units of measurement which permit comparison at any time and over time for historical review.

There are also the one-of-a kind objects, precise instrumentation, or other means of exact comparison that are established to provide the final confirmation of the accuracy of methods of measurement used regularly. A well-known example is the meter, which is defined in the dictionary as "the distance at the temperature of melting ice between the centres of two lines traced on a platinum-iridium bar deposited at the International Bureau of Weights and Measures", or "1,533,164.13 of the wave lengths of the red light emitted by a cadmium vapour lamp excited under certain specified conditions". There are more recent and much more exact scientific measurements.

The adoption of standards for widespread or universal use does not happen readily as a consequence of logic or "good sense". In the late nineteenth century in the United States, the government was undecided whether to continue supporting many different local "sun-times" and regional "railroad times" in different parts of the country, or to adopt Greenwich Mean time as the standard for the nation with several time zones. Today, we are still divided between our traditional Imperial System (inches, feet, miles . . . ) and the Metric System standard throughout most of the world (centimeters, meters, kilometers . . . ). Continued advances in science and technology, and increasing interactions around the world encourage the adoption of standards.

## Simulation of Society

As discussed previously, religion symbolizes our progress along the path leading to civilized behavior. It simulates the extent to which we have achieved a personal integration of our intuitions, emotions, and reasoning which produce an inner sense of well-being, societal harmony, constructive collective action, and peaceful resolution of differences. We have a long way to go. Government symbolizes our total state of affairs, not only the extent to which we have achieved a state of well-being, but whether we have also accumulated the knowledge and cognitive capability to develop a societal system and a government which functions effectively and will endure. The best humanistic aspirations will not be realized if the means and methods of attaining them are inadequate or basically flawed.

Government simulates our total human condition most completely. Its form represents what the populace wants, is willing to accept, or must endure, ranging from democracies with the most freedoms to absolute dictatorships with a subservient population and few if any freedoms. Democratic governments operating according to civil law, religious governments directed by canon law, and autocratic regimes ruling by arbitrary decree represent, effectuate, and perpetuate very different kinds of societies. The populations involved are very different in their aspirations and willingness to accept directive controls by a supreme authority. If they are to exist and function, however, different forms of government must perform the same basic operations. But the nature of these operations and the way they are conducted are as different as the types of regime. The objectives of their comprehensive planning will also be very different, but the analytical techniques employed will be substantially the same.

There are forces in a democratic society which favor reducing the role of the central government and decentralizing as much of its power and as many of its responsibilities as possible. The central government may have undertaken more than public, private, and special interests are willing to accept at the time. It may be ineffective, corrupt, arbitrary, or dictatorial. Other units in the total political system or power structure may want to take control. In a federal system, elected representatives of the central government may realize that they cannot perform as expected and accomplish what most people want and their constituents know is needed.

If the federal government transfers certain of its controversial and difficult societal responsibilities to the states and they do not object, it also transfers accountability and blame if the states do not perform. Whether the transfer is successful will not be known for some years. Everybody involved will have disassociated themselves from the decision if it proves mistaken, or moved on to other things. Whether or not they agreed with the transfer at the time, people will have forgotten who said and did what. This was the situation in the United States in the mid-1990s when Congress elected to transfer several of its responsibilities for heath care and social services to the states. The wisdom of such a move will not be known conclusively for many years.

A federal or national government should perform those functions it alone can execute, and those which it can carry out most successfully in the general public interest. If it is not fulfilling those national responsibilities, it should not be dismembered by untested legislative action. It should be restructured, manned, and managed so that it performs successfully in the public interest.

## Freedom

Governments represent and exercise the degree of authority people want or will accept. There can be no societal entity if everybody has complete freedom to do whatever they want, whenever they want, regardless of the effects on others. In democracies there is continuing debate concerning freedom of action and expression. In some countries, if people are assured acceptable secure employment and a pension by the government, they will accept its absolute authority and its direction of many aspects of their lives. Other countries are accustomed to a ruler or "strong man" and accept his dictates; people reason that this is how it was in the past and is fated to be today, or there is no other choice. Another nation may minimize the role of government because private political powers object to any limitation on their actions.

Both permissive and restrictive views concerning individual freedom would agree that legalizing criminal acts such as murder or theft by anyone at any time he or she desires would produce chaos rather than community. A society cannot exist as a functioning entity without some restrictions on individual behavior. Even with sound policies and the best of intentions, every society abandons its professed policies at times. Some religious governments ostracize disbelievers and call for the assassination of those they consider blasphemous. At times, avowedly Christian governments execute political opponents without trial or explanation, or with trumped-up charges. Democracies may knowingly engage in unlawful acts; some conduct violent and destructive "ethnic cleansing". The prescribed behavior of every government is different in time of war, civil emergency, revolution, and religious exorcism. Certain freedoms are not tolerated in wartime. Every government symbolizes the negative and abhorrent as well as the positive and laudable aspects of the society it simulates.

In the United States, one group claims that any limitation on individual "freedom of speech" including writing, art, music, and demonstrative acts violates the First Amendment of the Constitution. In other democratic societies, without a constitutional referent, complete freedom of expression would presumably be argued as an inherent and inalienable right of human beings as well as other animals. A second group maintains that a society cannot tolerate certain deliberately destructive statements and acts, such as deliberately disseminating false allegations difficult or impossible to refute, inciting people to illegal violent acts, or intentionally causing panic which injures or kills people. Differences between the two groups are exacerbated when the freedom under debate involves a personal concern, special interest, or monetary gain or loss for those involved. When this is the case, the first group finds any detrimental effects on society less compelling or nonexistent. The second group is motivated to reaffirm its convictions concerning restrictions it believes benefit society.

We have become so mired in what we have a right to do that we rarely give a thought to what we ought to do. And the press and electronic media are at the extreme.[3]

In the final analysis, there should be as much freedom of expression as is consistent with the needs of the society. But this does not provide specific answers to crucial and controversial questions. When are intentionally hateful, "rabble-rousing" expressions societally destructive? When is recorded history falsified in a personal interpretation by an author or producer which misstates documented facts? When is the repetitious portrayal of violence and aberrant behavior detrimental for children? When is art so obscene or pornographic in the eyes and minds of the great majority of people that it should not be widely disseminated? When are moral values and ethical views so right and so true that opposing viewpoints and convictions should not be allowed?

The answers to such questions are properly the subject of intense debate. They have to do with vital aspects of a society and determine certain characteristics of its government. They represent for every person another of the continual choices that must be made in real life, between childhood desires and parental admonitions, between individual preferences and permissible family behavior, between personal conclusions and those of a teacher, spouse, employer, or role model encountered in everyday life. In a democracy, such choices are resolved collectively when a consensus produces political decision and governmental action. The answers vary with different conditions. In general, the need for limitations on complete freedom of speech increases as telecomputing provides immediate intercommunication, reaction, and collective action by hundreds of millions of people. Television and computer video screens provide immediate and simultaneous exposure of dangerously disruptive and societally damaging misinformation broadcast by an individual or a single organization to an entire nation and much of the rest of the world.

### Corruption

The success of societies depends in large part on their central government performing effectively. The characteristic of government most endemic and most corrosive of quality performance is corruption. A concept which is different in different societies.

In the United States tipping is an established way of acknowledging personal services that are part of certain enterprises or operations such as restaurants, baggage handling, and taxi services, so much so that a place for tips is designated on some bills. They are not part of most operations and are considered inappropriate in connection with government activities and public services. Tips are not regarded as bribes. Quite to the contrary, expected income from tips is taken into account in determining regular pay.

In every country there is a word for gratuity: pourboir, trinkgeld, mancia, propina, drikkepenge, drick, spets.

There have been nations in which all tipping was forbidden. In some countries, tips are part of almost all services and most public and private operations which require approval, permission, or other procedural and documentary paperwork. So pervasive are those tips that American companies include them as a normal cost of doing business in these countries. They are considered bribes by American businessmen who are unaccustomed to this system and resent the added costs. To those within the foreign country, they are part of the pay, salary, or other income of ordinary workers and lesser officials, as tips are for waiters in American restaurants. Whether they add to total costs depends on whether without them living wages and salaries would have to be raised to avoid serious civil unrest.

The societal system is corrupt when bribes reach higher managerial levels in government and in business, and large sums of money are expected by officials in connection with contract awards, purchasing agreements, and other actions. Small bribes become large exactions. The public believes or wants to believe that higher officials are above corruption because they occupy what the public regards as positions of implicit trust. These personages count in the social scheme of things, and are counted on by ordinary folk to perform properly because of their relative importance. The leaders in a society are expected to adhere to the high moral and ethical standards which people aspire to but rarely achieve themselves.

Public confidence in government and business leadership, integrity, and concern with society is eroded by corruption. Cynicism rises. Consuming interest in one's personal affairs becomes the only realistic objective as concern for community and society becomes less credible. The consequences of corruption weaken the nation and its prospects. The nature and degree of the corruption simulates the condition of the society.

### Public Service

Employment by government can be established and conducted as a privilege, as a respected opportunity for public service, with compensation comparable to what is available in the private sector. The likelihood of corruption is reduced if core personnel in government are selected for their probity as well as their competence, and integrity is emphasized throughout their training and employment. And a sense of personal and professional pride can be engendered and encouraged by various administrative procedures which discourage misdemeanors. Several countries have established a tradition of competent professional public servants, most of them trained in schools of public administration.

There are a dozen or so such schools in the United States. There are also over 60 accredited schools awarding graduate degrees in urban and regional land-use planning. Most of their graduates are employed by federal, state, and local governments, or by private consulting firms which provide public services not regularly included in governmental budgets. In addition, schools of engineering, law, medicine, and the sciences supply people with the special knowledge required in connection with many governmental activities.

Unfortunately for enlightened government, the practice of most nations is to use public services for political purposes. Elected and appointed officials reward their political supporters, or act to obtain new advocates, by getting them government jobs where they can rest secure until a new regime takes over with its political clientele. They support their benefactors at work and at election time. A block of such votes and other forms of political support can make the difference in closely contested elections.

In general, the competence of political appointees is less than those selected on merit. They are less motivated to improve themselves while employed. The politics behind their appointments do not represent or encourage a sense of public responsibility and personal probity. United States ambassadors are often appointed as a reward for contributions to the political party in power. If they have neither the competence nor the motivation needed, the position is transformed into one of social amenities, with the embassy work performed by civil service deputies.

Private enterprise can contribute to superior public service. It can pass on to government new and improved management methods and analytical techniques developed in the private sector. It can arrange for certain of its executives to serve in government for a time, contributing their expertise, experiencing public service, and applying what they learn when they return to private enterprise. Law firms can donate *pro bono publico* the services of lawyers to advise or represent those who cannot afford legal services and when there is no public defender or other office to help them. Business and universities can provide as a public service expert knowledge which is needed by government and is not otherwise available. The differences between the purposes and processes of business and of government should not prevent cooperation where it is appropriate, is in the public interest, and benefits both parties.

Since television and radio are the most influential forces in a society when they can reach all parts of the country, they can impugn and rapidly discredit the public services in the minds of the people, if they wish and are allowed to do so. If the derelictions of the public service are not obvious, the mass media can extol an incompetent, corrupt, and politicized bureaucracy, which deserves opprobrium rather than praise. Except when people have enough direct experience or education to form accurate personal judgments, the mass media determine how they view many subjects. How the mass media treat the public services determines in large part their reputation, and affects the morale, motivation, and performance of public servants and the agencies they populate.

Investigative reporting is important to unearth inefficiency and corruption whenever and wherever it exists. The mass media are also in a position to express objective appraisals: to indicate the pros and cons of a controversial issue, the strengths and weaknesses of an organization, or the merits and demerits of actions by an individual. And they can point out operations that are well-conducted, organizations and individuals that are performing effectively. Explicit opinions, advice, and recommendations are expressed on the editorial and "op-ed" pages of newspapers, as editorial statements on television and radio.

Despite the equal opportunity to express approval and support, the prevailing practice is to emphasize the negative because it is more newsworthy, attracting more attention and revenue. The mass media seem to assume that well-managed organizations are recognized by those who benefit from their success, and this favorable view filters through to the public at large and positive performances are widely acknowledged. Unfortunately, this rarely occurs outside the financial community.

What are the roles and responsibilities of the mass media in a democratic society, when communications determine more than anything else the nature and success of government and private enterprise, public reactions and actions, the political situation, and the prospects of the society for the future? Whether the performance of governmental services is considered beneficial or unneeded, commendable, ordinary, or poor depends on how they are reported in the mass media more than anything else.

*Minorities*

The central government reflects and affects public attitudes toward minorities, the disadvantaged, the disabled, and the poor. If there is no concern on the part of the public for those in need, only an unusually altruistic controlling authority would take the initiative to help them. And unless the government advocates and promotes tolerance and concern for the less fortunate, it is unlikely to arise spontaneously among the people of a nation. Ethnic differences are deeply imbedded. Overcoming misunderstanding, stereotype prejudicial reactions, or active intolerance takes time. It may take many years to heal or at least ameliorate ethnic differences with tap roots in a violent past. Most people are too concerned with their current problems and questions concerning the future to dwell on the worse problems of the less fortunate.

The nature and number of minorities affect government in many ways: politically, as groups tending to vote as a block responsive to their treatment and their hopes for a future in mainstream affairs; socially, as people with distinct traditions, customs, values, attitudes, particular needs, and often different native languages and religions. These differences are reflected in specific provisions in many governmental actions: police practices, dissemination of public information, special educational requirements, affirmative action, fair employment procedures and opportunities.

Imagine 50 state governments, each or many of them with significantly different policies and programs relating to the minorities and the disadvantaged within their borders. In addition to the societal discontent created by unequal provisions, it would be difficult to justify the inefficiencies of servicing and the greater overall costs brought about by minorities and the disadvantaged moving from state to state seeking better conditions.

As with most of the major problems confronting the nation, progress toward harmonious societal relations in an increasingly racially mixed nation requires positive action by government and the mass media of communication to explain cultural and other differences that give rise to misunderstanding and antagonism. The treatment of handicapped groups symbolizes the interest and societal concern of government, the mass media, and the body politic.

### Technology

There are vast differences among nations. For some the average family monetary income is the equivalent of several hundred U.S. dollars. This does not include the value of the agricultural produce and products obtained from living off the land. In the United States, median household income is over $30,000. As noted elsewhere in this book, nations vary greatly in the area they occupy and the size of the population, in their climate, geography, history, and just about every other characteristic including their use of technology.

In a nation with an agricultural economy in the early stages of its economic development—and in some "backwoods" areas of industrialized nations—cash income is low because most people derive their livelihood directly from the land. Most of the few fabricated articles needed can be acquired by barter. Obtaining machine-powered agricultural equipment and the fuel to run it, and perhaps a single electrical outlet in the home, are likely to be the first technological acquisitions as industrialization gradually takes place.

The labor force, productive, service, and educational facilities, and people's lifestyles change accordingly. Contact with other nations increases as external trade becomes an important part of economic development, and monetary transactions part of an emerging financial system. As transportation, communication, productive processes, and other activities incorporate advanced technologies, the characteristics of the society change as markedly as they did when industrialization replaced an earlier form of economy.

As population increases because of better health services and medical facilities, more and more people move from rural areas to towns and cities seeking employment. People live longer. The knowledge and skills required for employment become greater and more specialized. Education is available to more people and essential for more and more jobs. Electronic communication is widespread, immediate, and affordable for most people. Almost all households in the United States have a telephone, television, and radio. A billion or more homes in the world are so equipped today. More and more households will soon have a computer. There is more business and commercial travel. Borrowing, credit, bank accounts, methods of payment, types of investment form a monetary system and market economy with more and more transactions electronically conducted, recorded, and stored.

The size and functions of government simulate the stage of economic and technological development of the country. In a subsistence economy with most of the population living off the land, less government is needed than in industrialized and technically complex societies, unless the governments are deliberately bloated for political purposes. If it is functioning successfully, government reflects the managerial and service needs of the society as it develops.

As populations increase and human affairs become organizationally more complicated and technically more complex, governmental administrative operations and service activities require more people, although probably not in direct proportion to the population increases. Better managerial methods, artificial intelligence, and robotics may substitute for people in certain routine situations. The competence of public service must keep pace as the intellectual content of government advances; instant communications and operational interrelationships require quicker reactions and responsive actions than ever before.

*Military Forces*

As human populations increased and encroached on each others' domains some thousands of years ago, competition and armed conflict became part of the human scene. War became then and continues today to be the scourge of humankind: the greatest threat to the welfare and survival of Homo sapiens.

Governments have had to determine the military forces required to defend themselves against attack, to mount an offensive against another nation, or to survive both events. This always involved a significant portion of the nation's assets: people, money, equipment, and facilities. Solutions have ranged from large to small armed forces, to none at all, from volunteer citizen to paid professional armies, from commandeered vessels to permanent navies. All the while, destructive weapons, tactics, and logistics developed until they have reached the awesome capabilities of today. For the first time in human history, we can, with nuclear, biological, and chemical weapons, eradicate ourselves as a species from the face of the earth.

In the United States today there are more than 1.5 million men and women on active duty in the armed services. There are probably as many or more civilian employees working for or dependent on the military. A significant percentage of the nation's scientific and engineering personnel are associated directly or indirectly with military activities. There is the "military-industrial complex", so designated by President of the United States and General of the Armies Dwight D. Eisenhower, composed of installations and facilities of all sizes and descriptions which serve the military forces in one way or another. Military expenditures account for close to one-third of the discretionary national budget. There are about 25 million military veterans of U.S. wars living today. Since the turn of the century, they have received more than $100 billion in compensation and pension benefits.

Worldwide, the thirty nations with the largest armed forces maintain about seventeen million troops on active duty, with two and a half times as many on reserve. One of every ten people on earth is connected with the military. Estimating Russia's defense expenditures as two-thirds of those of the United States, these 30 countries spend over $625 billion every year for military purposes. Six of them have "known strategic nuclear capability". Several additional nations may have now or will have this superdestructive capability in a few years.

It is clear that military activities and costs are an essential governmental concern. They provide direct and indirect employment for many people. Military research and development produce scientific and technological advances which can be applied in the civilian sector, or will in time, when released from security classification, benefit the population at large by adding to existing knowledge. Some military installations—such as hospitals, barracks, supply centers, or special port facilities—serve a useful purpose for a long time, for military personnel or when adapted for civilian use.

Armored vehicles, naval vessels, aircraft, missiles, guns, and other weapons systems are replaced as new, more deadly versions are created at greater unit cost, in a never-ending escalation. They do not add as much to the national stock of fixed assets as if the money have been spent for nonmilitary purposes, unless the country conquers additional territory and acquires assets worth more than the cost of the military action.

Certainly, the prospects of societies would be enhanced if military pressures, conquests, or annihilation were not a constant concern, requiring large expenditures which could be applied directly and more beneficially for civilian purposes. In many countries this would also reduce the ever-present threat posed by military and heavily armed police forces to democratic forms of government.

Wars started long before the present population explosion. Presumably, they are not therefore nature's way of controlling our population growth, which we appear unable to do ourselves, by implanting within us irresistible self-destructive instincts. And presumably the virtues of disciplined behavior, coordinated action, loyalty to a community and a nation can be instilled or acquired other than by being a soldier. And impulses accentuated in learning how to kill and conquer can be sublimated into constructive civilian behavior. Epidemics of unknown diseases could turn out to be nature's method of controlling our reproduction rate.

Governments determine national policy with respect to military defense and offense. Do they need to protect themselves from neighbors? Is there a world power which will protect them against military attack? If not, does a nation have the resources to aspire to becoming a global power? Can coalitions of nations committed to collective self-defense preserve international peace, or does the government decide to maintain a minimum or no armed forces at all, and compete economically and diplomatically in the global marketplace?

Such choices are made all the more difficult by the sale of sophisticated weapons systems by the leading military powers to nations around the world. Or they are smuggled among nations by criminals, dissidents, and others for profit or any one of many sane and insane motivations. The number of nations with nuclear capabilities will surely increase. With each passing year, the practicality of clandestinely concealing enormously destructive weapons increases as they become smaller and more difficult to detect. One or more nuclear bombs, together with biological nerve gas and poisonous chemical bombs, present a threat with potential consequences difficult to imagine.

By hiding such devices with remote-controlled detonation in countries they fear or dislike—or even as a strategic deterrent against some future eventuality—nations would defend themselves by threatening to detonate the hidden devices if attacked. It is conceivable that the nations of the world could be held in terror-stricken but peaceful coexistence by such "mutually assured destruction". Or they could engage in joint annihilation.

Governments will find it increasingly difficult to relate successfully with a world so militarily uncertain, precarious, and dangerous.

## National Simulation

Since governments engage in or are concerned with all human activities, they employ all of the various simulations noted in the previous pages of this book. Their unique responsibility is the overall direction of the political entity they control or represent. In the United States, the laws passed by Congress and the executive orders of the president, together with those of the 50 states, indicate by words and numbers the lawful behavior of individuals and the nature and permissible activities of organizations, in accordance with our Constitution. The master simulation required to fulfill the responsibility of governing in a democracy is the subject of this section.

In its brief history compared to most countries, the United States has developed from a sparsely populated land to a powerful nation of some 265 million people. It is economically and militarily preeminent among nations, with the highest average living standard of any country. It has functioned successfully as the leading democracy, with noteworthy advances in humanity despite a violent and societally disruptive civil war, ethnic diversity, religious and ideological differences. It has led the world in scientific and technological advances. We have much to be thankful for and to aspire to.

There are major problems, however, to be resolved if the United States is to maintain societal harmony and civil stability within its borders, and function effectively in an increasingly complex and potentially self-destructive world. The most serious of these is the poor performance of Congress. As the nation's highest representative and directive institution—charged with determining policy, enacting legislation, and controlling the public purse—Congress is the most crucial decision-making body in a land ruled by law.

Several developments threaten its capability to perform successfully. First and foremost is its size. When there are 535 individuals involved in directing anything, effective organization of their individual and collective activities and efficient operating procedures are essential. Otherwise, constructive performance is limited if not impossible. Over the years Congress has fragmented itself into some 300 committees and subcommittees. On the average, each senator is a member of eleven committees or subcommittees. Because this is more than any one person can handle together with other duties, the overload guarantees superficial or neglectful performance with respect to most of them. Furthermore, many committees have so many members that it is next to impossible to act effectively. Their members accept overassignment to committees because they present opportunities for public exposure and provide political prestige. They are assemblies rather than deliberative groups.

The result of this proliferation of oversized committees is wasted time and energy by all concerned, not to mention unproductive expenditure of money. The substantive product is usually the lowest common denominator of superficial consideration, rather than thoughtful analysis of a problem and how best to resolve it. In addition to this organizational and procedural inefficiency there has been a change in the motivation of our political representatives. Rather than an opportunity for a limited period of public service, as was once the case, political representation has become a profession with prestige, power, perquisites, tenure, generous pensions, and postretirement employment opportunities.

The requirements nowadays for election and reelection make constructive analytical performance by Congress next to impossible. Most of our representatives' time and effort is spent raising larger and larger sums of money to meet increasing political campaign costs. Candidates are now coming forth with the publicly avowed purpose of spending millions of their own dollars to be elected to public office. And the chances of incumbents being reelected are judged as much by the campaign funds they have accumulated as by their capability and performance in office. Costly television exposure is critical. The time is approaching when the person with the most money and the most exposure on television is assured election and reelection. Attention if not deference to special interests is required because they provide almost all the campaign funds. Some special interests give money regularly to members of both political parties to ensure special treatment or at least "the privilege of being heard", regardless of which party is in power.

The difference between political posture and legislative performance is reflected in the fact that only some 3 percent of bills introduced in Congress are enacted into law. Most are introduced to fulfill political obligations for personal purposes, without serious interest in them or efforts at adoption. Together with news releases, videotapes, and statements inserted in the *Congressional Record,* most legislative proposals are used to claim positive performance in office. Prepared speeches are a form of political currency delivered with calculated body language at podiums in the halls of Congress, recorded and made available to supportive groups at home. They may be delivered to an empty hall.

Attention to the above political realities has consumed the time and energy required and devoted not long ago to legislative performance in the public interest. To be non-partisan today with an independent vote is to be politically inconsequential in an era of fierce partisan politics and majority power. To a large extent Congress has set aside its collective responsibility of constructive leadership to meet the demands of the political marketplace.

This situation does not bode well for the future. In a technically complicated, fast-acting, and internationally interactive world, successful performance at the top requires the selection and election of the most capable people committed to public service. The electorate must look beyond political promotional strategies and advertising tactics devised by paid political consultants. Representatives must be able to concentrate on problem analysis and legislative action, without having to devote themselves to raising money, attending to special interests or private privilege. They should be concerned with the wishes of their constituents, but speak out and act contrary to current public opinion when they believe that it is transitory, too parochial, or not in the general public interest. They should not live, breathe, and vote according to the latest public opinion poll. They should be willing and able to plan ahead as necessary and desirable.

Altogether, these precepts are not Utopian or impractical. Rather than adopting the organization and procedures required to perform effectively, Congress is considering transferring to the 50 states responsibility for national public health, welfare, educational, and environmental programs, claiming that they will be more successfully carried out without the "heavy hand of big government". Or because in this way Congress passes on to state governments the onus, public exposure, and the political responsibility associated with these programs. This restructuring was presented as "balancing the budget" and getting rid of bureaucratic "rules and regulations".

So significant a proposal merited more thorough consideration and widespread debate than it was accorded. Important questions are involved. What will happen when the provisions and administration of these programs, intended to benefit people equally, differ markedly among the 50 states? Some will perform with outstanding success, will innovate and find better ways of carrying out their part of national programs. Some will provide less and administer poorly. Will there be migration between states by people seeking the programs which will benefit them the most? Can those who are not allowed to do this claim "unequal treatment" under the national intention? Will so many unjust discrepancies develop over time that federal standards and other requirements must be reinstituted? Should the original federal programs have been revised, improved, and retained?

Improving the performance of the federal government requires improving the performance of Congress. This will not come about by spontaneous enlightenment. It requires some compelling event or condition. For example, consider the partisan political deadlock over the federal budget in 1996 between the president and Congress. If shutting down parts of the federal government had lasted longer, might the electorate have considered this so politically inexcusable and needlessly disruptive of many people's lives that it would have forced changes preventing such stalemate occurring again? Might our elected representatives have become so frustrated, so disturbed at not being able to reach a collective decision as a governing body, that they might have acted on their own initiative to prevent such deadlock? Or believing that neither of these developments would occur, might the body politic in a subsequent election have accepted the assurances of a demagogic candidate decrying such stalemate, claiming that he would "put matters right" if elected and granted temporary legal power to do so? Would temporary political power be relinquished when its special purpose was attained?

Such a critical situation would not develop if Congress managed its affairs more responsibly and adroitly. To direct their activities and plan ahead as they must, most organizations require some simulation of their operations and functioning as an informational basis for decisions. Small businesses employ the four accounting statements referred to in a previous section to provide the information needed to manage the enterprise and avoid such fatal mistakes as not having enough money available to meet a payroll date or to pay interest on debt when due. Most large companies employ simulations on computers which represent the operations and condition of the principal components of the company and their interactions. The consequences of a decision or proposal concerning one component on the others can be quickly determined. The current and predictive reliability of the simulation is compared with what actually occurs, and continually improved to more closely represent the corporate entity and its functioning.

Such simulations are not used by our elected representatives and chief governmental executives in making the most vital determinations affecting our present and our future. The evaluations they make, the conclusions they reach, their decisions, and the actions they take relate to the specific matter under consideration. Its relations to other matters with which it is connected, and its interactions with the nation as a whole, are not taken into account. There is no simulation or portrayal of the nation at large permitting such analysis; no display of data concerning the principal elements comprising the nation, their interrelationships, the socioeconomic and legal situation, population characteristics and projections, trends, commitments, prospects, and relevant history.

Simulations are employed in many business and governmental activities, but not by federal and state legislatures, which make the most crucial decisions affecting the functioning, welfare, and prospects of our society. Simulations require relating decisions and resulting legislation to a common reference and analytic formulation rather than a vague statement or platitude. All too often it is possible to disregard major problems and take no action. By avoiding as many decisions as possible, our elected representatives can claim that they are not directly accountable if things do not work out or public opinion changes. The public is fickle. A proposal or endorsement by an elected official, favored by his constituency at the time, may haunt him later when he seeks reelection and the electorate has changed its mind, opposing what was done earlier with their concurrence. There is no escaping accountability when positions, commitments, and decisions are revealed in the public record.

Our representatives have avoided simulation because it requires thoughtful consideration, realistic analysis, definite conclusions, decisions, and specific actions concerning the many questionable and controversial matters that arise in directing large organizations. There are enough troublesome issues involved in ordinary affairs. Many more when planning ahead into the indefinite future. Directive management and planning take deliberate effort, and time which politicians would prefer spending eliciting the large sums of money required for election and reelection to public office.

The electorate might demand a higher order of governmental management if there were an adequate means of evaluating the performance of those holding elective office. In the business world, chief executives, boards of directors, and company management are judged by their specific achievements. Their performance is revealed in corporate reports, financial statements, and statistics published as part of market analysis and reporting.

Investors may focus on short-term profits and stock value, market considerations, long-range prospects, or any one of the methods of evaluation
constantly devised. In the United States, we have judged the performance
of our elected representatives according to the precept "What have you
done for me lately?", rather than their achievements in general for their
constituents and the public welfare.

As long as we are only interested in what our elected officials have done
for us personally, they are not likely to adopt simulation as a means of
performing constructively in the general public interest. And until we have
a common reference with which to evaluate their performance, we are not
likely to act wisely and well in our political choices and decisions. We must
be able to look through the blizzard of television pronouncements and
other paid political promotions: "glittering generalities" claiming much but
meaning little, allegations, misinformation, and deliberate falsification. We
must want a better indication of the intentions and performance of those
we elect, and to be better informed concerning the state of our society and
nation.

There are economic and technical forces at work which call for a higher
order of governmental management in the United States. As has occurred
in business, government has become more complicated, faster acting, connected with activities and conditions in other parts of the nation and other
countries around the world. Both require superior directive management
and longer-range planning. Efficient production and distribution of electricity, for example, requires comparable managerial competence whether
it is a public or private utility. Public health services require essentially the
same medical knowledge and skills as health maintenance organizations
and physicians in private practice. Modern communications involve the
same technical and administrative capabilities whether they are designed
and operated by business or by government.

However, in a democracy, governance is by its nature more difficult and
more complex than any business enterprise. It involves more numerous
considerations, broader concerns, an entire population rather than a segment or a smaller set of customers; the full range of public reactions and
opinions, rather than the preferences and condition of a specific market;
the desires and aspirations of an entire society, rather than a customer or
client group; a wider range of political, economic, and social factors. Simulative analysis is more difficult because the broader scope and more numerous societal responsibilities of government include many more indefinite
and intangible elements.

Budgets are abbreviated simulations which show the allocation of expected income among major categories of expenditure during a given year.
They are employed by almost all governmental units and private enterprises
in the United States. Several budgets covering successive years indicate income and allocations of expenditures over the longer period of time re-

quired for certain projects and activities. Not all activities of the functioning entity are included in most budget statements. Important aspects of the operation which cannot be expressed numerically are not treated at all. In practice, the amounts allocated to different categories may be changed, provided the total amount of money budgeted remains the same. Budgets are short-term, "bare bones" approximations if they are used to simulate the functioning of a governmental entity.

The national budget, which was the centerpiece of the impasse between the president and Congress in 1996, illustrates its features and limitations as a simulative device. It enabled proposed expenditures in different major categories to be identified and debated separately, and in different combinations, year by year over a period of seven years, resulting in "balancing the budget". But it did not include substantial outlays for national defense, interest on the debt, and the social security trust fund. Despite its incompleteness as a simulation, the ease with which alternative expenditures could be seen and considered supported firm partisan positions.

On the Internet's World Wide Web . . . a computer model called the National Budget Simulator allows browsers to emulate the budget negotiators. . . . [It] divides the budget into two dozen categories. . . . One can cut or increase spending in each category. . . . A computer . . . calculates the results revealing the size of the resulting deficit or surplus.[4]

When numbers can be associated with different alternatives, they can be compared and changed in many combinations. It would have been possible, for instance, for the contending parties in 1996 to simply agree "to split the difference" between their respective proposals. The difficulty, of course, was that the numbers reflected very different conclusions concerning what the federal and state governments should be doing, and their respective roles in administering the funds appropriated.

Many people think the federal budget is a more complete simulation of the nation's activities and functioning than it is. Even if they know it is incomplete, they may consider it sufficient to reach conclusions. Or they may want to use it to put disagreements to rest whether it is complete or not. It serves the limited purpose of indicating the monetary values associated with alternative expenditures by different units of the federal government over a period of one year.

All of the primary elements of the national entity must be included in a simulation if it is to be used by elected representatives as a basis for their deliberation, conclusion, and action. Data representing different elements— such as transportation, communication, housing, and finance—are interrelated. Changes in one affect the others. The effects of proposals or assumptions concerning one of them on the others can be determined. This analytical expression of elements and their interrelationships is projected year by year into the future, showing the probable consequences of growth, trends, and decisions made today. It can be used to portray as a national simulation the likely results of a proposed plan on all the elements together.

The simulation includes elements that are vital in the functioning of the organism but cannot be expressed in numbers: political, legal, sociopsychological, personal, and historical considerations. Significant differences in the quality of elements represented by almost the same numbers are shown. For example, differences in the quality of several medical services with about the same personnel, equipment, and facilities might be indicated by comparing the mortality, morbidity, disability, or other pertinent rates for the comparable population groups they serve.

Historical information included in the simulation reveals trends and the outcome of past events and conditions. It is adjusted to take into account how the data were collected, precisely what they represented, and how they were affected by inflation. Relating what is being considered today with comparable decisions or developments in the past reduces the chances of repeating past mistakes; at the least it induces more careful consideration of the present and future in the light of history. Technical and other expert opinion, special studies, and other supplementary information which is not outdated is maintained and indexed for ready reference.

Since a nation is the most complex of human organisms, formulation of an analytical simulation of the state of the United States is an intellectual challenge indeed. There are more political, legal, public attitudinal, and other vital elements that cannot be expressed substantively with numbers than for any other human entity. They must be taken into account because at times, for most organisms and on occasion for some, they are crucial elements. Once the decision to proceed is made, it would take several years to develop a simulation which is the best possible analytical representation of the nation as a functioning entity, formulated by the best minds available, and improved continually as its reliability is checked against reality. It could be used by all three branches of the government to provide a consistent factual and analytical reference for their respective decisions and actions.

Because of the volume of data required and their analytical complexity, the national simulation would be composed, programmed, and maintained on computers. It would be displayed and viewed on large, flat computer screens along the walls of a room specifically designed for presentation to groups of people as well as individuals. Discussion taking place in this "simulation room" would be less fragmented than is usually the case, and more focused, because definitive reference material would be at hand for everyone in the room at the same time. Important decisions by legislators and others would probably be considered and made here, acting collectively rather than separately at their personal computers. Except for security classified and confidential personal information, the simulation and related material would be available to the mass media and the public at large on computer networks, and in abbreviated form as printed documents for those who do not use computers.

Adoption of a national simulation as the key referent in governmental management and planning signifies that rational analysis prevails over partisan political, special interest, parochial, or personal concerns as the primary determinant in decision-making and legislative actions. It favors thoughtful rather than superficial consideration. It is employed for overall direction and planning, not for operational management, which is the responsibility of each governmental unit involved. With simulation, the focus shifts from almost exclusive concern with parochial matters to the societal entity as a whole. It discourages casual treatment of important subjects, careless conclusions, and irresponsible decisions. It leads to a more accurate and realistic determination of priorities, to comprehensive rather than piecemeal planning. Longer range planning is more likely to be undertaken because the simulation provides an analytical justification for legislative action, reducing any political risk involved. In general and in its particulars it is conceived and expressed in the simplest possible terms, comprehensible and available to as many people as feasible.

Governmental operations conducted in the United States provide partial precedents for a national simulation which could be employed by Congress as the basic reference in its analysis of conditions, directive decisions, and legislative actions. City and county "master plans", authorized by state enabling acts, designate major categories of land use within their governmental jurisdiction. Local zoning ordinances indicate the types and intensities of industrial, commercial, residential, and public land uses permitted on a recorded parcel of property. These plans project for the next twenty years or so the spatial pattern of different land uses which the political community endorses as desirable. They are a reaction to the completely permissive land use in the early 1900s which allowed heavy industry or a 24-hour commercial activity to locate next door to a single-family home or an apartment building in an established or developing residential neighborhood.

In the United States, city and county land-use plans are formulated and administered by planning commissions appointed for this particular purpose as an advisory body to the local legislature. These master plans are subject to adoption, revision, and specific approval and legislative enactment of every zone change by the local legislature which has the police power to regulate land use. Land-use plans do not treat the basic responsibilities and operating activities of the local government, such as taxation, financial and legal affairs, public safety, sanitation, water and power, public works, transportation and communication, recreation and parks, or the public school system. City and county "master plans", despite the inclusive adjective, are advisory statements concerned solely with land use and its relation to the economic development and physical form of the community.

These land-use formulations could be expanded into true master plans by incorporating the functions and plans of the operating units of the municipal or county government. They would serve as the basic reference for determining policies, making decisions, and taking legislative action. Depicting the principal elements and aspects of the community, they would constitute the local equivalent of the national simulation discussed in previous pages.

The United States has no comprehensive national simulation of different land uses throughout the nation. Certain units of the federal government maintain records of land use relating to their activities and plans for the future: for example, the Department of Housing and Urban Development, Environmental Protection Agency, National Park and Forest Services, Geological Survey, Bureau of Land Management, Federal Highway and Railroad Commissions, and the Army Corps of Engineers in connection with its responsibilities for navigable waterways in the nation. The scope of functional operations and planning represented by these and other federal inventories of land is nationwide. Together, they constitute a portion of a complete simulation of existing, intended, and proposed land uses.

Land use is but one aspect of the national condition and situation. Information concerning every aspect and element of the United States as a functioning society is maintained by some organization—probably more completely than in any other country. The aggregate amount is enormous, often requiring a choice among alternatives or distillation of existing data.

Numerous government agencies maintain historical and current data relating to their area of concern. For example, those which provide information directly about the economy include the Bureaus of the Census, Labor Statistics, and Economic Analysis, the Federal Reserve System, Internal Revenue Service, Securities Exchange and Communications Commissions, or military Program Analysis and Evaluation. Add to such units the many federal agencies that maintain operating information concerning the kind of activity they perform and the facilities they maintain throughout the nation.

The private sector also maintains extensive data concerning its myriad substantive interests and activities. They comprise critical elements in the functional representation of the United States, since private enterprise fulfills a greater role in the economy and activities of society than in any other nation.

The sum total of the governmental and private entrepreneurial information available is more than enough—if carefully selected, distilled, and organized—to provide the factual basis for a national simulation which can serve Congress, other legislatures, and the American people as a basic analytical reference. Determining the interrelationships between disparate

Institutions 143

components of the simulation would be far more of an intellectual challenge than providing information descriptive of each element.

Considering the recent record of legislators and elected government officials, they must be induced to improve their performance. They must not disregard or postpone indefinitely acting on critical problems, nor act piecemeal. They must proceed thoughtfully and analytically in reaching conclusions and making decisions, lead the nation in directions that circumstances and the general public interest require, rather than according to transitory public opinion, partisan politics, self-interest, and reelection at all costs.

The increasing complexity of human affairs, brought about in large part by scientific and technological advances, requires competent direction and management of governmental affairs. Just as "seat of the pants" management is no longer feasible in most business, present-day legislative practices cannot cope with the major problems of society. Both business and government are being shaped by inexorable forces which not only call for superior management separately, but suggest that they must act together in the future, rather than adversarially, as is often the case today and was usual in the past.

Societies are becoming increasingly technical in nature. Almost every human activity requires particular knowledge, special competence, continuous monitoring, and skillful management if it is to operate successfully, or in many instances to function at all. In the United States, increasing technical complexity is to be seen on all sides: in communication, transportation, production, services, education, entertainment, and even our use of leisure time. Many of our activities are more closely interrelated as they employ a core of common knowledge, use the same analytical techniques, and similar equipment. The same sources of energy and computer processes are used in many human operations. Technical advances in either of these common provisions produce immediate and widespread effects. Financial markets, once separated in time and space, are tied together today in one giant complex by instant intercommunication.

Human affairs are linked in depth as well as breadth. Threats to the supply and increases in the price of crude oil not only have repercussive effects far and wide, they have led to war. Thousands of oil spills every year affect the ocean environment, which is the primary determinant of the global environment. The economies of some nations are founded on their crude oil resources. Some are immediately raised to a higher-level economy by the discovery of oil within their borders. Petroleum is probably still the most critical substance in the world. Oil and energy are dominant international political concerns.

The "Information Revolution" made possible by science and technology is affecting everyone and will change the way people live and work in the future, as much or more than the Industrial Revolution 150 years ago; no one knows now in what specific ways and how disruptively. Science and technology are a driving force affecting people's behavior. For example, recent advances have made possible new weapons systems sold to countries around the world, increasing the cost of defense for some and tempting others to attack or terrorize. The vast increase in the sophisticated weapons in the hands of individuals and groups contributes to actual and potential crime and localized destruction. A million and a half people are in prison in the United States. Unlawful activities are widespread. Areas in our large cities are battlegrounds of drug activities and juvenile violence. Many families are disintegrating. Terrorist, financial, and computer crimes are additions to a long list that has existed throughout history. Government has been unable to develop a consensus and formulate a set of coordinated policies and action programs to reduce and to prevent crime.

It is clear that superior business and governmental management are essential if human activities are to function successfully in increasingly complex societies. As now constituted and with present procedures, legislative government in the United States cannot constructively consider and act to resolve our most serious societal problems.

As more people learn of this situation through electronic systems of direct intercommunication, television, videotapes and disks, radio, newspapers, and personal contacts, public pressure will develop for better legislative government. People can see, hear, read, ruminate, and conclude for themselves how their elected representatives are performing, if reliable information concerning governmental affairs in general, specific events, actions and inaction, successes and failures is made available to all concerned and interested.

As people hear about successful comprehensive planning by corporations, some governmental agencies, and organizations directing large, multipurpose projects, they will ask why legislators and other elected officials cannot carry out their governmental responsibilities in like manner. In time, if our democratic system is hale and hearty, people will insist that elected representatives perform responsibly in the general public interest. The mounting costs of campaigning will have to be curtailed, as will undue perquisites, excessive travel at public expense, larger staffs than needed for legislative support, rewarding private interests with public dollars, costly organizational inefficiencies, political stalemates, procedural subterfuges, and seniority as an automatic right to a committee chairmanship. This is a formidable list of practices and privileges to be relinquished. If everyone conformed, no individual elected official would be hurt. Collectively, they could perform responsibly and effectively in the general public interest.

A major force for the formulation of a national simulation could originate on the Internet World Wide Web. As noted previously, in 1996 a university research center organized a National Budget Simulation page showing the federal budget divided into many categories. One can decrease or increase spending in each category. For example, the section on tax breaks allows you to close loopholes or raise corporate taxes. The simulation is an excellent means of testing preconceptions and wishful thinking. If serious and lively debate were to develop on the Internet regarding the allocation of funds in the federal budget, and there was a clear-cut consensus among many people concerning what is best for the nation, this would be reported by the mass media. Some organizations and individuals would want to air their own specific proposals. Continuing serious evaluation of the federal budget in cyberspace could cause Congress or the president to explain or elaborate their official positions.

Since a budget by itself is an entirely inadequate representation of the functioning and state of a nation, some individual, organization, or the federal government may be induced to formulate a more adequate national simulation. This would replace the budget as the basis for inquiry, discussion, and analysis on the Internet. As its usefulness was demonstrated in the minds of a growing group of interested individuals and organizations using it on the Internet, they might promote its use by government. Or the availability of a national simulative statement might support other forces pressuring legislative government toward a higher level of directive management.

## SCIENCE—TECHNOLOGY

During the past several centuries, remarkable advances in science and technology have brought about great changes in every element and aspect of most countries. The invention and development of modern means of rapid transportation of people, goods, and services, of global communication, and new manufacturing technologies have transformed the way people in industrialized countries live and think. Science had added enormously to human knowledge; no period of such short duration in human history has produced such profound changes in rapid succession.

Scientific advances and their pervasive effects will continue. As the means and methods of conducting human activities become more complex technically, they must be maintained in good working order, and there is constant pressure by those who use them to improve them. The advances in scientific knowledge required to improve existing systems trigger new systems which in turn call for further knowledge. This compound rate of progress should continue if major intellectual breakthroughs are made as frequently in the future as they have in the past, during the early stages of the current age of science. Nuclear fusion may become as practical a source of energy as fission. Superconductive methods of distributing electricity may be developed. So far there has been no asymptotic limit to the rate of growth of scientific knowledge.

Scientific thought and research have brought into question some religious beliefs that have existed in the minds of men and women for thousands of years. The belief that human beings were created *de novo* at one time by a supernatural force, spiritual, anthropomorphic, or other being confronts the Darwinian theory of evolution which postulates a very different picture of our creation. Religion has been regarded as the only and best basis for determining desirable individual moral values and human behavior. Some people maintain that scientific observation and research also provide a basis for defining optimum individual behavior and spiritual fulfillment, constructive interaction among people, and positive prospects for society that favor its survival. Its proponents believe that it would be less likely to justify war, individual cruelties, and genocide promoted or allowed by religious ethics at times in the past and present. Ecclesiastical certainty and infallibility contrast with scientific research, intellectual consensus, and gradual refinement and improvement in our moral beliefs and behavioral conclusions.

Science also confronts politicians with a basic choice. Those concerned with the public interest incorporate scientific knowledge in their political statements, conclusions, and actions, and seek scientific input if it is needed to resolve the matter at hand. Those who put election and reelection above all else ignore or try to refute scientific knowledge that does not support their personal and political self-interests. As noted in several connections in this book, this is the situation at present in the United States. Congress is not performing its responsibilities of directive guidance and planning national affairs. Its application of rational thought, the lessons of experience, and scientic method is minimal.

Sometimes it seems that Congress's utilization of scientific knowledge is limited to paying close attention to scientific sample public opinion polls. But it also makes use of the results of surveys that are anything but scientific, and some that are deliberately conducted to promote false or exaggerated public preference. As activities throughout the nation reflect scientific and technological developments more and more, Congress appears to consider them less and less in its own operations. Our elected representatives are not likely to employ scientific analysis and a national simulation in their deliberations unless public opinion focuses specifically on what is needed for constructive performance in the general public interest. This is not likely to occur unless Congress's failure to exercise sound directive leadership is exposed repeatedly by the mass media, or until the increasingly complex operating systems of the nation necessitate rational legislative decision making if they are to continue to function. Politicians know that the American public will not tolerate drastic curtailment or discontinuation of essential public services.

Almost all of the simulations noted in the sections of this book on videoelectronics and medicine are instruments made possible by scientific discoveries and technological developments. Legal, literary, and religious representations are almost entirely verbal, with relatively little mechanical or scientific simulation. Government and business employ both.

As a field of investigation and knowledge, science is intellectually distinct in several ways that are crucial to its use and significance in human affairs. It shares with religion the purpose of seeking the "truth". Some of their respective truths are similar, most are different, and some are contradictory. They are determined in different ways. Religious verities are the result of divine beliefs and spiritual reasoning. Scientific precepts are the product of "scientific method", which seeks truth in several ways: by experiments formulated to produce information or to confirm a hypothesis, which can be repeated and confirmed by scientists other than those who conceived and conducted the original experiment; by concepts in the mind which constitute logical constructs expressed mathematically or by other abstract symbols. They are confirmed by peer scientists following the same logical reasoning and reaching the same conclusion, or by confirmation of a condition or event in the physical world postulated in the mental concept. Science is simulation of cause and effect in situations and conditions observed or imagined in the physical world or formulated within the mind, which are consistent and meaningful in themselves and with other related concepts. Science is the field of analogs par excellence.

In both religion and science, beliefs and knowledge attained in their respective ways accumulate and aggregate into an established and generally accepted body of knowledge, which provides a basis for further exploration and discovery unless everything done before is to be done over again. In science, this basis is revealed in the citations which represent the substantive roots of a scientific paper. At times the established body of knowledge can delay acceptance of new knowledge which contradicts what has been accepted as fact for many years. The earth was considered flat for a very long time. Plate tectonics, reporting a different geological structure of the earth's mantle, was rejected by almost all geologists because it was so different from previous conclusions. Evidence of the existence of prions was resisted by biologists for twenty years because of their belief that only viruses and bacteria cause disease. After every such instance of people's resistance to radical change, new areas of investigation have opened up and additions made to the existing body of scientic knowledge.

Mathematics imposes on itself the rigorous statement and reproducibility of the hard sciences. It is the most powerful analytical instrument in the store of human knowledge. As the means of quantitative expression and interactive calculation, it is employed in both hard and soft scientific applications. As mathematics develops methods of calculating probabilities and dealing with uncertainties, it can be used in some way in connection with most human activities. Even the most theoretical and abstract mathematics can lead to practical uses.

Math researcher finds way to organize chaos, leading to better air-traffic control, smarter missiles . . . a good example of how very abstract mathematical theory might turn out to be an important practical tool for the solution of real-life problems.[5]

As the sciences and mathematics leap forward, aided by fantastically fast calculations by computers, they become progressively more complex and specialized. This is demonstrated by the multiple authorship of most scientific papers reporting the results of research today. Papers with one author are few and far between in scientific publications. Not too many years ago, single authors predominated. Nowadays, scientific papers can have ten or more authors each responsible for a particular part of the research. This subdivision into smaller and smaller segments of knowledge or expertise among fewer and fewer people accentuates the disparity between the highly educated "haves" and undereducated "have-nots". Coupled with the differences in income and wealth between the top several percent of the population and everybody else, increasing scientific specialization exacerbates an already potentially disruptive societal situation.

Advances in the hard sciences are so numerous, significant, and often newsworthy nowadays that they are covered or at least noted by one of the media of communication. Physics delves deeper into quantum theory, the search for the ultimate elementary particle, and a grand, unified theory of "everything". Mathematics extends its own substantive perceptions, employing the increasingly high-speed calculations and simulative capabilities of the computer which have made possible or hastened scientific advances in general. Meteorology is discovering more about the global formation of atmospheric conditions, and specific events such as tornadoes, hurricanes, and earthquakes. Chemistry explores the composition and dynamics of matter and bodily functions, producing new materials and medication. Medicine has developed non-invasive diagnostic and surgical procedures, and replacements for more and more parts of the human body. Astronomy looks further and further into the universe and its evolutionary history, with new instruments on earth and the Hubble telescope in the sky. Biology is making the most dramatic advancements with cellular and genetic discoveries following one after another, posing ethical and social problems never before encountered.

The public is made aware of the more dramatic accomplishments of science by the mass media, but is not yet alert to the nature and requirements of the scientific method, its employment in human affairs, and its implications for the future development of society. There has never been such a burst of new knowledge, new mechanisms, and new processes. Coincident with advances in each field of science there has been a corresponding increase in the functional interconnections between them. Physics, chemistry, biology, and mathematics, for example, are interlocked in a single, functional comprehension.

The soft sciences have not matched the theoretical and applied achievements of the hard sciences because human beings are critical components of economics, sociology, political science, public administration, and other fields having to do with people who are far more indeterminate, variable, and unpredictable in their reactions and actions than the forces involved in the inanimate objects and non-human creatures treated by the physical sciences. Generalizations can be made concerning matters relating to people based on existing knowledge. They are helpful guideposts for certain purposes, but rigorous analysis of human behavior employing scientific methods is just beginning. Research efforts and supporting funds have been directed for the most part to the physical rather than the social sciences because of their more precise and positive results, which are immediately available for military and potentially profitable private use in ongoing operations.

It is time for exploratory science to be equally divided between the physical and the social sciences, and between basic and applied research. Remarkable advances in the hard sciences cannot be realized if people incapacitate themselves by civil conflict, war, societal disintegration, environmental contamination, or their inability to act collectively to counter plague, pestilence, terrorism, or natural catastrophes. Some scientific advances could prove harmful if they facilitate the disintegration of societal organisms or make them more vulnerable to disruption; for example, those that increase the lethality and transportability of massively destructive weapons, decrease their size, and reduce their cost, or those without safeguards that make it easier to act and profit illegally.

Most scientists prefer to devote themselves to basic research. Not only do they consider it more important than applied research, but they are more likely to be applauded and remembered for fundamental rather than operable contributions. It is applied research concerning human behavior, however, which is urgently needed today. By learning more about human attitudes and motivation, science can contribute to persuading the American people to act positively in their own best interest, favorable prospects, and survival as a species.

Few people question whether science is essential for the successful functioning of the United States. Its operational systems depend directly on scientists for their design, maintenance, improvement, and eventual replacement, or on engineers, physicians, law enforcement personnel, and other professionals and specialists who apply scientific knowledge and principles in their work but are not themselves engaged in scientific research. To make use of this knowledge and perform in the general public interest, legislators must appreciate the contributions and the limitations of science, and recognize its role in modern American society. Their attitudes, policies, and actions with regard to science affect the national, state, and local welfare. For its part, planning must take into account the science incorporated in the form and functioning of the entity being planned. And it must employ scientific knowledge and method in its own operation, and in research designed to improve the methods of analysis used in planning.

Planning is an art and a science. It is an art in that certain considerations in the functioning of an organization or activity are simulated, examined, and resolved in the mind by observation, subjective judgment, and intuition. This could involve evaluating political influence or governmental policy, the consequences of a particular personality in the hierarchy of management or in the chain of command, or the exposure of an organization to legal action. Matters that cannot be expressed in numbers and calculated mathematically may be more important at times than elements which can be treated scientifically. Research supporting these aspects of planning can be directed toward improving the simulations and judgments which are made within the mind by helping individuals to identify their subjective predilections, misconceptions, and prejudices, in favor of more objective and more accurate attitudes and conclusions.

Planning is primarily a science, applying rational thought and rigorous analysis whenever possible. Continuing research is needed to improve the mathematical integration of diverse variables with different significance and uncertainties, and projecting them in concert into different periods of future time. The planning process will be strengthened by finding ways of improving the range of reliability of scientific sample opinion surveys, statistical sampling and correlation in general, determining and comparing risks, and other analytical techniques employed in planning. Computer programs need to be researched and written to record, store, and integrate large quantities of different forms of information, analyze it scientifically, and display the results clearly and concisely on video screens. Methods must be developed to prevent disclosure of information employed in planning which must be classified by government for security reasons, or restricted by business for competitive reasons.

As science advances, so does simulation. Each step forward requires a hypothesis to be proved or disproved by experiment or abstract reasoning. Scientific knowledge advances by a progression of such simulations, each based on its predecessor. The history of the development of a scientific idea or element of knowledge over the years is a series of conceptual simulations and tests in the past which led to its present form. The tests may have been carefully designed experiments, or corroboration demonstrated in the physical world or out beyond in the universe. Some concepts are conceived and tested entirely within the mind, as the chess grandmaster Tartakower did in the mental exercise described earlier, and mathematicians do regularly. They are expressed by abstract symbols, or by other visualizations which are transformed into symbols so that they can be made available for peer

review and publication. They may have had to do with the world of ordinary human experience or a purely imaginary entity of time, space, elements, and interrelationships. As noted above, purely imaginary
formulations can turn out in time to have practical application.

## Technology

The word "technology" or the words "industrial science" represent the
"systematic knowledge of the industrial arts". They simulate very generally
the capability of a nation to engage in activities producing goods and services, which is the economic base of most countries, particularly of developing countries seeking to move from an economy based on subsistence
farming and agriculture to one providing the material, mechanical, technical, and foreign trade advantages derived from domestic production and
manufacturing. The state of the basic and applied sciences and of engineering indicate what is possible and practical in the way of technological
development.

As happens with words subject to change in the content they signify,
some dictionary definitions of technology do not incorporate the transportation, communication, and information sciences, services, and related
manufacturing which have emerged during less than the combined life ex-
pectancies of a father and son. They are now the dominant technologies of
the United States, so familiar today that it is easy to forget that they have
developed since the invention of the principal object involved, in each case
not long ago. In the chronological order of their invention, they include
the incandescent lamp, camera, gasoline-powered automobile, telephone,
motorized airplane, radio, television, radar, transistor, and fiber optics. It
would be hard to exaggerate the economic, societal, and cultural impact of
the new technologies, and the effects of the billions of dollars involved in
the research, production, operation, and use of these systems.

While agriculture, manufacturing, and the productive activities are an
important part of its economy, the United States is the first nation shifting
to an economy based on the new technologies. This has had and will continue to have far-reaching consequences. It indicates the kind of education
and special occupational skills that are required for employment in emerging sectors of the economy. It is clear that the requirements for employment
in farming, ordinary manufacturing, and heavy industry are different from
those needed for miniaturized manufacturing of electronic products, software products, and robotics. Some requirements are becoming universal.
Computer literacy will soon be essential for almost all human activities.
And a much higher minimum knowledge of mathematics will follow in the
United States in the future.

The new technologies are affecting many aspects of our society. They are
bringing about changes in the English language. Special vocabularies are

being formulated to facilitate electronic intercommunication. And as networks interconnect more and more people and involve a wider and wider range of subject matter, ordinary words that are needlessly inconsistent, confusing, or with markedly different spelling and pronunciation are simplified, corrected, and adapted by common use. If automatic and immediate translation of language is perfected, people around the world will be able to communicate without using a common language.

Television and telecomputers provide visual and verbal communication among hundreds of millions of people in different countries, opening up new awareness, desires, attitudes, reactions, and resentments among people previously separated in space and cultural contact. Will these developments promote uniformities and huge common markets, or greater pride in differences that do not threaten common characteristics favoring human prospects and survival? It will be some years before the range and depth of the societal effects of the new technologies are revealed.

The higher the scientific content of the technology, the higher and more specialized the education and training needed. Yet many people believe that everyone is entitled to gainful employment whether or not they make the effort to keep up with changing requirements in the workplace. The existing educational establishment resists such change. Many teachers and educational administrators find it easier to continue to do the same thing rather than learn new subject matter or different teaching techniques; all the more if the changes are to be made rapidly, rather than by someone else in the future early in his or her career with less awareness of forthcoming retirement.

Changing technology challenges the existing educational system to develop new techniques to teach new and different subject matter. Specially designed telecomputer programs will be needed, very different from the professorial lecture and laboratory classes conducted today. Self-education programs must be available to everyone everywhere at any time. Universities as we know them today may become telecomputing centers, providing reference resources and interaction among off-campus students engaged in continuing self-education, and between people located anywhere and teachers, experts, and intellectual authorities located on campus or elsewhere. This may be the only way of educating an increasing population worldwide, meeting the educational requirements of new technologies without excluding entire classes of people from many areas of employment.

As the scientific content of technology increases, the layers of simulation increase accordingly. Artificial intelligence, intelligent software, virtual reality, and so-called intelligent materials are several steps removed from the physical realities they simulate. They involve substitutes for human sensors, sensual coordination, and substantive conclusions reached *in situ*. And they seek to improve on these by incorporating more sensitive artificial sensors and the lessons learned from the accumulation of analytical experience.

Such intelligent systems are part of other new technologies such as satellite surveillance, high-speed rail transportation, commercial airliners, spacecraft, and robotics. And the new fields of gene therapy, solar energy, and fusion extend the investigation of cause and effect to the most fundamental levels of animate cells and elementary particles.

Television is a specific example of the layers of simulation which can be involved in a new technology. The camera lens and microphone record the visual image and sound in geometric or digital form on a videotape or disk. This is transmitted by wire, wireless, ground or air transportation to the broadcast station where it is received and stored as is or in a different form. It is reviewed and edited on an instrument designed or modified for this purpose, and a series of visual images and sound accompaniment is prepared for broadcast. For certain programs, teleprompter texts are prepared for human announcers or commentators. A half dozen or more simulations are incorporated in this routine procedure.

## NOTES

1. *Webster's New International Dictionary of the English Language,* 2d ed. (Springfield, MA: Merriam, 1960), Vol. II, p. 2105.

2. *Encyclopaedia Britannica,* 14th ed. (London: Encyclopaedia Britannica, 1929), Vol. 6, p. 463.

3. David R. Fine, "Some Things Are Better Unseen", *Herald Tribune,* 27 March 1996.

4. Laurence, Zucherman, "A Virtually Balanced Budget", *New York Times,* 1 January 1996, p. Y27.

5. Eric Mankin, "Ending a Reign of Error", *University of Southern California Chronicle,* 25 March 1996, p. 1.

The majority of Americans spend most of their time sleeping, working, and watching television and video.

*New York Times*, 6 September 1995, p. zB1

# Chapter 6

# Simulation, Planning, and Society

## SIMULATION

The ability to imagine events and visualize activities within the mind was a critical cognitive development in human evolution. Being able to conceptualize internally real and imagined happenings in the external world enabled early man to analyze and plan, rather than rely entirely on his instincts. Simulation is an essential cognitive mechanism in humans as thinking animals.

Throughout history, people have progressively extended their capabilities to formulate actual and proposed thoughts and images within the mind, or externally by means and methods developed to represent objects, events, situations, and processes. There are cave paintings portraying primitive hunting thousands of years ago; descriptive hieroglyphics depicting various activities of Egyptian pharaohs and gods; Hammurabi's law code prescribing behavior in the Babylonian empire; and the simulative designs of Leonardo da Vinci for war machines and other fabrications during the Italian renaissance.

The numerous examples of simulations discussed in this book indicate the extent to which they permeate society today: mechanical devices such as wind tunnel and flight simulators for specific tests; art, literature, movies, and television entertainment for expressive purposes. Simulations have become so universal in medical diagnosis, so operationally essential in engineering, and the modus operandi of law that they are in fact an integral part of the substance of these professions and activities.

## Growth

As knowledge advances, so does the use and representative content of simulations that facilitate comprehension and research. The means and methods of representation advance. Graphical expression of the double-helix form of DNA led to such expression in biology generally and also in particle physics. For example, Feynman diagrams, mentioned earlier in this book, portray the interaction among certain fundamental forces and particles of matter more clearly and usefully for most purposes than the complex equations from which they are derived.

Simulations contribute to basic knowledge. As the electronic scanning machines employed in medical diagnosis are improved, they reveal more of the internal structure and dynamic interactions within the human body. The recent use of high resolution magnetic resonance imaging (MRI) to produce an anatomical simulation of the human body, millimeter by millimeter, has disclosed a small muscle in the head and a patch of fibrous tissue near the top of the spine never before noted during several centuries of dissection and anatomical study. Remote sensing from aircraft and orbiting satellites has contributed to basic geographic, geological, and other fields of knowledge by revealing features of the earth previously unknown. Their discovery has in turn extended the scope and improved the accuracy of remote sensing by confirming their appearance and identification on the simulative images.

## Computers

Since the first computer only 50 years ago—the mammoth ENIAC with 17,000 vacuum tubes—they have increased vastly in speed, and decreased markedly in size and price. Mathematical advances have greatly expanded calculative capabilities. Computers now permeate industrialized societies. They account for much of the simulation produced, since the images displayed on their screens are representations of things located or created elsewhere. They make possible a range and speed of simulation inconceivable not long ago. Objects can be viewed from different directions, shown at different sizes, moved about and manipulated in various ways, and with extra equipment viewed in virtual reality on the computer screen. Data, text, and graphics can be displayed and altered, stored and retrieved in an instant.

As telecomputers become a central element in most households, a wide range of informational material, personal intercommunication, news, governmental and public announcements, business and financial data, and much more will be received, processed, and decisions reached on the basis of what is shown on the telecomputer screen. This visual display will be an operational and activity center of the home: sight and sound for the household collectively and its occupants individually. Everything that appears on the telecomputer screen is a simulation, one or more steps removed from the state-of-being or reality it represents. The original form or image of what is reproduced can be abbreviated, enhanced, or otherwise changed. By simply selecting and repeatedly using an atypical image among many, a false impression, a wrong conclusion, and a mistaken action can be engendered. Images can be modified at the original recording, during transmission, or as they are displayed.

Digital technology for manipulating images has subverted the certainty of photographic evidence . . . can easily trick us into false beliefs. . . . The information superhighway will bring us a growing flood of visual information in digital format, but we will have to take great care to sift the facts from the fictions and the falsehoods.[1]

Unless accuracy is assured or special provisions are made, those receiving and using information on the telecomputer will not be able to verify its content without special inquiry, which few people will undertake.

We are all subject to being misled, confused, and reaching wrong conclusions if the information that determines our reactions and subsequent actions is falsified as a hacker's prank, an individual's hostility, an institutional falsification, or an "honest" mistake. The effects of misinformation are no longer local and limited. They can affect many people far and wide connected by computer networks. On the afternoon of the 1996 Super Bowl football game, misinformation would have reached 138 million people watching the television broadcast, immediately and simultaneously. In the intensely intercommunicative world of tomorrow, more and more people will view the same material on their telecomputers. If the power to tax is the power to destroy, telecomputer communication has the power to misinform, confuse, mislead, and subvert large numbers of people or entire populations. The possible consequences range from inconvenience to disaster.

Transactions as well as single subjects are simulated when multiple actions conducted separately are combined and new features may be added. Not long ago, we paid cash, wrote a check, or were billed by the gas station if we were a regular customer. We could use credit cards when they became available, signing the receipt and retaining a copy for our file. Later, our credit cards were confirmed by wire and the money due deducted from our bank accounts and credited to the account of the gas station. These separate actions by the customer, gas station attendant, and several bank employees are simulated today at the automated gasoline pump. Multiple actions have been reduced to inserting an acceptable credit card, selecting the type of gasoline desired, and requesting a receipt if it is wanted. A simpler example of transaction simulation is the automatic toll booth, where the vehicle licenses of cars are recorded without their stopping and the toll charge immediately deducted from an associated bank account or credit balance.

### Surrogate Intelligence

Surrogate or artificial intelligence is potentially the most complex form of simulation, most likely to affect human activities dramatically in the future. A simple and familiar example is the thermostat, which simulates the desired atmospheric conditions within the home by automatically maintaining the furnace heat and air conditioning at different average temperatures within prescribed limits during the day and night hours of one's choice. Control and maintenance of inventories consisting of many items is a more complicated example. If a record is made of each item withdrawn, the number desired in stock, who supplies each item and how quickly, and each item received, a computer program can record, monitor, reorder, and maintain the inventory as desired, with an automatic alarm or signal system indicating when human intervention is needed. Additional features can be incorporated, such as recording slow-moving and less profitable items which could be replaced by more profitable products.

Possibly the most complex simulation of human intelligence today is the parallel-processing supercomputer nicknamed "Deep Blue", developed by the International Business Machines Corporation (IBM). The objective is to design and program a machine which can out-think and outplay the world chess champion. To suggest its complexity and the simulative significance of the endeavor for those who are not familiar with the game of chess, a brief description of the primary components, moves, rules, and characteristics of the game is required.

The square chessboard has 64 "squares". There are 32 named "pieces", 16 for each of two players on opposite sides of the board. Three of the eight primary pieces placed on designated squares along the side of the board in front of the player at the beginning of the game have a different set of permissible "moves": straight, diagonal, or an odd combination for the "knight". The "king" can move only one square at a time. The "queen" can make the most moves of any of the chess pieces in any direction. Lined up in front of these eight primary pieces are eight "pawns", each of which can make the same moves.

The object of the game is to capture or "checkmate" the "king". Usually, this does not occur until each side has "taken" some of the opponent's pieces and removed them from the chessboard and remaining contest. The game begins with an "opening", a sequence of beginning moves identified by name which have proved most successful over the years. The "middle game" is devoted to strategic and tactical development of the pieces and their position on the board as they advance. The "end game" is when the few pieces remaining on the board maneuver to checkmate the opponent's king, or to tie or "draw" the game if the king cannot be checkmated with the pieces at hand. If, at any time during the game, one of the two players believes neither can win, he can propose a draw; if accepted, the game is terminated. "Speed chess" games lasting either 10 or 50 minutes seem almost frantic compared with the more contemplative pace of regular games lasting hours.

Additional features of chess produce more complications, but it is clear from this partial description that there are astronomically large numbers of possible combinations of the different pieces, with different moves, in different positions on the chessboard. Chess is one of the most difficult intellectual analyses undertaken by man. It simulates complex human activities very generally. The chess pieces are like people acting individually in different ways. They dispose themselves on the chessboard space in an almost limitless number of strategic and tactical combinations. Their activities are directed toward a known objective which determines the success or failure of the entire operation. The logical aspects of the endeavor favor careful thought. Competing against an active opponent produces an emotional, psychologically hostile, environment. Time limits force continual action. In such ways chess simulates certain aspects of human activities, decisions, and behavior.

The most successful openings and winning ways, demonstrated in thousands of games between foremost players, have been recorded over the years. Chess sets are produced with built-in electronic mechanisms which advise the player concerning his or her beginning moves. And for some years scientists interested in artificial intelligence have been developing computer programs simulating the play of the best chess players. "Deep Blue" is the latest of these efforts, linking 32 computers in "parallel-processing", which enables it to examine 50 *billion* chess positions in three minutes.

It considers every possible move, every possible reply to each move, and all the possible replies to these moves to the depth of about twelve levels in the average position.[2]

Human grandmasters analyze each of their moves and those that can be made by their opponent through several successive cycles of moves and countermoves. They also rely on their intuitions, which reflect their intensive study of the game and what they have learned from playing thousands of games that are stored in the billions of neurons within the brain. Some chessmasters can play entire games in their minds. As mentioned earlier in this book, Tartakower—one of the foremost players in the world in the 1920s—maintained he could recall every game he had ever played. The minds of foremost chess players may be as different from those of most people as the computing capacity of "Deep Blue" is from most computers.

Supercomputers usually win at speed chess because their computational speed enables them to analyze almost instantaneously many more possible plays and positions than the most skilled individual can accomplish mentally in the short average time allowed for each move. The machine also has the advantage of being able to store in its memory information concerning how the champion is likely to play, based on many years of previous play. The champion cannot do this because the machine has engaged in few if any such competitive matches. Although Garry Kasparov won a highly publicized match against "Deep Blue" in early 1996, he lost the first game ever to the machine, regarded as a "historic victory" by its designers. Kasparov acknowledged that "to beat this machine, you have to fight really hard, for as many hours as it takes". "The machine does not make many mistakes".

One illustration of how far software has come in reproducing complex human decision-making ability [is the development of] computer "agents" that can match wits with top human jet-fighter pilots in simulated dogfights conducted in virtual computer environments.[3]

Scientists believe that it is a matter of time until a supercomputer is developed which will regularly win matches with the best chess players. The contest is between a lone individual with his knowledge, experience, judgment, intuition, and creativity, and an opposing group who integrate accumulated information concerning the most successful chess play with the ultra high-speed analysis possible with supercomputer parallel processing.

If machines triumph in certain situations, it demonstrates that they are superior to human intelligence in these particular applications. It does not suggest that surrogate intelligence is superior in general to the human mind, which is far and away the best organic computer with a range of capabilities which a mechanical computer cannot and probably never will approximate. A computer can simulate chess with increasing success. But it cannot identify and smell a particular rose, compose a poem that is more than doggerel, evaluate a law, play Mozart on the violin, or perform the thousands of very different things a fine and educated mind can do in never-ending combinations.

It remains to be seen if surrogate intelligence will reign supreme in chess and comparable situations. It is, of course, already in use for certain activities. For example:

[Artificial intelligence] has been in regular use by the staff of the Commander in Chief of the U.S. Pacific Fleet since August 1987 . . . to coordinate the movements of nearly 300 ships, including aircraft carriers, submarines, destroyers, and tankers, together with more than 2000 aircraft, spread over 95 million square miles of ocean and 2450 ports of call.[4]

If the supercomputer can also be programmed to identify its own successful and unsuccessful decisions, learn from its mistakes without outside assistance, and improve its performance accordingly, it can provide a higher level of directive intelligence. It could duplicate the feat attributed to Tartakower against an amateur opponent who picked before the game began, the piece with which Tartakower would checkmate him, the square on the chessboard where this would occur, and Tartakower played blindfolded.

If evaluations, judgments, and decisions by people are incorporated in powerful surrogate intelligence computer systems, the range of productive analysis will be expanded to include a higher level of executive planning and management. If successfully developed and thoroughly tested, a combination of human and synthetic intelligence could analyze, reach conclusions, and make decisions in situations which conform to its conceptual and operational characteristics. As an advanced form of simulation it would be employed in more and more human affairs as they become technically more complex, including the development of a national simulation for widespread use, proposed in the previous section. This is why the IBM research laboratory has invested time and money developing supercomputers to play chess, and the Association of Computing Machinery provided a half million dollars in prize money for the match between computer and man in 1996.

## PLANNING

### Attitudes and Reactions

A plan can be a concept in our minds, such as how we intend to conduct our daily activities or by what route we intend to reach a destination. Or it can be a detailed document simulating an object, a structure, or a multipurpose project. Planning and accompanying conceptualizations are intrinsic in our every act and activity, consciously and deliberately, or intuitively without our being aware of the internal process.

Perhaps it is because planning is so ubiquitous and inevitable that most people do not realize that they engage in forethought all the time, that it is a crucial process in their lives. They are aware of the results of some planning, but rarely have occasion to consider the process as such. As a consequence, or for whatever reasons, there are misconceptions concerning the process that make it difficult for society to derive the full benefit of looking ahead. Some people say that there should be no organized planning, that individuals can decide what to do when the need arises, that spontaneous action produces better results than deliberative forethought.

Some simply fulminate against the idea of planning, as if a process intrinsic in our thinking and actions can somehow be eliminated. Many people may disagree with a particular application of planning or a specific proposal, and conclude therefore that there should be very little of it or none at all. Some believe that it means excessive or even autocratic controls, although in fact it may involve few or many restrictions, imposed or voluntary, as democratic as desired or as arbitrary as those who are affected approve, are willing to accept, or must endure because of the political or emergency situation.

Most people question planning because they have given the subject and process little or no thought. They may find it difficult or impossible to accept the necessity of planning, or they may depreciate its value by associating it with the empty promises and glittering generalities by politicians concerning what they say they can do in the future if elected or reelected, but rarely accomplish. The public is aware that most governmental programs turn out to cost far more than indicated at the time the decision to proceed was made. Costly programs that prove far less effective than touted may be abandoned or discarded as useless.

There are innate resistances in all of us to certain characteristics of planning, which must be overcome by those undertaking planning and those affected by it. Planning requires extra effort, taking on a set of concerns and responsibilities most people would just as soon avoid. We may decide we have enough immediate problems to resolve. Planning means looking ahead into the indefinite future, which we do all the time but formalize for only a few objectives, such as a mortgage on the home; a pension plan; life, disability, and other insurance if we can afford it; our children's education; and funeral arrangements. Most people cannot afford all of these. We resist allocations of money for use in an uncertain future, it could be used for purposes benefitting us immediately. Let the next generation take care of its own problems. They are not likely to appreciate what we did for them years earlier.

These attitudes and reactions refer for the most part in the United States to the higher levels of planning by government and private enterprise: legislative bodies, corporate America, and the chief executives of both. Although we may complain about some local public service or business practice at the local level, we are aware that a lot of successful planning must be going on. Water, electricity, natural gas, telephone service, and sanitation are provided with few serious and prolonged interruptions. We accept those caused by natural disasters as unavoidable. Stores are well supplied with goods, orders filled, and services supplied. Business delivers most of what it offers. Many major projects are undertaken and successfully completed.

Planning—like engineering, medicine, or mathematics—can be used for good or bad purposes. It can be conducted graciously or cruelly. There are no inclinations inherent in "administration", "management", or "planning" toward the constructive or destructive, the beneficial or harmful, moral or immoral. There are those who maintain that planning can and should be conducted so that everyone involved or affected benefits and is satisfied. This is rarely possible. Activities which benefit almost everyone will almost always disadvantage a few people who are subject to an unusual set of circumstances or have needs and desires different from everyone else's. There are no activities or plans involving numbers of people that benefit everyone equally and do not displease someone. There are optimists or enthusiasts who believe that planning is a process which in and of itself can solve our most pressing problems if only people would act as required for the plan to work and its objective to be achieved.

Economic theory, methods of management, and questions of law are discussed generally as subjects and as recognized elements of society. Planning is rarely conceived and discussed in the same way. It is almost always reported in newspapers and by other mass means of communication as connected with and limited to a particular application, with its proponents and opponents. It rises or falls as a general subject, a valid concept, and desirable activity on the merits and demerits of the particular case. This evaluation is not only misleading, it is difficult or meaningless where there are great differences between countries, cultures, and values. To believe that planning can or should be the same in societies that are dominated by established religious beliefs or at different stages of development, is to defy reality. At the same time, to deny that there are certain basic principles that apply to all planning is like maintaining that management or mathematics have no fundamental features in common in different countries and cultures. There are both important differences and basic similarities which affect their employment in different places and situations. There is a nucleus of knowledge in every field which is universally applicable.

At present, education in planning in the United States has to do with its application in different areas of activity, such as land use, in urban and regional planning schools and a few schools of architecture; government, in schools of public administration; corporate planning, in business schools; and special uses of planning associated with different specializations in engineering. There is no educational or research program in planning as a distinct intellectual discipline with its own particular methods of examining an organization or situation, conducting analyses, reaching conclusions, determining objectives, formulating and implementing plans, obtaining political or other support. The specifics of planning vary with each application, but there is a body of knowledge and a set of analytical and operational principles and procedures proven in practice that are the core of successful planning.

## Capabilities and Problems

During many thousands of years we have gradually increased our capability to plan our activities in significant ways. During the past several centuries we have conceived, planned, and constructed transportation, communication, military, space exploration, industrial, and commercial production and distribution systems which were inconceivable not long ago. It appears that scientific and technological advances will continue as existing fields of knowledge are expanded and new knowledge is acquired.

The products and mostly positive consequences of planning are to be seen on all sides, except at the topmost level of our society where the most crucial decisions for the nation are made. In government, where politics reigns supreme, legislators and elected officials in the United States resist performing at a higher level of planning and management for political and personal reasons noted in various connections in this book. These reasons do not apply to the same extent to chief executive officers in the business world, who do not resist analytical corporate planning as they once did. When they do, it is usually because they are performing satisfactorily without it in the eyes of those who judge them. Or they do not believe analytical staff support would assist them in their decision making. They do not accept a societal responsibility beyond what is required in conducting the business successfully.

Public pressures and the necessity of a higher level of directive management in an increasingly technical and complex society will require gradual improvement in governmental performance. Business planning will develop in whatever ways are necessary for it to function profitably as operating conditions and the business environment change. Superior planning is certainly required to resolve the very serious societal problems which afflict the United States today. They are not going to simply disappear, or be resolved in a generally undirected course of affairs by some fortuitous force.

The public in general and most of its leaders are well aware of what must be undertaken and accomplished to prevent further deterioration of society: full employment without a large number of disaffected unemployed; general educational programs that reach every individual at every level of society; special training and retraining programs enabling people to keep up with the changing requirements for employment; eliminating to the extent possible the need and use of addictive drugs and drug trafficking; reducing the crime rate and the prison population, making communities and countryside safe for normal life and human affairs; strengthening the family unit to fulfill its parental, educational, and other supportive responsibilities within the household; providing alternatives for constructive social bonding when it is not available within the family; developing a mutually sustainable relationship with the natural environment which prevents indiscriminate pollution, use, and destruction of natural resources.

## Television and Planning

If these critical national problems are recognized by the body politic and its leaders, why is there so little constructive discussion and explanation in the mass media of communication concerning specific actions proposed and being taken to resolve them? Why do politicians at all levels of government—continuously campaigning nowadays for election, reelection, or higher office—describe the better state-of-being they will bring about without indicating specifically how they will do so?

Because explicit public statements concerning their desires and intentions can directly and indirectly affect politicians' exposure and treatment by the mass media. Favorable or at least neutral treatment is essential for their political survival, aspirations, and future success. What is done specifically concerning critical and controversial societal problems affects important interests of many kinds, including advertisers who support television stations, newspapers, and other mass media. Important and controversial issues involve proponents and opponents. Politicians do not want to take the chance of antagonizing any influential interest by being more specific than necessary.

Television is the most powerful directive force in the United States. The primary campaign and presidential election in 1996 confirmed that the nature and extent of television exposure determine, more than any other factor, who is elected to government office. Most of America gets its news and much of its entertainment from television sets turned on an average of more than seven hours a day in the nation's households. What news is foremost in the public's minds, what entertainment it sees, its reactions to current events, problems, personalities and people, and proposed activities are influenced by television more than anything else. Role models, entertainment stars, popular and unpopular figures are created and as regularly remembered or forgotten by television. Cultural and behavioral attitudes, political preferences, and personal values are affected significantly.

To know and evaluate what is shown on television requires viewing as many stations as possible over a period of months, preferably a year or two: so-called "browsing". Many of those who have opinions concerning television have not spent the viewing time required to fully comprehend the object of their opinion. Those who say that they have not seen enough television to have an opinion are disregarding potentially the most powerful societal force in the nation today. Comprehending television requires examining its content; its selection and treatment of subjects; the means and methods of presentation; the technical recording, transmission, and delivery of images; special effects and image manipulation; repetition; and the consequences of audience ratings.

Newscasts, news commentaries, and interviews occupy a significant percentage of network broadcasts in the English language in the United States in 1996. "Soap operas", "talk shows", and "gossip" programs are a major component. Sports are an important part of entertainment, together with "old movies" from the large inventories available. Features concerning police activities, detective and courtroom fiction are much in evidence. Special programs concerning nature and the environment are shown occasionally. Cartoons and animated films fill much of the time required for children's programs. Advertising spots—interjected before, during, and after most programs—aggregate a substantial percentage of television time. Half-hour periods are purchased for direct sales of a product or "infomercials" incorporating the "sales pitch" as part of entertainment or news. Cable television offers the menu shown in television guides, ranging from informational and reportive subjects to family, child, and adult entertainment.

Supported by federal funding, memberships, and contributions from "viewers like you", the Public Broadcasting System (PBS) is unique in television. It presents programs on governmental, environmental, economic, social, scientific, technological, historical, and cultural subjects. Children's programs are specifically designed to entertain and educate an age group. Cultural presentations include operas, orchestral music, dance, art, and literature. The movies shown are selected for their high quality. News programs incorporate opposing views, commentary, interviews, and essays. Culinary and other household activities are presented. The documentary programs on PBS stations concerning sociopolitical and governmental subjects of current concern account for congressional threats to cut off federal funding.

Certain facts concerning television in the United States today are clear to the impartial observer. The medium reflects a built-in motivation to transform all programs into "shows". Astute listeners will have noted that people connected with television use the word show as a more accurately descriptive term than program or presentation. This showmanship is most apparent in the numerous sports programs. In football, multiple announcer/commentators, interviewers on the field and in the grandstands, graphical explanations, other chatter, and advertising takes as much as or more than the time required for the game itself. The rules of the game have been adjusted to accommodate television coverage, and half time has become a free-for-all observational, reportive, or promotional opportunity.

The same showmanship is taking place in basketball. Even in golf, one of the most sportsmanlike and gentlemanly of games, television commentators are following golfers and seeking comments. "Skin games" have been introduced with the players sometimes wearing walkie-talkies, emphasizing the prize money won hole by hole more than the game itself. Advertising and other promotion take more and more of sports broadcast time. Athletes are now often rated and acclaimed as much by their prize money earnings as the quality of their games. Aided and abetted by television, all sports are becoming more professional and pecuniary. Television has played the leading role in this change.

Financial and investment success in television broadcasting and the political power it provides requires programming which attracts more viewers than competitors also seeking advertising dollars. Subject matter, personal preferences, and other considerations being equal, programs with high emotional content attract more people. Built into us are emotional sensitivities established during several million years when we evolved from animal-like humanoids into human beings several hundred thousand years ago. These sensitivities guarded us against external threats which required immediate instinctive reaction and intuitive action.

Rumination and thoughtful deliberation are relatively recent developments. Without being consciously aware of it people are attracted and intrigued by emotional events and situations. Accordingly, wittingly or unwittingly, television favors programs with high emotional content. As competition for audience ratings intensifies, programs are produced and newscasts are treated more emotionally. This built-in dynamic is one reason there is so much violence on television.

Anyone observing network television will note the violence incorporated in the movies shown and programs produced specifically for television. It is most conspicuous and extreme in those starring three well-known and successful actors. They feature continuous gun play, violent conflict, cruel and sadistic behavior, and disregard of any restraints on human behavior. Not only do they indicate or imply that violence is appropriate in certain personal and local situations, but they suggest that punishment or retribution for unlawful and extremely violent behavior is rarely forthcoming. Several of these films may incite violence by viewers so inclined, justified in their minds by seemingly similar conditions in their communities. Violent movies are often broadcast one following another on the same day, on successive days, or repeated every few months, producing a cumulative effect on those who view them.

Violent programs affect the attitudes of many adults and the behavior of some people. They disturb children who view violence on television continually despite parental prohibitions and efforts at supervision. Very young children may accept exaggerated and abnormal situations as normal and permissible, until they reach the age when they can differentiate between fantasy and reality, fact and fiction.

There is considerable repetition on network television. Comedy, science fiction, westerns, and other continually popular and exceptionally successful programs and movies are shown time and again. They must be viewed by enough people and produce enough profit to justify the time allotted to them. This must also be true for the second-rate material that is shown and repeated occasionally. Presumably these programs would not be aired if they were unprofitable, unless there was no other market demand for the broadcast time and they are used to fill the schedule. There is always the question of the best use of the finite broadcast time available. Are entertainment and market demand or audience acceptance the desirable criteria? Or would the combination of television and telecomputer, as the primary means of transmitting information and interactive communication, serve the public better if the broadcast time were divided among major categories of content, such as: entertainment, news, education, public information, public participation, evaluative reporting, and interactive services.

## Coverage and Content

Besides the question of whether the combined television and telecomputer system should serve major categories of market demand and national need, there is the question of what would be covered in each category and how it would be presented. News programs are an example. Which of the enormous number of news items available will be covered and presented in the time at hand? There is never enough time to cover more than a tiny fraction.

This is a crucial choice. It determines what the public will be made aware of by their primary source of news. Events, situations, and subjects that are not covered remain unknown, unless they filter through to public awareness by other mechanical means or by word-of-mouth. Single events that are repeatedly broadcast and subjects that are continually covered are fixed in the public mind far more than topics covered once briefly. Material presented emotionally has a stronger and more immediate impact than if it is voiced "cool, calm, and collected". The subject matter of many local newscasts is selected for its dramatic content and reported in an excitative rather than "matter-of-fact" manner.

The mass media are subject to what can be called "reportive frenzy". A mass of microphones and reporters confront an individual at close range, pressing for information, comment, and newsworthy reaction. At times this constitutes an intrusion, an invasion of privacy, or a deliberate attempt to evoke a photogenic emotional response. Newsy events may be covered by a small army of reporters and commentators representing local, regional, national, and international news media driven by the fear of missing out on some noteworthy happening or not justifying their presence. A reportive "feeding frenzy" can dominate the news for weeks or months, affect current activities, and pervade the public consciousness for a long time, obliterating other news of importance. Large sums of money, which could be used to advantage for other purposes, are squandered since one or two reporters could cover the story for everyone. The costs of television escalate as intense competition forces more dramatic and special treatment of ordinary events, transforming many of them into expensive shows.

In the early stages of the communication revolution now underway, the information, images, and interactions available will be more than most people can absorb and comprehend. Competing interests will be scrambling for preferred positions. Some will drop out, others will combine, and a few will survive to become the preeminent producers and transmitters of information to the American people. They will channel the output of the mass media of communication to the television-telecomputer screen in the home, at the workplace, and just about everywhere else. A vast array of interactive services and contacts will be available. This electronic concentration of information and visual display will affect individual and collective reactions, attitudes, and behavior, which will in large part determine the "state of the union" and the prospects for the nation and society. The significance of the forthcoming electronic concentration of communicating information can hardly be exaggerated.

### Accuracy and Reliability

The information which will be transmitted on the television-telecomputer system must be accurate if the nation is to function successfully. Democracies need information as a basis for informed and knowledgeable voters, effective governmental and business operations, professional and academic activities, and people's personal affairs. The ordinary viewer has no way of knowing if what is displayed on the electronic screen is accurate. Occasionally, he may be able to detect false information or question the accuracy of data which seems too exceptional to be correct. The ultimate responsibility lies with the originator of the information and with those who transmit and disseminate it to hundreds of thousands or millions of people, unless a disclaimer or an indication of the range of accuracy accompanies transmission of the information.

In the maze of informational interconnection which is developing, ensuring accuracy will be difficult. More people will be involved and there may be several intermediate steps between the original source and the recipient of the information. There will be more people and more procedural steps enabling those so inclined to exaggerate, misinterpret, or sometimes to falsify data. Accuracy includes indicating the range of error inherent in the data, and any altering of the initial visual image or sound in one or more of the many ways this can be done. For example, events, and situations should not be broadcast if applause or other response was dubbed in when there was none, or audience reaction pro or con was artificially enhanced.

The informational system must also be reliable. If widely and persistently disseminated, misinformation can produce severely disruptive or even destructive societal results. We know from experience that a hypothetical or unfounded announcement can cause thousands of people to act in panic or false expectation. Misguided or careless broadcast of potentially disturbing information can create civil unrest, outbursts of emotional over-reaction, or a "slow burn" of prejudicial feelings leading to hateful actions. Potentially disturbing events, such as the Simpson trial in 1995, can produce disruptive, profound, and lasting effects if they are broadcast intensely and continuously over a prolonged period of time.

Electronic means of communication are also subject to disruption by "hackers", fraudulent schemes, criminal activities, and complete invasion of personal privacy. Encryption is required to prevent unauthorized access and misuse of information during transmission. While the best way of doing this is being debated in Congress in 1996, many systems have failed to provide the protection needed and remain vulnerable to misuse. Prevention of fraudulent and criminal activities on the television-telecomputer broadcast system is the responsibility of its owners and operators, as well as law enforcement and other governmental agencies. Ensuring the accuracy and reliability of the primary communication and information system of the nation requires attention, research, and planning which it has not yet received. Cooperative action by government, private enterprise, and the public is required.

### Trends and Developments

Network television today is incorporating more and more violence, gunplay, implicit and explicit sex, aberrant behavior, and emotionalism in its programs. Local newscasts are devoted largely to reporting crime and police actions, with brief reporting of other news, sports, and the weather. The emphasis is on negative happenings, almost to the exclusion of positive societal actions and events. The powers-that-be in television maintain that these developments do not affect viewers individually or collectively in any societally significant way. They are part of the entertainment most people want. Television is a commercial business providing entertainment broadly defined, with minimal societal impact and no pretensions of social purpose or service. It responds to but does not create audience demand. The absolute and relative value of television programs is determined by audience ratings and profitability.

Research indicates, however, that the selection and content of television programs does impact viewers, especially children. Its increasing use by those campaigning for election or reelection to public office, and the continuous scramble for television exposure in connection with all sorts of public and business affairs confirms its significance as an instrument of persuasion. There are those who maintain that if it is not now, it is potentially the most powerful directive force in the United States. It is the main source of news now, and coupled with the computer it will soon be the main source of information and means of interactive intercommunication.

Television has in fact become a public utility, an activity as crucial to the functioning of the nation as providing potable water, electricity, natural gas, and sanitation is for localities. As such, it must be examined as an essential element of public life, operating to the advantage or disadvantage of the public at large as well as those who own the stations or control them through the purchase of television time. As a public utility it should not become an unconstrained commercial monopoly nor an overwhelming informational and political force controlling the nation.

The mass media are discussed in this section on planning because, together with science and technology, they will determine more than any other force the nature and extent of planning by each and every individual, and by government agencies and business organizations. Planning will continue as inherent in human existence and activities. What kind and how much planning is necessary or desirable for a society to function effectively in the general public interest is the key question.

If people are unaware of planning as a societal process, the subject is of little or no public interest. People will have no opinion pro or con. When only failures in planning are reported, public opinion is negative. If successes are also reported, opinion is likely to be balanced. If planning is disparaged or presented as a process which involves means, methods, and consequences inimical to most people, it will be limited to the minimum required for the organization or activity to function. If it is regarded as an essential and neutral process in itself, whether it is desirable or not will depend on what it seeks to achieve and how it is conducted.

In which of these ways planning progresses depends on how the subject is treated by the mass media as part of their reporting of situations and events, particularly by television, which informs and influences most people. Planning, television, science, and technology are closely interrelated.

### Societal Situations

The serious and pressing problems in 1996 noted above will not disappear or be resolved by the competitive processes of the socioeconomic marketplace. Carefully formulated plans are required to reverse the societal deterioration that is taking place at an increasing rate. Will the nation adopt a policy, formulate plans, and carry them out over a decade or more to restore the nation's societal health? The past record of such actions and perseverance is not encouraging.

The structure and habits of democratic states, unless they are welded into larger organisms, lack those elements of persistence and conviction which alone give security to humble means . . . even in matters of self-preservation, no policy is pursued for ten to fifteen years at a time.[5]

For half a century we have known that long-lived radioactive nuclear waste must be stored so that it does not leak and kill people, contaminate underground water supplies, and render land areas uninhabitable for the many years of half-life of the radioactive material. No one in his right mind disputes the scientific fact of lethal radiation, nor the societal imperative of finding a permanent storage site and facility as temporary storage places pose increasing hazards. A solution has not been determined, although scientists; political, governmental, and business leaders; and those of the public who have informed themselves agree that containment or possibly counteracting injurious radiation is necessary. Numerous studies have been produced, sites proposed, and hundreds of millions of dollars spent constructing a massive underground storage facility which is now being challenged as geologically unsafe. The situation is distressing testimony to the difficulties of planning successfully. The many-trillion-dollar question posed is whether human societies can plan and act in their own best interests before a "clear and present danger" becomes a killing crisis. By that time, lives are lost, the costs of containment have multiplied, a successful solution is uncertain, and the possibility of societal catastrophe is evident.

Other such situations exist. The "sword of Damocles" continues to hang heavily over our heads. The possibilities of nuclear, chemical, and biological warfare increase as the capability of nations to engage in catastrophic conflict proliferates. Global warming and ocean pollution threaten the welfare and possibly the survival of the human species, if rising earth temperatures are scientifically confirmed and we continue to despoil two-thirds of the earth's surface containing invaluable marine resources and linking continents and countries together environmentally. Both involve everybody everywhere in the world. Doing something about them requires international agreement and collective action in perpetuity by vastly different societies and national entities.

Last and temporally the least urgent is the probability that the earth will be hit by a comet or asteroid from outer space. This has occurred in the past and devastated areas surrounding the point of impact. Some scientists conclude that a massive celestial body struck the earth during the era of the dinosaurs many millions of years ago, causing their disappearance and ushering in the era of mammals and the evolution of the human species. They believe that it will be possible to calculate the collision course of the celestial body with the earth years before the collision. A guided missile with a nuclear warhead might intercept and throw off course the incoming comet or asteroid before it hits the earth. This would require planning with the survival and possibly the extinction of the human species at stake.

## SOCIETY

Simulation began a very long time ago when our oldest human ancestors found that they could comprehend a condition or situation, and exercise rudimentary thought with respect to it. This might have had to do with finding food, constructing shelter, or meeting some threat which required forethought. The mental concept simulated the intended outcome of thinking ahead. From such a conceptual beginning, the different forms of simulation and their widespread use have come about, facilitating the conduct of human affairs and enabling people to anticipate and plan ahead successfully. Simulation is an instrument of analytical reasoning, a means of determining what to do and how to do it: incorporating rational thought as well as intuition and emotional reaction in decision making.

As indicated throughout this book, different kinds of simulation are employed in almost all human affairs. They have progressed from simple concepts in the minds of primitive people to flight simulators which mimic as closely as human ingenuity and accumulated knowledge permit the physiological and psychological experience of piloting aircraft under routine conditions and emergency situations; from direct barter between buyer and seller to a multilayered monetary and credit system including currency, stock certificates, book and computer entries, as evidence of ownership; bank and brokerage statements depicting a particular financial condition; credit cards and credit balances. These simulations are a means of establishing monetary value and ownership, exchanging assets, and determining liability. None of them are valuable in and of themselves. Their value lies in people's acceptance of what they represent as currency and its purchasing power in an established marketplace.

News is processed through several layers of simulation. Except for people who were there and experienced what is being reported directly, everyone else must rely on the reporter's view of what transpired: his or her memory, notes if any were taken, and any questioning of people who were present. The reporter's story may be altered by the news editor who reviews its content, emphasis, length, treatment of subject matter, and its relative importance compared with other news items competing for the limited space in newspapers and broadcast time available. It may be altered to conform to general publication policies by the editor in chief, the publisher or producer, or the owners of the mass medium of communication. The impact of the final representation on the reader, listener, and viewer is also affected by its location in the newspaper, its treatment as prime or secondary news in a television broadcast. The impact is increased if the item is repeated several times in slightly altered versions and followed up over a period of time.

By their nature and for particular purposes, simulations separate the user from the original or basic form of what is being represented, and from the initial event which is depicted. As societies become more complex, there are an increasing number of simulative steps between what is actually being transferred or depicted and its representation by one or more of the mass means of communication and reference. At each of these steps, the representation may be modified, changed by choice or events, inadvertently altered, deliberately disrupted or falsified. Other than what we view and experience directly, what we read, hear, and see as communicated by the mass media is what we perceive, accept, and believe to be the reality.

Those who are alert, knowledgeable, and well-informed may be able to note simulative discrepancies. But the public at large has no reason to question, no motivation to investigate, nor the means to determine the representative validity of what we read, hear on the radio, and especially what we see and hear on television and the telecomputer. "Seeing is believing". As human affairs become technically more complicated and more specialized in their content, what appears on the television-telecomputer video screen will be what is believed to be and referred to as real.

## Reality

Reality in its most fundamental form, relating to the physical world in which we live, is what we perceive through our sensory organs and process in our minds into a conscious concept. The same event or situation, however, is perceived differently by different people. In legal proceedings, witnesses often describe the same event differently. The initial reaction of people who are optimistic by nature or want to believe in new ideas or experiments is usually more favorable than the first judgment of those who are inclined to be critical and skeptical. The most objective reality is the common denominator of different perceptions, although the correct view may turn out in time to be the one held by the lone individual disagreeing with everyone else.

An ultimate resolution of a perceived reality is reached when almost everybody accepts a particular perception. This is not final and conclusive because new knowledge may further define the reality in the future. Generally accepted realities stabilize human affairs and human behavior. People could not function effectively if they continuously adjusted their every move and decision to take into account ever-present and never-ending uncertainties concerning everything.

There is also the reality of misconceptions, illusions, delusions, and fantasies. Hateful attitudes, prejudices, and other unalterable beliefs imbued in a person since childhood are realities for those who harbor them, even if they are incorrect in most people's opinions or the proven product of deliberate misrepresentation. We are all subject to illusions: misleading images which we create in our minds for personal fulfillment rather than descriptive accuracy. An example in the physical world, which many of us have read about and a few people have experienced, is the illusion of an oasis or the mirage of a body of water far-off in the distance in desert land. We may have illusions about ourselves which can become self-fulfilling delusions: Hollywood is associated with creating and maintaining illusions; scenarios and public images supercede realities.

Delusions provide the mental image which some people require to satisfy a compelling emotional need. Resentment, disappointment, or anger engendered by some event or situation affecting us may be transformed and redirected from its source to a scapegoat, which had little or nothing to do with what occurred. This transference relieves us of the feelings that disturb us, by unconsciously associating them with someone or something else. We delude ourselves and often hurt others. Most of us have fantasized ourselves in all sorts of situations we wish existed or would like to experience. People with strong and active imaginations may conjure in their minds images that are emotionally and intellectually important for their peace of mind. When these fantasies are no longer recognized as such, but are regarded as real, they become delusions with negative effects. Emotionally derived and emotionally dependent concepts and images are as real for those who cherish them as perceptive and scientific simulations are for other people. Shared beliefs provide a strong bond among members of political, social, and religious groups.

Throughout human history societies have been spiritual, religious, royal, or autocratic in nature. Democratic societies as we conceive them today have been few and far between. Scientific knowledge as a basis for individual, collective, and societal action and behavior is a recent arrival on the historical scene. And the mass media of communication are just now emerging as the dominant force in technically advanced countries. The key question confronting the United States today is what sort of society will emerge in the future from a melding of the primary elements existing at the present time. There are our many democratic institutions established only 220 years ago. There is a religious component consisting of different faiths rooted in the more distant past. During the past century science and technology have become a major factor in our society. And most recently, the expanding communication and information system has emerged as the dominant directive force in the nation.

## Television—Telecomputing

If actions are not taken, specific objectives adopted and attained, the serious societal problems confronting the nation today will worsen, and give rise to civil unrest which threatens our democratic form of government. Whether these actions are taken depends on the mass media of communication more than any other factor. Among these media, the television-telecomputer system of communication, information, and reference is dominant today and will become more so in the future. It is the central nervous system which transmits the signals that direct the nation.

At present, the major problems threatening social stability and the national welfare receive scant attention on the networks. Television is devoted almost exclusively to commercially profitable entertainment and news. Our congressional representatives, elected to guide the nation, depend on television for the public exposure which decides their political fate. Favorable and repeated exposure can transform them into national figures. Unfavorable or infrequent appearance on the video screen can erode or eradicate their public image. As a consequence they avoid any and all questions concerning this powerful medium of communication, which can support or destroy them. Audience ratings, advertising, and other promotional revenue determine the subject matter and the content of what is transmitted through this primary nerve cord of the nation.

Television is considered a commercial enterprise rather than a public service which provides news for most people and entertainment broadly defined which influences how they react to events and situations, what they think, and how they act. Those who control television do not acknowledge these determinative effects. And those who depend on it do not publicly concede this reliance for fear of alienating an essential element of public exposure in their affairs. The result is legislative stalemate: an almost total absence of critical review of television in the halls of government and business offices, a dearth of constructive discussion, and inaction in the development of television as a public service functioning in the general public interest.

A first step in addressing the serious problems confronting the nation is acknowledging that they exist, rather than largely ignoring them as is now the case, and open discussion by both government and private enterprise concerning what to do. The respective roles of these two primary directive forces in the nation must be determined, specifically defined, and made clear for everyone. The television-telecomputer system can no longer be regarded as the private preserve of commercial interests. Nor can it be the political mouthpiece of government. It is in fact a national public utility, enjoying an informational monopoly, concerned with a societal function far more important than local public utilities supplying water, natural gas, sanitation, and other essential public services. It is the primary instrument of communication, information, and reference; the main means of explaining and implementing public policy; a force in mitigating or resolving major problems and developing constructive attitudes and behavior; and a provider of self-education as part of or in addition to the traditional educational system.

If ownership and control of television and telecomputer networks remain in private hands but are treated as a public utility, broadcast time, subject matter, and content would be divided between commercial and public service programs. The informational stem of the nation will function most successfully and productively as a joint operation or partnership between government and business, both fulfilling their respective roles in our society. If the divided responsibilities are not clearly defined and understood by the public, one of the two partners will end up predominant and affecting the nation as it wishes.

When irreconcilable disagreements arise, the government must prevail. It cannot abrogate its basic responsibility of directing the nation in the general public interest without a formal or de facto change in our type of government. This would have to occur were a small group of private entrepreneurs or business organizations to control the primary system of communication and information in the country. As powerful a political and socioeconomic force as television-telecomputing cannot be controlled by business or by government without jeopardizing our present form of democracy. Unless their partnership is formalized and clearly explained for the watchful eye and ear of the public, government or business will obtain operational control with far-reaching governmental and sociopolitical consequences for the nation. The partnership agreement would be monitored and enforced by a national public information utility commission with members representing the government, the television and telecomputer industries, the public at large, education, social psychology, and macroeconomics.

### National Information System

A national information system requires resolution of certain basic considerations in our society. Most of these did not exist or were related to very different circumstances when our founding fathers formulated the Constitution and its first amendments. "Freedom of speech" is the term used today in connection with many considerations concerning television, telecomputing, radio, and the press. What does the key word "abridging" signify in the first amendment, enacted long before the enormous changes brought about during the past two centuries by global events, population growth, societal developments, and scientific and technological advances? Does the dictionary definition "no reduction in compass with the retention of relative completeness" require or justify the dissemination to millions of people simultaneously anything and everything spoken and written? Should it include information intended to incite civil disruption or violent overthrow of the existing societal system and government, to promote illegal and antisocial action, cause public panic, publicize specific instructions explaining how to fabricate explosives and virulent weapons from readily available materials? Should the enactment of prurient behavior, explicit, pornographic, and deviant sex be broadcast worldwide for anyone and everyone?

It is often argued that men, women, adolescents, and children do not have to watch television programs they find personally objectionable or societally detrimental. This assumes that programs harmful for children and hurtful for other categories of people will be forbidden by parents and others concerned, or automatically rejected by technical devices. It presumes that there is no built-in dynamic in television and perhaps also in telecomputing, created by the direct relationship in commercial programs between advertising and other promotional revenue and the system of audience rating.

In fact, intense competition promotes television programs with emotionally enticing, exaggerated, and violent subject matter and human behavior to increase or maintain their instinctive appeal and their audience rating. There is a steady escalation of this emotionalism as television station owners seek to outdo each other. Ordinary events are often transformed and sometimes distorted into "shows" to make them more alluring and entertaining. This showmanship now includes most sports and is gradually being applied to more and more events and situations. We are attracted to such treatment by the emotionally sensitive, strongly reactive, and spontaneously aggressive aspects of our behavior established during eons of evolutionary time. Civilization seeks to sublimate these more primitive impulses into behavior that is more rational and appropriate to modern times and our prospects as a species.

These are crucial questions concerning the public responsibilities of mass communication networks serving and affecting an entire nation and other parts of the world. Are there obligations other than advertising and entertainment, such as public and participatory information, education, supportive and critical investigative reporting of human affairs? Should there be a maximum percentage of time devoted to direct advertising and other promotion during different periods of the day and night? Who determines the allocation of broadcast time, the responsibility for different subject matter, program content and treatment? Is it the small group of station owners, operating executives, producers, directors, and scriptwriters who make these decisions now with little or no governmental oversight? Who is accountable for the accuracy of information affecting millions of people? Can misrepresentation, alteration, and falsification of data, language, visual images, and actual events be detected, prevented, or minimized? There are other important questions relating to the permissible and desirable functioning of the nation's most important informational system.

The structure of our government was formulated by a small group of people dedicated to the effort. The Constitution, Bill of Rights, and Amendments have guided the nation ever since. An organizational structure and operational requirements for a national information system can also be formulated by a group of the best minds representing the principal interests involved. By forswearing adversarial confrontation which produces the lowest common denominator of implacable self-interests, the group could develop a consensus concerning the information system which would best serve the general public interest for years to come. Such an undertaking would take time, and should be the primary concern of the participants until the task is completed and their collective recommendation presented for congressional review and public response.

## Planning

In today's fast-moving world it is no longer feasible to wait for political pressures or crisis conditions to induce legislatures to think ahead and provide the directive leadership required for their constituencies and the nation, state, or locality they represent to function successfully. To wait for such forces to operate ensures that major problems will not be addressed, policies adopted, and specific programs formulated in time to be most effective, before a crisis develops with its disruptive consequences. Planning ahead is required.

Congress has performed poorly in planning. Rather than anticipating obvious needs and serious problems, it reacts to them after they become critical and can no longer be disregarded. And then it often abrogates to a special commission the task of formulating and recommending policies and plans concerning controversial subjects it wants to avoid debating and deciding, and knows it cannot cope with under its present practices. It will be a long time before societal, scientific, and technological advances force Congress to plan comprehensively, or to bring about institutional changes which enable planning in the general public interest to be performed and effectuated by a special governmental institution in the name of Congress.

## Scenarios for the Distant Future

The ultimate question which overarches all others is whether we are capable of thinking, concluding, and acting in our self-interest to ensure our survival as a species. Some scholars maintain that there is within us an unconscious drive to self-destruct, which will in time produce the desired result. Ecologists fear that we will alter or contaminate our planetary home until it is no longer habitable for us. Some scientists are concerned that a worldwide viral epidemic or catastrophic collision with a celestial body will eradicate animal life on earth. There are those who believe that we are anointed by invisible powers-that-be to prosper, dominate the globe, and survive in perpetuity as the preferred animal species. Most people believe or at least hope that we will have the foresight and the capability, the motivation, and the will to do what is necessary to prosper and survive in our earthly and atmospheric environment, whatever adversities may develop. Which it will be remains to be seen in the far distant future.

In one way or another, simulation would be involved in each of these scenarios. If we harbor an unconscious drive to destroy ourselves, it could relate to a mental-emotional image or simulation within us of a nirvana or supremely desirable afterlife achieved only upon our demise. This is the basic motivation of those accepting sacramental sacrifice for themselves, the self-destruction of Kamikaze pilots, terrorist bombers, and self-immolators for a current cause; and to a lesser degree by flagellants and penitents wounding themselves in various ways. If a self-destructive urge does exist in all of us rather than only a few people, it is at the present time totally beyond our awareness, comprehension, and explanation.

If we allow ourselves to contaminate our planetary home, we will have simulated the conditions required for our disintegration or extermination. This could occur by radioactive contamination were it carried around the world in the atmosphere, deadly to humans and absorbed by plants. The global effects of the nuclear disaster at Chernobyl in the Ukraine are not widely known. The possibility that a number of the existing nuclear plants producing electric power or plutonium for explosive purposes could "melt down" at about the same time, threatening human life on earth, seems remote now. But the possibility of a deadly pandemic from an unknown organism is much greater—particularly if it is airborne or cannot be successfully quarantined—because of the continuous transportation of more and more people, goods, and services far and wide throughout the world. Experimental simulations would certainly be required to identify, isolate, and neutralize the deadly organism.

Ideas are being advanced concerning what could be done to avoid or reduce the destructive effects of an asteroid or comet striking the earth. This possibility has been brought to scientific attention by geological research which suggests that the extermination of the dinosaurs some 90 million years ago was caused by a large celestial body striking the earth at what is now the Gulf of Mexico. Before any human action could be taken with respect to such a forthcoming event, the present and projected path of the threatening celestial body would have to be simulated exactly. This could be done by astronomical observation and mathematical calculation of its collision course with the earth and the time of its arrival. One proposal suggests that a guided missile or rocket with a nuclear warhead and proximity fuse could be dispatched to destroy or deflect the approaching celestial body into a path no longer threatening the earth. One scientist estimates this counteraction would require five years' advance notice to plan and execute successfully with today's technical knowledge.

Another scenario presumes that people conclude they cannot deflect the oncoming crash, and can only act to reduce its catastrophic effects and prevent the possible annihilation of the human species as is believed to have occurred with the dinosaurs. This would involve simulative analyses concerning the destructive effects of the collision on the earth's surface and environment which could make life on earth difficult to sustain for years or decades after the crash. The only recourse would be to plan to protect as much human life as possible, perhaps with hundreds of thousands of "air-raid shelters" around the earth, other protective measures, or accepting the likely decimation of most of the people on earth and concentrating on preserving enough people to save the human species from extinction. Perhaps enough genetic material could be protected for preprogrammed and undamaged robots to start up our species again for us; a desperate scenario, indeed, which would require many kinds of preparatory simulation while waiting and planning for the fateful event.

Those who believe that the future for human beings is predetermined by a supernatural force or godly being will continue to engage in those activities and the planning which come about in the daily course of events. Some people contend that planning indicates people do not really believe in predestination because they are trying to change what is inevitable. But if whatever planning is done is considered predestined, there is no contradiction in not limiting human activities intended to affect the future. "Come what may" does not preclude planning because it is an essential requirement for human existence and a fundamental aspect of human behavior. But too much directive effort might contradict the faith of those who believe that the present and future have always been and will always be planned and directed by an immutable and irresistible force beyond human understanding. For those who not only believe that the future is preordained but human beings are doomed, whatever people do in the meantime is irrelevant. So why worry about the future and planning?

Finally, there are those who maintain or hope that we can improve our prospects by not leaving things to random, disordered, or preordained development, but by planning as wisely and well as we can. We may or may not be as successful as we would like. We may or may not be able to survive unexpected events or catastrophes occurring in the world we inhabit. But as the species which has attained self-consciousness and acquired considerable knowledge, we will have done what we could in our current self-interest and in favor of our survival in the future. This will require organized forethought, planning, and collective action which has not yet been achieved in most nations, much less on a worldwide scale, which would make possible global collaboration to meet global adversities. Simulation is an essential part of this planning. Consensus and collaboration will certainly be necessary if people want to increase their chance of surviving worldwide epidemics or celestial collision.

## Generalizations for the Present

We have heard people declaim that the government should cease and desist planning, because of some experience they have had or have heard about. We cannot cease planning because it is inherent in human behavior. It is an intrinsic aspect of human life and part of our deep-rooted instinct to survive.

The vital question for the individual and for society is what kind of planning and how much. The answer defines the form of government, the nature of the society, and its prospects. Most people are not aware of the universality and inevitability of planning. The planning involved in conceiving and completing the vast number of projects which enable societies to function will become more apparent as human affairs become technically more complicated. Planning is so ubiquitous that the importance of intensive and continuing study of the process is not yet widely recognized. It has not received the attention it deserves in research and education.

Since planning is ever-present, a political decision "not to plan" means that the government will not encourage the best planning as an organized method of directive management or promote its use in business. Its employment in government can be minimized by executive order or legislative action. Restricting its use in business is difficult or impossible because business people know from experience that successful operations producing profits require planning. A decision by a society to minimize planning means that governmental affairs will be conducted day-by-day as the circumstances of the moment suggest or require, as political powers or market forces dictate, by guess and by God, or in some other unorganized way. Some countries at an early stage of their development do not have the managers or accumulated knowledge needed to conduct more than rudimentary planning. The characteristics and functioning of a society reflect the presence or absence of organized planning.

Simulation is an essential part of planning, first, as the analytical formulation which represents in a simplified and abbreviated form the major elements and interactive dynamics of what is being planned. It is the evaluative reference for examining and deciding questions concerning planning and operational management. The second simulation is the comprehensive or master plan for the organization or activity which results from using the analytical simulation to develop the plan and specific programs to achieve designated objectives. The comprehensive plan may be a printed document, a computer program, or a conceptualization in the minds of those directing small enterprises. The same process of formulating an analytical reference and an operational plan is carried out by each of the component units within larger organizations and complicated activities. Fitted together they comprise the comprehensive plan for the parent entity. This process of planning is practiced, knowingly or unknowingly, formally or informally, in connection with innumerable human activities and projects.

### Developing Systems of Simulation

As indicated in this book, millions of mechanical devices, analytical formulations, and other kinds of simulation are used regularly in the United

States. They constitute in some applications a societal system of interconnection and transaction which is becoming more multilayered and complex as science and technology progress. Consider the system of consumer credit to pay for ordinary goods and services and "unexpected purchases or emergencies"; and our communication system for providing news, entertainment, and other information via television.

### Credit Card System

Not so long ago, goods and services were paid for in cash or check handed to a salesperson or to an individual or organization supplying a service, or by a check mailed to the mortgage holder, a public utility, a few department stores, or mail order houses. For the most part, daily affairs were conducted by direct one-to-one contacts and transactions, between individuals or with a few people. Only several parties were involved in each transaction, and they were known to each other. Fault or failure in this simple system of payment was readily identified. The situation is far different today. More than one-quarter of the almost $5 trillion of consumer purchases in the United States every year are paid by credit card, rather than with cash or personal check.

Several companies provide to those who subscribe to their services information having to do with the credit record of individuals and organizations. These data are collected and exchanged among those concerned with the capability, willingness, and record of repayment of present and potential credit card holders. This includes the credit information companies themselves, companies that issue their own credit cards, establishments that accept them as payment, and financial institutions which issue, distribute, and underwrite general purpose credit cards and provide the necessary supportive services. Each of these may determine a credit rating based on its own information and that available to it as a subscriber to a credit information service. Or the information service will provide a credit risk score derived from a statistical analysis of the information it has collected.

Credit services are required by law to investigate the accuracy of information in their files which is challenged by the person or party whose credit is affected. They will provide a free credit report once a year to anyone requesting it in the United States, in order to provide this opportunity to note and correct any mistakes.

Some well-established organizations conduct their own credit card operations for those buying their products or services, such as oil and telephone companies and department stores. They provide the accounting, billing, and collection service. They must have sufficient financial resources themselves, or by affiliation with a bank, to carry unpaid cardholder debt until it is repaid.

Product and service credit cards are being gradually replaced by general purpose cards. These are accepted by most retail and wholesale establishments. They are issued, underwritten, and serviced by banks, in their own name or as distributors for organizations wanting their own name on the credit card. The distributing banks may obtain the VISA, MasterCard, American Express, or another imprint or logo for a fee, because, as one of them advertises "You will find your card welcome at over twelve million locations across the country and around the world . . . at more than 250,000 automatic bank teller machines, and 305,000 financial institutions worldwide".

Failure to make full payments on a credit card account when due accumulates interest on the unpaid balance at about 10 percent above the current prime rate. Since late payments are potentially very profitable, and secure because they are a lien against the cardholder, credit is rarely denied or cancelled. "If your income is . . . at least $8,000, your application will be processed for a silver card . . . with all the information you need to transfer your balance". There is active competition among issuers to increase the number of holders of their credit cards, by offering rebates on everyday purchases, lower than the usual interest rates on overdue payments for a promotional period of time, frequent-flyer airline miles, and a variety of other incentives including t-shirts and mugs. The total of all overdue payments for all cardholders in the United States is a large enough accumulation of personal debt to be taken into account in analyzing the national economy. The outstanding debt on a particular credit card is an asset which is bought and sold.

Establishments accepting general purpose credit cards pay several percent of the amount charged to the financial institution carrying the account. With each purchase, the cardholder agrees "to perform the obligations set forth in the cardmember's agreement with the issuer". Millions of transactions take place every day. Not only are new cardholders being recruited, but increased borrowing is encouraged by approving larger "credit lines" and "advance payments". The entire system is based on the attraction of credit card purchases and deferred payment.

It is clear from even this minimal description that credit operations comprise a simulative system which extends throughout our society and affects it in many ways. It is widespread. Credit cards can be used almost anywhere in the United States and in other nations around the world which have the necessary communication networks. Issuers of credit cards compete for a larger share of the business. And new cards are issued by those wanting to participate in the lucrative market of consumer debt incurred with credit cards.

The credit card system is also multilayered. Payment with a general purpose credit card at a gas pump is recorded by the oil company's credit accounting system. It must be collected from the cardholder's account in another credit card system. The oil company's credit card can be used for corporate purchases. Soon it will be possible to pay taxes and almost any obligation by credit card. This proliferation in breadth and depth creates a vast societal system of simulation many steps removed from payment by cash and occasional check: a "house of credit cards" with myriad interactions among a great variety of transactions.

An additional element to the credit card system is being market tested. Cash drawn from bank accounts is recorded on microchips imbedded in "stored-value" credit cards, replacing the cash carried in a wallet, purse, or pocket. Payment for purchases is made by inserting the card into a terminal on the store counter, a slot in a vending machine or gasoline pump, or a small, calculator-like device held by the restaurant waiter or taxi driver. The correct cash payment as shown on a small display is transferred from the purchaser's cash card to the seller's card. The seller credits the accumulation of cash on his stored-value card to his account at the bank by wire at his convenience. This could be another step in the trend toward an almost totally electronic monetary system. Is the day coming when a "smart card" will as advertised "replace almost anything in your wallet: a list of phone numbers, an identity photo, a subway token, credit cards and cash".

Each credit card purchase is a simulation one or more transactions removed from direct payment in cash, or a convenient substitute for payment by personal check. Purchases and payments with different credit cards and their "fine print" can produce accounting complications and repayment difficulties, which may require some cardholders to seek the "professional credit repair and counseling" advertised in the yellow pages of telephone books. A worldwide system with so many participants, transactions, and interactions becomes an electronic complex which borders on the artificial and unreal. The individual cardholder finds it difficult to deal directly with such a simulative system.

The credit card complex is exposed to error, interruption, and disruption: unintentional and otherwise. Spotting mistakes in such a maze of information in motion is difficult, hence the laws requiring credit services to provide a free credit report once a year on request, so the individual or organization can check it for accuracy. It may not be easy to check a claimed error, or to determine how or why it occurred. Deliberate misinformation may be more difficult to detect and to discontinue. Once found, it may have to be traced back and corrected on many transactions.

The present credit card system transmits almost all information on telephone lines which are subject to legal and illegal wiretapping or malicious interference. Unless information is encrypted, wireless communication is readily intercepted. Credit card numbers are embossed on every card, and bank account numbers are printed on every check. They are disclosed to everyone handling these means of making monetary transactions. Fraud is relatively easy for those so inclined who have obtained someone's credit or bank account number, in one of the many ways this is done. So much so that banks and issuers of credit cards are urging account holders to accept cards imprinted with their photographs and other personal identification.

Its vulnerabilities also expose the credit card system, accounting for more than a quarter of consumer purchases, to deliberate manipulation, misuse, disruption, or temporary interruption for political or even insurrectional purposes. To make and maintain the system safe from operational misuse will require a permanent team of technically skilled specialists, working with the cooperation of all the major interests involved. Unless this is done, the mounting losses from fraud will continue to increase. Rather than absorb the reimbursements they must make to cardholders for their losses through fraud, issuers will pass these costs on to others. Ultimately, this means you and me.

## Television, Telecomputing

Television and telecomputing constitute a societal system which is simulative from beginning to end. Essentially, it records information of many kinds and transmits or transforms it into what millions or hundreds of millions of people view on their television or computer screens. All except the original event, situation, or abstract information is an electronic representation in photographic, graphic, written, or other form, with accompanying sound. The system extends around the world. Its influence is widespread and profound. In many areas it is the main source of information. If it is not now the most powerful force in the world affecting individuals and society, it certainly will be before long. It has enormous potential for encouraging constructive or destructive actions and activities, for good or for evil, peace or war, the survival or extinction of the human species.

Simulation on television begins in the mind of the reporter or cameraman before the first image and the first sounds are recorded. There are questions to be asked and choices to be made concerning whether the time is right to fulfill the intent of the televising. Is what is being portrayed as it normally exists, or is it in an unusual state or condition? Would proceeding immediately show the person as he or she usually appears and behaves, or with an exceptional demeanor and acting atypically? Should the picture be close-up or taken at a distance, posed or informal? Most of us have sat or stood for a group picture when the photographer tries one of the ways devised to make us smile, look pleasant, or at least less self-conscious. And some of us have made sure that the portrait negative is destroyed which shows us blinking our eyes, because it is an inaccurate simulation of our good looks. Of course, in dire emergencies and momentary events when seconds count, any clear recording of what is happening is acceptable, but may require explanation.

Different means and methods are employed to record the wide range of images that may be shown on television or the telecomputer. Cameras recording the electromagnetic wavelengths visible to the human eye are the usual means. But there are also the infrared camera recording heat, the multispectral camera sensitive to a number of different wavelengths, and radar and sonar producing special images. Each has technical features which produce particular characteristics in the image. For example, photo images taken through a lens have optical distortions toward their edges, which are not noted normally and noteworthy only if they are being used to measure distances on the ground simulated in the photograph. Photos can be cropped to show only part of the original image, highlighted during processing to attract or divert attention from part of the picture, cut and pasted back together again so that the change is undetectable except in the original. For certain purposes, infrared photos are transformed into "false color infrared" images which appear different than the usual photograph taken with the visible range of light.

Images recorded in digital form, microscopic dots with photographic values ranging from white to black, are becoming the favored method of reproduction because of their advantages in electronic transmission and the many ways they can be used in scientific research. There is almost no limit to the changes that can be made in the original image without it being apparent. Digital technology permitting the manipulation of images has subverted the certainty of photographic evidence. What we see and believe on the television and telecomputer screen "ain't necessarily so".

When sound is an integral part of television, as is almost always the case, it can be employed in different ways to produce different effects on viewers and listeners. Music can be used or composed which is calming or exciting, romantic or bombastic, melodic and emotionally appealing or discordant and irritating for most people. Sounds can be manipulated while music is being recorded or broadcast. We have seen pictures of the array of sliding switches in recording studios and broadcast stations that are used to produce the precise sound desired. The overall impact of sound can be increased or decreased by amplifying or lowering its volume. Its timbre can be modified. Sound can be added to or subtracted from a television program. Rousing applause can be "dubbed in" when in fact none occurred, or it can be the response of handpicked studio audiences to signals from a prompter at live television shows. Applause can also be reduced or eliminated, suggesting disinterest or negative response by the audience. Dramatic and horrifying events can be portrayed most vividly by including the disturbing sounds which are often part of such happenings: screams, moans, and other sounds. The effects of sounds are subtle in that they are absorbed subliminally more than they are noted consciously.

Manipulation and misuse can occur at any one of the operational steps involved in preparing and broadcasting network television programs, such as when it is determined what kinds of subject matter will be aired, how it will be treated in general, and approximately what percentage of total broadcast time will be allotted to different categories; film is reviewed and edited after it is received at the television station, and at subsequent reviews before it appears on the television screen; it is decided which movies will be shown, and what is cut out to shorten them to fit the air time allotted; "handout" materials, including regular advertising and infomercials are accepted; teleprompter writers and scriptwriters decide what they will write; and it is decided how regular announcers and special reporters are to deport themselves on television.

Underlying all such decisions are audience ratings. If this generally accepted measure of successful performance is low, the television station has lower advertising revenues and less profit than its competitors with higher ratings in the same market. It will act to improve its lower audience ratings as best it can. In the United States this has resulted in many more newscasts reporting mainly local crime and exciting events; increased sports coverage; and entertainment programs with greater emotional and violent content, or treated as enticing "shows". This built-in competitive dynamic, or syndrome, referred to in several connections in this book, constitutes an overall form of manipulation to attract more viewers and longer viewing. Almost everyone making decisions of consequence in network television participates: managers, producers, directors, editors, writers, announcers, actors, and others. Television viewers did not give notice of their awareness of what was occurring until the prevalence of violence, gunplay, sex, aberrant behavior, and emotionalized content became conspicuous. People began to wonder about its effects on individual and societal behavior, on actual events, and particularly on the development of children.

Intentional alteration of visual images, sounds, statements, and other means of recording and transmitting information is difficult or impossible for people viewing the broadcast to detect. It can occur at any or all of the operational steps noted above where decisions concerning program content are made. Misrepresentation is most likely to be noticed at each successive stage in the handling of information on its way to final broadcast, since comparison with the immediately preceding version of the information may reveal any change. Misuse is minimized by a firm organizational policy against tampering; and making sure that those in decisive positions observe general admonitions and specific prohibitions against altering information. Random checking and occasional investigation help to prevent misuse. Because of its vast extent and instant transmission, the television and telecomputer system may require a mechanism or form of surrogate intelligence to detect alteration of information which distorts its intent and content.

Television and telecomputing constitute a simulative system with greater potential to benefit society than any other development in human history, including such major achievements as the discovery of the wheel, igniting and controlling fire, the emergence of written language, mathematics, and particle physics. Each had great impact on the human population at the time. Today, television and telecomputing relate to a population of 5.5 billion people around the world, increasing in number at a rapid rate.

Such a system can serve as the primary source of broadly representative, accurate, and reliable news—a tremendously important societal function by itself. It can also be a primary purveyor of information concerning public affairs in general: important political actions, economic developments, major social problems and opportunities, individual and collective responsibilities; material not normally covered in newspapers or delivered electronically in the home. People can obtain through the Internet and other networks an incredible volume and variety of news. And they can communicate directly and immediately by the Internet, e-mail, telephone, and facsimile.

Networks, cable, videotapes, and videodisks can provide accredited self-education programs enabling individuals and groups to acquire the skills or additional knowledge required for employment in rapidly changing economic marketplaces; to fulfill continuing education requirements; and enjoy adding to one's personal store of knowledge. Effective techniques will be developed which will allow formal education to be acquired by television-telecomputing. A vast accumulation of knowledge and experience—true and false, current and age-old, good and evil—is available over the Internet, including every conceivable interest, belief, attitude, unlawful activity, and perversion.

Different cultures can be viewed as represented by major works of art and folk art preserved in museums, galleries, conservatories, religious structures, and special collections around the world. Viewers can walk through many of these repositories in virtual reality, and examine color photographs of individual works of art. Selected music can be ordered up in the home, in addition to the programmed music available on radio. Dance, drama, and other artistic forms of cultural expression can be called up on the video screen. And the beliefs, tenets, and operating features of different faiths and organized religions can be examined in exploratory documents, or as seen on moving pictures of cultural events, religious services, ceremonies, festivals, and other observances. Cultural information available to everyone with a television set or computer should reduce the lack of information and misrepresentations concerning the history and habits of other people, which can lead to prejudice and hate, with its societally destructive consequences.

The Internet was conceived and established originally by the military services in the United States to provide immediate intercommunication among scientists at various locations in the country and in different nations. By enabling them to collaborate closely without delay, research was speeded up and better results were attained. This can continue, apart from the heterogeneous activities occurring on the Internet, with the additional feature of face-to-face video conferences between individuals and groups. The same forces that have created the Internet can be used for ecological planning that addresses problems of education, food, water, and political stability. Informal studies by ordinary people, organized research by professional specialists, and operational activities by any number of engineers at different locations can be conducted simultaneously as interactive video conferences.

Entertainment is broadcast in its many forms. Movies are selected from stored collections of thousands of films of every kind and description, produced during a century of moviemaking. Which movies are selected for broadcast and how often they are shown affects viewers' preferences for entertainment, their reactions to some situations in real life, and their attitudes toward certain events. Programs prepared specifically for television have similar effects. Sports are entertainment for many viewers, increasingly as "shows" with multiple announcers, associated statistics, and interviews, emphasizing money awards and players' annual income as measures of athletic capability and achievement. Talk shows, soap operas, and celebrity programs titillate and influence those who watch them in various ways. Audience ratings determine the selection of what is broadcast on television as entertainment.

This vast television-telecomputer system affects most people in the world in some way. As the primary means of selecting, processing, and disseminating information throughout the United States, at least some part of it will in time be installed in every household. Computer literacy will be as essential in human affairs as being able to read and write. The system is simulation from the acquisition of information to its display on a video screen. Its use will determine more than any other factor the conduct and prospects of human society.

It requires actions by government to establish and maintain technical standards and operational requirements permitting direct integration of different parts of the system. Political, governmental, and commercial arrangements between nations must be worked out and negotiated. Features must be incorporated to prevent complete loss of personal privacy, fraud and other illegal use, and manipulation of the system which could threaten a nation's stability. Whether additional governmental action in partnership with private enterprise is needed to structure the simulative system in the general public interest depends on whether maximizing private profit or power is the best criterion for a national information system.

Should network television be considered an information service which is more basic to a community's welfare than the public utilities now provided? To meet the needs of a community, should equal time be devoted to news, entertainment, public information, education, and political-societal affairs? Should advertising be concentrated within one proportionate part of each hour or half hour of broadcast time? If the money required to produce quality television programs requires too much advertising time at current prices, should part of the cost of the system be paid from the public exchequer or directly by the viewer, or by government agencies? For example, if information broadcast on television during the time allotted for public information makes it unnecessary for many viewers to come to the agency for explanations, requiring more staff and increasing operating costs, should the cost be paid by the agency. Viewers may conclude that a national system provides information and opportunities that are worth more to them than the unidentifiable services which now add more than 10 percent as surcharges to many utility bills.

If television networks were treated as a public utility monopoly, a national information public utility commission would determine the net return on investment for the private enterprises operating the system, and bill the television viewer for any difference allowed between the cost of operations and the income derived from the sale of television time. The commission would include a member representing the general public interest, government, the television industry, the telecomputer industry, information-communication economics, international relations, and television-telecomputer users.

In the present political climate the problems and possibilities of the television-telecomputer system will not be raised and debated, much less seriously considered. Congress is unable to address complex national problems and needs constructively, and act effectively in the general public interest. There are no well-known and generally respected leaders in government or private enterprise concerned above all with the welfare of the nation as a societal entity. The public appears confused by the serious problems confronting the country and the changes brought about by advances in science and technology, with little confidence in the nation's capability to handle them successfully, or that competitive market forces will produce the right resolution. Sooner or later in a democracy, how best to manage the primary public information system must be addressed. How long it will take to face societal realities and decide what, if anything, to do about them and what circumstances will bring this about, remains to be seen.

The credit card and television-telecomputer systems as described briefly above are examples of the complicated simulative systems we have created. The modern military establishment is another such system, even more technically and organizationally complex. They are of our own devising, brought about by our fast-developing scientific knowledge and technological capabilities.

They signify an increasing disassociation of human affairs from the physical world. More and more we function in a complex of simulative actions and activities, several steps removed from direct interrelationship with nature. The ties that bind us to nature are not as close as they once were.

And our concept of nature changes as we learn more about the most fundamental forces underlying the natural world.

Art not only imitates life, it sometimes is better than life. . . . Driving these new attractions is technology such as virtual reality, big-screen projection, motion simulation and increasingly computerized rides . . . "you can recreate history, scenery, culture through the flip of a switch". . . . While some tourists use the movies, rides and such to enhance their visits to the real thing, others stick entirely with the synthetic.[6]

Such simulative developments can lead us to the favorable future imagined in some science fiction. Or they can lead us to the type of political society described by George Orwell in *1984,* or to gradual societal disintegration as we disconnect ourselves from the restraining forces of the natural world from whence we came and which will determine our evolutionary destiny. If we apply organized forethought including simulation to our societal affairs, and plan to the extent experience indicates we have an appropriate probablility of attaining designated objectives, we can maximize the progress and prospects of society within the constraints established by evolutionary forces and the natural environment.

## NOTES

1. William J. Mitchell, "When Is Seeing Believing?", *Scientific American,* February 1994, p. 68.
2. Jack Peters, "Kasparov Bedevils Deep Blue with First Win", *Los Angeles Times,* 12 February 1996, p. A13.
3. Eric Mankin, "Computers Learn to Match Wits with Humans", *University of Southern California Chronicle,* 26 February 1996, p. 7.
4. M. Mitchell Waldrop, "AI Is the Able Assistant", *Science,* 2 June 1989, p. 1045.
5. Winston S. Churchill, *The Second World War, The Gathering Storm* (Boston: Houghton Mifflin, 1948), pp. 17, 18.
6. Susan Carey, "Unnatural Wonders, Simulated Tours Beat Real Thing", *Wall Street Journal,* 3 May 1996, p. B1.

# Selected Bibliography

This is an illustrative bibliography, rather than a list of sources confirming specific statements in the text. Each reference incorporates information on some form or aspect of simulation, or on its present and future use in planning. The subject matter and relevance of many of the references is indicated by the descriptive subtitle which follows the title proper in parentheses. All together, these references represent and support the contents of this book. For the most part, they are selected from generally available journals and newspapers.

Ahmed-Taylor, Ty. "Behind the Scenes, Where There's Smoke, There's (Possibly) Profit" ( . . . simulated photo realism . . . How it was done). *New York Times,* 3 July 1995, p. Y27.

———. "Visual Feats." *New York Times,* 25 September 1995, p. zC7.

Allakhverdov, Andrey and Daniel Clery. "Testing the Psychology of Would-Be Astronauts." *Science,* 7 October 1994, p. 24.

Anonymous. "Chrysler and French in Design Project." *New York Times,* 3 August 1995, p. zC2.

———. "High Altitude Photos from NASA: The Applications Aircraft Program Began as an Internal Project." *Functional Photography,* May-June 1984, p. 26.

Axel, Richard. "The Molecular Logic of Smell" (Mammals can recognize thousands of odors, some of which prompt powerful responses. Recent experiments illuminate how the nose and brain may perceive scents). *Scientific American,* October 1995, p. 154.

Bak, Per and Kan Chen. "Self-Organized Criticality" (Large interactive systems naturally evolve toward a critical state in which a minor event can lead to a catastrophe. Self-organized criticality may explain the dynamics of earthquakes, economic markets and ecosystems). *Scientific American,* January 1991, p. 46.

Baker, Molly. "Playing the Stock-Market Symbol Game." *Wall Street Journal*, 6 November 1995, p. C1.

Baldwin, Neil. "The Laboratory Notebooks of Thomas Edison" (The raw visual and textual evidence of his imagination, Edison's notebooks were the unrevealed talismans of the inventor's career). *Scientific American*, October 1995, p. 160.

Batten, Mary. "Making Waves to Build Better Harbors: USC Engineer Simulates Effect of Tidal Waves on Structures Such as Ships, Mooring Facilities and Sea Walls." *University of Southern California Transcript*, 14 October 1985, p. 9.

Beardsley, Tim. "The Cold War's Dirty Secrets" (Radiation experiments ignored ethics guidelines). *Scientific American*, May 1995, p. 16.

Bell, Ted. "Beale's Fortunes Soar with Spy Planes." *Sacramento Bee*, 4 September 1995, p. B1.

Blakeslee, Sandra. "Brain Locates Source of a Sound with Temporal, Not Spatial, Clues." *New York Times*, 10 May 1994, p. 235.

———. "Tracing the Brain's Pathways for Linking Emotion and Reason" (An emotion like fear has been conserved through evolution, a researcher says). *New York Times*, 6 December 1994, p. zB5.

Blier, Suzanne Preston. "The Place Where Vodun Was Born" (At a West African crossroads, devotees of an ancient religion welcome each appearance of the gods). *Natural History*, October 1995, p. 40.

Bradsher, Keith. "Greenspan Says the Fed Uses Anecdotal Guides." *New York Times*, 11 August 1994, p. C2z.

Branch, Melville C. "Analytical Core." In Melville C. Branch, *Continuous City Planning: Integrating Municipal Management and City Planning*. New York: Wiley, 1981, p. 108.

———. *Comprehensive Planning, General Theory and Principles*. Pacific Palisades, CA: Palisades Publishers, 1983, 199 pp.

———. "Conceptualization in Business Planning and Decision Making: The Planning Control Room of the Ramo-Woolridge Corporation." *Journal of the American Institute of Planners*, Spring 1957, p. 13.

———. *Telepower, Planning, and Society: Crisis in Communication*. Westport, CT: Praeger, 1994, 203 pp.

Brenman, John. "How Is It That 'Scientific Surveys' Results Can Be Polls Apart." *Los Angeles Times*, 17 July 1994, p. D2.

Bressi, Todd. "The Real Thing? We're Getting There" (Environmental simulation has come a long way). *Planning*, July 1995, p. 16.

Broad, William J. "Map Makes Ocean Floors as Knowable as Venus" (Widely held views on plate tectonics will have to be revised). *New York Times*, 24 October 1995, p. zB9.

Browne, Malcolm, W. "New Form of Ice Is Invented to Batter Hulls of Model Ships." *New York Times*, 14 January 1986, p. 17.

Brugioni, Dino. "Aerial Photography: Reading the Past, Revealing the Future" (With new tools and techniques, a young science is flying high, and proving useful in unexpected and peaceful ways). *Smithsonian*, March 1984, p. 150.

———. "The Art and Science of Photoreconnaissance" (In the 1950s and 1960s, photointerpreters devised ways of extracting valuable information from recondite images. Oftentimes, their work profoundly affected international re-lations). *Scientific American,* March 1996, p. 78.

Bryant, Adam. "The Art of Car Styling Adapts to Computers." *New York Times,* 4 December 1991, p. zC5.

Bulkeley, William M. "Business War Games Attract Big Warriors." *Wall Street Journal,* 22 December 1994, p. B1.

Buzbee, John. "People Movers at Work: Caltrans Nerve Center Tracks Pulse of Traffic." *Outlook Mail,* 8 September 1993, p. A1.

Calvin, William H. "The Emergence of Intelligence" (Language, foresight, musical skills and other hallmarks of intelligence are connected through an under-lying facility that enhances rapid movements). *Scientific American,* October 1994, p. 101.

Canby, Thomas Y. "Satellites That Serve Us." *National Geographic,* September 1983, p. 281.

Carley, William M. "Fare Game, Did Northwest Steal America's Systems? The Court Will Decide, AMR Unit Says Rival Hired Its Experts and Filched Vital Planning Formulas." *Wall Street Journal,* 7 July 1994, p. A1.

Carter, Bill. "New Report Becomes a Weapon in the Debate Over TV Violence." *New York Times,* 7 February 1996, p. zA1.

Chevers, Jack. "Sky Wars Chamber: High-Tech Southland Facility Vies for Funds." *Los Angeles Times,* 19 September 1994, p. B1.

Cleave, Richard. "Satellite Revelations: New Views of the Holy Land." *National Geographic,* June 1995, p. 88.

Clough, Michael. "Why Nations Could Fear the Internet." *Los Angeles Times,* 4 February 1996, p. M1.

Cole, Jeff. "New Satellite Imaging Could Transform the Face of the Earth, Com-panies, Cities and Others Would Get Views of Land, Traffic—and Your Yard, Big Worries about Security." *Wall Street Journal,* 30 November 1995, p. A1.

Csere, Csaba. "The Steering Column: Computers Are Our Co-Pilots." *Car and Driver Magazine,* October 1995, p. 6.

Cushman, John H., Jr. "10 Governors in West Agree to Create On-Line College." *New York Times,* 25 June 1996, p. zA9.

Damasio, Antonio R. "Descartes' Error and the Future of Human Life." *Scientific American,* October 1994, p. 144.

d'Aulaire, Per Ola and Emily d'Aulaire. "Freight Trains Are Back and They're on a Roll" (Thanks to engineers with "choo choo U." degrees, computers and new locomotives, more goods than ever now go by rail). *Smithsonian,* June 1995, p. 36.

Department of City Planning. "Citizen Images of the City." In *The Visual Envi-ronment of Los Angeles.* Los Angeles, April 1971, p. 8.

Dubbink, David. "Interactive Sound Information System Explains Noise Control." *California Planner,* January-February 1995, p. 8.

Engelberger, Joseph F. "Robotics in the 21st Century: Automatons May Soon Find Work As Subservient Household Help." *Scientific American,* September 1995, p. 166.

Evans, Diane, Ellen R. Stofan, Thomas R. Jones, and Linda M. Godwin. "Earth from Sky" (Radar systems carried aloft by the space shuttle *Endeavor* provide a new perspective of the earth's environment). *Scientific American,* December 1994, p. 70.

Fallows, James. *Breaking the News: How the Media Undermine American Democracy.* New York: Pantheon, 1995, 296 pp.

Fancher, Carol H. "Smart Cards" (As potential applications grow, computers in the wallet are making unobtrusive inroads). *Scientific American,* August 1996, p. 40.

Farmelo, Graham. "The Discovery of X-rays" (One hundred years ago this month, William Conrad Röntgen cast the first x-ray images by chance). *Scientific American,* November 1995, p. 86.

Fisher, Lawrence M. "Despite Engine Snag, G.E. Expects 777 to Be on Time" ( . . . bird-ingestion tests . . . ). *New York Times,* 7 June 1995, p. zC2.

Fishman, Charles. "Weirdest Science: The New Masters of Weather Prediction Have It All Figured Out (Well, Almost)." *Los Angeles Times Magazine,* 14 January 1996, p. 8.

Flynn, Laurie. "Virtual Reality and Virtual Space, Simulated Surgery on a Computer—This Won't Hurt." *New York Times,* 5 June 1995, p. zC3.

Gehrels, Tom. "Collisions with Comets" (The chances of a celestial body colliding with the earth are small, but the consequences would be catastrophic). *Scientific American,* March 1996, p. 54.

Gibbs, W. Wayt. "Profile: George F. R. Ellis, Thinking Globally, Acting Universally" (The foundational line of true ethical behavior . . . is the degree of freedom from self-centeredness). *Scientific American,* October 1995, p. 50.

Gilder, George. *Life After Television: The Coming Transformation of Media and American Life.* Rev. Ed. New York: Norton, 1994, 216 pp.

Gilovich, Thomas. *How We Know What Isn't So: The Fallibility of Human Reason in Everyday Life.* New York: Free Press, 1991, 216 pp.

Glaberson, William. "Press: Tantalizing Hints of a Brave New World Filled with Mirrors, the Path of 'All Media All the Time' Was Blazed by 'Imus in the Morning'." *New York Times,* 25 September 1995, p. zC7.

Glan, James. "Computer Processing Gives Imaging a Sharper View." *Science,* 8 September 1995, p. 1338.

Goleman, Daniel. "Brain May Tag a Value to Every Perception." *New York Times,* 8 August 1995, p. zB5.

———. "Delusion, Benign and Bizarre, Is Recognized as Common" (Researchers hope to gain new ways of spotting illness). *New York Times,* 27 June 1989, p. zB7.

———. "Hidden Rules Often Distort Ideas of Risk." *New York Times,* 1 February 1994, p. zB9.

———. "Insights into Self-Deception: Denial Masks Uncomfortable Truths" (This is one reason, say cognitive psychologists, why individuals and whole societies find a compelling need to lie to themselves. But there are risks to burying secrets). *New York Times Magazine,* 12 May 1985, p. 36.

———. "New Kind of Memory Found to Preserve Moments of Emotion: Adrenaline Makes Mind Take Snapshot of Fraught Events." *New York Times,* 25 October 1994, p. zB5.

———. "New View of Mind Gives Unconscious the Expanded Role." *New York Times,* 7 February 1984, p. 20Y.

————. "Study Finds Jurors Often Hear Evidence with Closed Minds: A Third Make Up Their Minds at Time of Opening Arguments." *New York Times,* 29 November 1994, p. B5.

Goodman, Walter. "Horror vs. Hindsight: A War of TV Images." *New York Times,* 4 December 1995, p. zB1.

Gore, Rich. "Neanderthals, the Dawn of Humans." *National Geographic,* January 1996, p. 2.

Hansell, Saul. "It's Coming: Your Pocket Cash on a Plastic Card." *New York Times,* 10 April 1996, p. zC1.

Haselberger, Lothar. "Deciphering a Roman Blueprint" (Scholarly detective work reveals the secret of a full-size drawing chiseled into an ancient pavement. The "blueprint" describes one of Rome's most famous buildings). *Scientific American,* June 1995, p. 84.

Havel, Vaclav. "Civilization's Thin Veneer." *Harvard Magazine,* July-August 1995, p. 32.

Hawley, John F. "Keplerian Complexity: Numerical Simulations of Accretion Disk Transport" (Supercomputer simulations have been used in conjunction with analytic studies to investigate the central issue of astrophysical accretion-disk dynamics: the nature of the angular momentum transport). *Science,* 8 September 1995, p. 1365.

Hays, Laurie. "PCs May Be Teaching Kids the Wrong Lessons." *Wall Street Journal,* 24 April 1995, p. B1.

Hendler, James. "High-Performance Artificial Intelligence." *Science,* 12 August 1994, p. 891.

"Highway Information." *New York Times,* 6 November 1995, p. zC3.

Holmes, Steven A. "Census Is Urged to Use Statistical Sampling: A Technique to Count the Uncounted May Prompt Controversy." *New York Times,* 18 November 1994, p. zA10.

————. "Even if the Numbers Don't Add Up." *New York Times,* 14 August 1994, p. E5.

Horgan, John. "The New Social Darwinists" (Psychologists and others try to side-step old pitfalls—both political and scientific—as they apply evolutionary theory to the clothed ape). *Scientific American,* October 1995, p. 174.

Ingrassia, Lawrence. "Minnesota Devises Early-Warning Index." *Wall Street Journal,* 12 May 1981, p. 25.

Jacobs, John. *A Rage for Justice: The Passion and Politics of Phillip Burton.* Berkeley: University of California Press, 1995, 577 pp.

Jensen, Elizabeth. "TV Beats Even the Polls in Illusion, Chicanery" ("Candidates are elevated, scrutinized, and discarded in a space of 48 hours," says one reporter, all as a result of the "churn of gossip and speculation"). *Wall Street Journal,* 21 February 1996, p. B1.

Johanson, Donald C. "Face-to-Face with Lucy's Family: The Dawn of Humans." *National Geographic,* March 1996, p. 96.

Johnson, George. "Why Unshakable Belief Isn't the Same as Truth." *New York Times,* 26 August 1991, p. B2.

Joseph, Christopher A. "Ars Scientia: Re-Imaging L.A." ( . . . computer program that displays and manipulates images of Los Angeles, as it is and as it could be . . . ). *Dispatch,* June 1995, p. 5.

Keizer, Gregg. "SimCity 2000." *Electronic Entertainment,* February 1994, p. 86.

Kolata, Gina. "1-in-a-Trillion Coincidence, You Say? Not Really, Experts Find: Statisticians Show That Events That Look Unlikely Are Almost to Be Expected." *New York Times,* 27 February 1990, p. zB5.

Kolbert, Elizabeth. "Americans Despair of Popular Culture: In a *New York Times* Poll, People Have Little Good to Say About TV, Movies and Pop Music." *New York Times,* 20 August 1995, Sec. 2, p. 1.

Lanham, Richard A. "Digital Literacy" (Multimedia will require equal facility in word, image and sound). *Scientific American,* September 1995, p. 198.

Laurel, Brenda. "Virtual Reality" (VR will transform computers into extensions of our whole bodies). *Scientific American,* September 1995, p. 90.

Lavin, Carl H. "Simulated Flights but Real Profits." *New York Times,* 6 February 1989, p. zC1.

Leary, Warren E. "Robot Completes Volcano Exploration." *New York Times,* 3 August 1994, p. A8z.

LeDoux, Joseph E. "Emotion, Memory, and the Brain" (The neural routes underlying the formation of memories about primitive emotional experiences, such as fear, have been traced). *Scientific American,* June 1994, p. 50.

Lenat, Douglas B. "Artificial Intelligence" (A crucial storehouse of commonsense knowledge is now taking shape). *Scientific American,* September 1995, p. 80.

Lew, Julie. "Making a Game of City Planning, Players, Beware: It's Possible to Be Run Out of Town." *New York Times,* 15 June 1984, p. B4z.

Lipin, Steven. "Risk Management Has Become Crucial in a Year When Strategies Proved Wrong." *Wall Street Journal,* 29 September 1994, p. C1.

Maes, Pattie. "Intelligent Software" (Programs that can act independently will ease the burdens that computers put on people). *Scientific American,* September 1995, p. 84.

Markoff, John. "A Satellite and Computing-Imaging to Join Search for Pan Am Dead." *New York Times,* 14 January 1989, p. 2z.

Maslin, Janet. "The New, Improved Virtual Reality." *New York Times,* 6 October 1995, p. zB1.

McCoy, Dr. Michael. "Virtual Radiology." *UCLA Medicine, Inventing the Future: Can Computers Humanize the Practice of Medicine?* Summer 1995, p. 16.

Meyerson, Allen R. "Superhuman Feats from a Subhuman Diver." *New York Times,* 13 July 1994, p. C4z.

Minsky, Marvin. "Will Robots Inherit the Earth?" (Yes, as we engineer replacement bodies and brains using nanotechnology. We will then live longer, possess greater wisdom and enjoy capabilities as yet unimagined). *Scientific American,* October 1994, p. 109.

Mukerjee, Madhusree. "Hidden Scars" (Sexual and other abuse may alter a brain region). *Scientific American,* October 1995, p. 14.

Nadis, Steve. "Computation Cracks 'Semantic Barriers' Between Databases." *Science,* 7 June 1996, p. 1419.

Naj, Amal Kumar. "Helicopter Whirls into Computer Age." *Wall Street Journal,* 9 November 1994, p. B1.

Neelin, J. David and Jochem Marotzke. "Representing Ocean Eddies in Climate Models." *Science,* 20 May 1994, p. 1099.

NOVA Videotapes. *Killing Machines,* 54 min.; *Top Gun & Beyond,* 55 min.; *Submarine,* 56 min. Corporation for Public Broadcasting.

Nowak, Martin A., Robert M. May, and Karl Sigmund. "The Arithmetics of Mutual Help" (Computer experiments show how cooperation rather than exploitation can dominate in the Darwinian struggle for survival). *Scientific American,* June 1995, p. 76.

O'Connor, John J. "Lush Music to Match Emotions on Screen." *New York Times,* 8 November 1995, p. zB3.

O'Neill, Thomas. "Irian Jaya, Indonesia's Wild Side." *National Geographic,* 7 February 1996, p. 1.

O'Reilly, Richard. "Software Can Map Out the Future, . . . to Redraw Political District Boundaries for the State." *Los Angeles Times,* 16 January 1992, p. D3.

Parfit, Michael. "Mapmaker Who Charts Our Hidden Mental Demons." *Smithsonian,* May 1984, p. 123.

Passell, Peter. "Life's Risks: Balancing Fear against Reality of Statistics." *New York Times,* 8 May 1989, p. 1.

Pentland, Alex P. "Smart Rooms" (In creating computer systems that can identify people and interpret their actions, researchers have come one step closer to building helpful home and work environments). *Scientific American,* April 1996, p. 68.

Peterson, Iver. "Turbulence Is Examined as Cause of US Air Crash: Investigators Undergo a Rough Test Flight." *New York Times,* 27 September 1995, p. A12z.

Pfeiffer, John. "The Secret of Life at the Limits: Cogs Become Big Wheels" (Researchers learn how complex organizations like aircraft carriers and electric utilities perform so well when everything has to go right). *Smithsonian,* July 1989, p. 38.

Phillips, Kevin. "Why This Congress Must Be Considered the Worst in a Half-Century." *Los Angeles Times,* 4 February 1986, p. M1.

Pine, Art. "Marines Get Taste of Urban Warfare Battling 'Enemies' at Home." *Los Angeles Times,* 8 July 1995, p. A15.

Pollack, Andrew. "A Cyberspace Front in a Multicultural War: Finding Alternatives to a World Where Only English Is Typed." *New York Times,* 7 August 1995, p. zC1.

Rabinovitch, Jonas and Joseph Leitman. "Urban Planning in Curitiba" (A Brazilian city challenges conventional wisdom and relies on low technology to improve the quality of urban life). *Scientific American,* March 1996, p. 46.

Raver, Anne. "Hatching a Novel Theory about the 10 Biblical Plagues: A Scientist Explores the Gory Part of Passover and the Exodus Story." *New York Times,* 4 April 1996, p. B6z.

Rentein, Alison Dundes. "Psychohistorical Analysis of the Japanese American Internment." *Human Rights Quarterly,* November 1995, p. 618.

Richelson, Jeoffrey T. "The Future of Space Reconnaissance" (As the superpowers continue to launch spy satellites, many nations are planning to orbit their own. Such extensive proliferation will complicate international politics into the next century). *Scientific American,* January 1991, p. 38.

Ricks, Thomas E. "How Wars Are Fought Will Change Radically, Pentagon Planner Says." *Wall Street Journal,* 15 July 1994, p. A1.

Rosenbaum, David E. "Internet Surfers Transmit a Mixed Political Agenda, 'Netizens' Would Take Money from Veterans, Give It to Endangered Species." *New York Times,* 8 July 1996, p. C4z.

Ross, John F. "Risk: Where Do Real Dangers Lie?" (We have always had to assess the chances that bad things will happen; now, new tools give us hard numbers but also raise new questions). *Smithsonian,* November 1995, p. 43.

Shaw, David. "The Shaping and Spinning of the Story That Hijacked America: The Simpson Legacy, Obsession, Did the Media Overfeed a Starving Public." *Los Angeles Times,* Special Report, 9 October 1993, Section S.

Sims, Calvin. "Advances in Skyscrapers: Defying the Wind with Less Steel." *New York Times,* 18 March 1987, p. 32.

Shogren, Elizabeth. "Population in U.S. Prisons Is Up Record 8.8%." *Los Angeles Times,* 4 December 1995, p. A1.

Small, Christopher and David Sandwell. "Sights Unseen" (Scientists are getting their first complete view of the midocean ridges, where two-thirds of our planet's surface was created). *Natural History,* March 1996, p. 28.

Solomon, Caleb and Peter Fritsch. "How Shell Hit Gusher Where No Derrick Had Drilled Before: Company Makes Huge Bet on Untested Methods to Tap Deep Well." *Wall Street Journal,* 4 April 1996, p. A1.

Steinmetz, George. "Irian Jaya's People of the Trees." *National Geographic,* 7 February 1996, p. 35.

Stix, Gary. "Boot Camp for Surgeons." *Scientific American,* September 1995, p. 24.

———. "Fighting Future Wars" (U.S. military planners hope to rely on improved versions of the technologies tested in the Gulf War to help fight the next Saddam Hussein. They may be preparing for the wrong conflict). *Scientific American,* December 1995, p. 92.

Strom, Stephanie. "A Wild Sleigh Ride at Federal Express." *New York Times,* 20 December 1994, p. zC1.

Swanbrow, Diane. "Computer Modeling: Despite Fears, Improved Decision-Making Process." *USC Trojan Family,* March 1986, p. 17.

Swerdlow, Joel L. "Information Revolution." *National Geographic,* October 1995, p. 5.

Taubes, Gary. "Taking the Data in Hand—Literally—with Virtual Reality." *Science,* 12 August 1994, p. 884.

Trachtenberg, Jeffrey A. "Zap! Smash! Aggressive Ads Plug Game Sequels." *Wall Street Journal,* 24 August 1994, p. B1.

Tufte, Edward. *The Visual Display of Quantitative Information.* Cheshire, CT: Graphics Press, 197 pp.

Waldholz, Michael. "Computer 'Brain' Outperforms Doctors in Diagnosing Heart Attack Patients." *Wall Street Journal,* 2 December 1991, p. A7C.

Waldrop, M. Mitchell. "The Visible Man Steps Out." *Science,* 8 September 1995, p. 1358.

Wallich, Paul. "Lies, Damned Lies and Models" (The NAFTA debate was conducted in terms of fallacies exposed 150 years ago). *Scientific American,* January 1994, p. 151.

Warton, David. "Aiming for the Stars" (Inside a million-dollar space shuttle simulator). *Los Angeles Times,* 4 December 1995, p. B1.

Weber, Bruce. "A Mean Chess-Playing Computer Tears at the Meaning of Thought." *New York Times,* 19 February 1996, p. A1.

Weiner, Tim. "Weapons of Mass Destruction Are Spreading, Pentagon Warns." *New York Times,* 12 April 1996, p. A4.

Wessel, David. "New Simulators Come Closer to Matching the Real World." *Wall Street Journal,* 7 November 1986, p. 33.

Whitney, Craig R. "Zap! Zap! The Allies Update War Games." *New York Times,* 10 November 1994, p. zA5.

Wiley, John P., Jr. "Phenomena, Comment, and Notes" (For millions with heart problems, an age of miracles has come. Doctors now routinely stop heart attacks and prevent recurrences in ways that would have been considered magic 50 years ago). *Smithsonian,* October 1995, p. 28.

Wilford, John Noble. "Lofty Instruments Discern Traces of Ancient Peoples: Silk Routes, Fossils and Lost Cities Yield to Shuttle Radar and Airborne Detectors." *New York Times,* 10 March 1992, p. zB5.

———. "Mapping in the Space Age" (Satellites, computers and new technologies are changing our views of the once-familiar world—shedding light on secrets as diverse as the nature of the ocean and the vegetation of the Amazon basin). *New York Times Magazine,* 5 June 1983, p. 46.

Wilson, James Q. *Bureaucracy: What Government Agencies Do and Why They Do It.* New York: Basic Books, 1989, 433 pp.

Wolkomir, Richard. "Sitting in Our Stead: Crash Dummies Take the Hard Knocks for All of Us." *Smithsonian,* July 1995, p. 31.

Zetsche, Dieter. "The Automobile: Clean and Customized" (Built-in intelligence will let automobiles tune themselves to their drivers and cooperate to get through crowded traffic systems safely). *Scientific American,* September 1995, p. 102.

Zorpette, Glenn. "War Games" (In the U.S. and Germany, wars are now being fought without firing a shot. The microprocessor revolution has spawned high-tech simulators that match combatants on a battlefield of technology. Their mission? Preparing for the real thing). *Los Angeles Times,* 7 October 1991, p. B3.

# Index

# About the Author

MELVILLE C. BRANCH is Distinguished Professor of Planning Emeritus at the University of Southern California in Los Angeles. His exceptional experience is reflected in the contents of this book. From 1961 to 1970 he was a member and officer of the Board of Planning Commissioners of the City of Los Angeles; from 1954 to 1962 he was Corporate Associate for Planning (West Coast) and Member of the Senior Staff at TRW Inc., a large business corporation engaged in automotive, electronic, and aerospace production; and from 1938 until 1941 he was on the staff of the U.S. National Resources Planning Board in the Executive Offices of President Franklin D. Roosevelt. Earlier he was Director of the Bureau of Urban Research at Princeton University. Dr. Branch has been a member of the Faculty of the University of Chicago and the University of California at Los Angeles, as well as the University of Southern California. His graduate education includes a master's degree from Princeton and a Ph.D. in Regional Planning from Harvard—the first advanced degree in Planning awarded in the world. In 1986 he received the National Planning Award for Distinguished Leadership of the American Planning Association, and in 1992 the Distinguished Planning Educator Award of the Association of Collegiate Schools of Planning.

ISBN 0-275-95403-X

EAN

9 780275 954031

HARDCOVER BAR CODE